Hometown Recipes

for the

Holidays

Also from the editors of *American Profile*

American Profile Hometown Cookbook

Hometown Recipes

for the

Holidays

From the Editors of American*Profile*

Candace Floyd, Anne Gillem,
Nancy S. Hughes, and Jill Melton

WM
WILLIAM MORROW
An Imprint of HarperCollins*Publishers*

HOMETOWN RECIPES FOR THE HOLIDAYS. Copyright © 2007 by Publishing Group of America, Inc. All rights reserved. Printed in the United States of America. No part of this book may be used or reproduced in any manner whatsoever without written permission except in the case of brief quotations embodied in critical articles and reviews. For information address HarperCollins Publishers, 10 East 53rd Street, New York, NY 10022.

HarperCollins books may be purchased for educational, business, or sales promotional use. For information please write: Special Markets Department, HarperCollins Publishers, 10 East 53rd Street, New York, NY 10022.

All photographs by High Cotton Food Styling and Photography, except Pitcher Punch (photo by Mark Boughton; styling by Teresa Blackburn); Georgia Corn Bread Cake (photo by David Damer, styling by Mary Carter); and Cream Cheese Cupcakes (photo by Mark Boughton; styling by Teresa Blackburn).

FIRST EDITION

Designed by Nicola Ferguson

Library of Congress Cataloging-in-Publication Data has been applied for.

ISBN: 978-0-06-125789-6
ISBN-10: 0-06-125789-3

07 08 09 10 11 WBC/QWF 10 9 8 7 6 5 4 3 2 1

Hometown Recipes for the Holidays is dedicated—with our gratitude—to the cooks across the country who read *American Profile* magazine each week. We especially salute those who are upholding food traditions of generations past as well as starting new ones. A special thanks goes to all those who contributed cherished recipes, sharing with us the special ways in which they celebrate holidays.

Contents

Acknowledgments

Like a recipe, every cookbook has many components—as well as numerous "cooks" who work together to assemble the finished product. Without the help of many people, *Hometown Recipes for the Holidays* would not have been possible.

Our thanks go to *American Profile* magazine's Stephen Duggan, chief operating officer; Charlie Cox, executive editor; Steve Minucci, director of business development; and the editorial staff: Stuart Englert, Richard McVey, and Jane Srygley. Special thanks to Kim Cornish, administrative assistant for Publishing Group of America, who opened and sorted hundreds of recipe submissions.

Sarah Durand, our editor at HarperCollins in New York, and her colleagues offered invaluable advice and expertise.

We are grateful to Betty Yandrasits, president of the Saint Vincent de Paul Society of Christ the King Catholic Church in Daphne, Alabama, who found recipients for the abundance of food prepared in our test kitchen. The elderly, sick, or those who just needed a good meal received the food.

For help with the testing of hundreds of recipes, we express our gratitude to Robin Brinker, Maura Dismuke, Jessica Hendry, Monica Davis, Maria Skinner, and Libby Allen. They were there for the shopping, chopping, measuring, and cleaning up—only to start all over again.

The beautiful food photography is a result of the talent of Karry Hosford of High Cotton Food Styling and Photography in Natchez, Mississippi, and Mark Boughton, photographer, and Teresa Blackburn, food stylist, in Nashville, Tennessee.

Bringing a nation's finest holiday recipes together in this cookbook was no small task, but it was a rewarding one. America's legacy of tradition, family, and food is alive and well. The table is set, and we're ready for a memorable holiday meal.

Icon Key

The recipes contained in this book have been labeled with an icon recommending holidays for which the recipes are appropriate.

New Year's Day		The Fourth of July	
Groundhog Day		Flag Day	
Valentine's Day		Labor Day	
St. Patrick's Day		Columbus Day	
Easter		Halloween	
Passover		Thanksgiving	
Cinco de Mayo		Hanukkah	
Mother's Day		Christmas	
Memorial Day		Category Winners	
Father's Day			

Hometown Recipes

for the

Holidays

Introduction

Postmarks on the dozens of recipe contributions that arrive at *American Profile* magazine's offices every week represent a map of hometown America. Cooks from all over the country are passionate about preparing good meals for their families—and never more so than for a holiday celebration.

No matter what the occasion—New Year's Day, Valentine's Day, Easter, Passover, Father's Day, Labor Day, Halloween, Christmas—favorite dishes bring to mind warm memories of past celebrations and the special relatives who prepared holiday fare. Whether the recipes are written on a scrap of paper in Grandma's shaky hand, inked on a well-worn recipe card, or typed on a computer, they all help define a family, a community, a region—and, in a broader sense, a nation.

Hometown Recipes for the Holidays brings together prized choices for the holiday table—from appetizers to desserts and breakfast to dinner. This collection grew out of a contest in which *American Profile* asked our readers to submit their favorite

holiday recipes. The nearly 1,500 entries we received were reviewed, culled, tested, and edited to result in the 250 recipes in this book, recipes that represent the best of America's hometown holiday celebrations.

Phyllis Willink of Baldwin, Wisconsin, won the Grand Prize with her Cranberry Cake with Hot Butter Sauce. The category winners were Gwen Swanson of Pukwana, South Dakota, for Smoky Salmon Spread; Doris Ann Rose of Eddy, Texas, for Summertime Bean and Corn Salad; Trisha Kruse of Eagle, Idaho, for Apricot- and Blueberry-Stuffed French Toast; Loyd Patton of Spokane, Washington, for Garlic Parmesan Rolls; Michaela Rosenthal of Woodland Hills, California, for Pan-Seared Pork Loin with Apples and Onions; Mary J. Lewis of Eatonton, Georgia, for Autumn Rum-Glazed Carrots; and Laura Frerich of Napoleon, Ohio, for Ooey-Gooey Caramel Turtle Cake.

Our heartfelt thanks go to these winners and to the hundreds of other readers of *American Profile* who submitted recipes and made this book possible.

Breakfasts

Whether it's Mother's Day, the day after Thanksgiving when shoppers are getting ready to hit the streets, or Christmas morning, breakfast is an important part of holiday celebrations. America's cooks take pride in preparing a special repast, far more festive than everyday fare such as cereal or toast. It might be a traditional dish handed down through generations or a new creation destined to become a family favorite.

When Trisha Kruse of Eagle, Idaho, serves her Apricot- and Blueberry-Stuffed French Toast on Christmas, she recalls the warmth and excitement of the holiday that she felt as a child, feelings that to her are more memorable than the gifts under the tree. Kruse was the winner in the breakfast category of the *American Profile* Holiday Recipe Contest.

Ever since Mary J. and Max Lewis retired to Lake Sinclair in Georgia, they have welcomed family and friends to their home. One dish that's sure to please their guests is Mary's New Year's Day Broccoli and Cheese Quiche. It pleases Mary, too, because it can be made ahead, frozen, and thawed to reheat for the meal.

Debra Amunrud of Glencoe, Arkansas, makes sure she's not going to be stuck in the kitchen when her children and grandchildren are looking in their stockings and opening their gifts on Christmas morning. Her savory Grandma's Christmas Casserole is a one-dish answer to "What's for breakfast?" once the presents are unwrapped.

Christina Wood of Martinsburg, Missouri, has found a way to carry a little of Thanksgiving dinner to the morning meal. Her Pumpkin Pie Pancakes can be enjoyed warm or cold with whipped topping.

Ruth Fuller Lature of Hopkinsville, Kentucky, starts Valentine's Day in a colorful way. Her Raspberry Cream Cheese Coffee Cake is not only a festive color but it's tasty as well.

Gay Martin of Albertsville, Alabama, plays not only with the color of her special morning dish but with the name of it. Her Green Eggs and Ham Cups appeal to the younger set. We think that Dr. Seuss would be proud.

Breakfast Granola

Kathie Junker, Lafayette, Tennessee

8 cups old-fashioned oats

½ cup plus 1 tablespoon olive oil

1 tablespoon vanilla extract

½ cup plus 1 tablespoon honey

½ cup each almonds, walnuts, and
  pecans

½ cup each raisins, cranberries, and
  other dried fruit

"This is the recipe my friend Debbie made when we
went on retreats twice a year in Kentucky."

1. Preheat the oven to 325°F. Combine the oats, olive oil, vanilla, and honey in a large bowl; mix well. Spread in a single
layer on a baking sheet. Bake for 30 minutes, turning and
stirring every 10 minutes. Add the nuts after the first 10 minutes.

2. Remove from the oven; cool. Stir in the fruit. Store in an
airtight container. Serve with milk, or cover a ripe banana
with peanut butter and roll in the granola.

Good Morning Oatmeal

Gwen Swanson, Pukwana, South Dakota

1½ cups apple juice

One 7-ounce package mixed dried fruit

⅓ cup packed brown sugar

½ teaspoon ground cinnamon

2 pears, cored and chopped

2½ cups milk

½ teaspoon salt

3 cups quick-cooking oats

Two 6-ounce containers vanilla yogurt

1 cup granola

"We eat this breakfast to help control our blood pressure, to improve the health of our arteries, and to lower our cholesterol. It is also very delicious."

1. Combine the juice, dried fruit, brown sugar, and cinnamon in a saucepan. Bring to a boil. Reduce the heat and simmer, covered, for 20 minutes.

2. Add the pears and cook, covered, for 10 minutes. Cool, drain, and discard the cooking liquid. Set aside.

3. Bring 2½ cups water and the milk to a boil in a saucepan; add the salt and oats. Reduce the heat to medium; cook for 1 minute; stir.

4. To serve, spoon the oatmeal into 6 cereal bowls and top each with the fruit mixture, yogurt, and granola.

Oatmeal Coconut Breakfast Bars

Trisha Kruse, Eagle, Idaho

SERVES 16

1 cup quick-cooking oats

1½ cups apple juice

1½ cups all-purpose flour

½ cup toasted wheat germ

¾ cup shredded coconut

2 teaspoons baking powder

½ teaspoon baking soda

1 teaspoon salt

1 cup packed brown sugar

½ cup applesauce

2 cups grated carrots

2 eggs, lightly beaten

TIPS FROM OUR TEST KITCHEN

Toasted wheat germ adds a nutty flavor and fiber to these bars. It's also often enriched with vitamin E and folic acid.

"These bars are a nice way to get kids (and grown-ups) to have a little extra nutrition from carrots, applesauce, and wheat germ. They're like a dessert for breakfast. A real treat in the morning with coffee, tea, or milk, they also pack well for lunch boxes and hiking snacks."

1. Preheat the oven to 350°F. Grease a 13 x 9-inch baking pan.

2. In a microwave-safe bowl, combine the oats and apple juice. Cover and heat on high for 2 minutes. Let stand for 10 minutes.

3. Combine the flour, wheat germ, ½ cup of the coconut, the baking powder, baking soda, and salt in a large bowl. In a separate bowl, combine the brown sugar, applesauce, carrots, and eggs; fold into the flour mixture. Add the oat mixture and stir until just blended.

4. Spoon into the prepared baking dish. Sprinkle with the remaining ¼ cup coconut. Bake for 50 to 60 minutes until a wooden pick inserted in the center comes out clean. Cool and cut into squares.

FEBRUARY
[2]

New Year's Day Broccoli and Cheese Quiche

Mary J. Lewis, Eatonton, Georgia

SERVES 4 TO 6

1 teaspoon vegetable or olive oil

1 cup chopped onions

1 small garlic clove, minced

2 tablespoons chopped fresh basil leaves
    or 2 teaspoons dried basil

1/2 teaspoon black pepper

1 1/2 cups small broccoli florets

1 frozen pie shell, thawed

1/2 cup grated Parmesan

4 eggs

1/2 cup mayonnaise

1 medium tomato, cut into 5 slices

4 pimiento slices, optional

Butter-flavored nonstick cooking spray,
    optional

"My husband, Max, loves broccoli, so this quiche was a natural for him. Since we retired to Lake Sinclair, we are fortunate to have friends and family who enjoy visiting. When company comes, I take a quiche out of the freezer to thaw."

1. Preheat the oven to 350°F.

2. Heat a medium skillet over medium heat. Add the oil and tilt the skillet to coat the bottom.

3. Add the onions and cook, stirring frequently, until translucent, about 4 minutes. Add the garlic, basil, and black pepper and cook for 15 seconds, stirring constantly. Remove from the heat and set aside.

4. Combine the broccoli and 2 tablespoons water in a microwave-safe bowl. Cover the bowl with plastic wrap and microwave on high for 4 minutes until crisp-tender. Drain well and transfer the broccoli to the pie shell. Sprinkle the Parmesan evenly over the broccoli. Top with the onion mixture.

5. Combine the eggs and mayonnaise in a small bowl and whisk until well blended. Pour over the onion mixture and arrange the tomato slices and pimientos, if using, on top.

6. Lightly coat the top with butter-flavored nonstick cooking spray, if desired. Bake for 50 to 60 minutes until the crust is golden and a knife inserted in the center comes out clean.

Breakfasts **7**

New Year's Day Blender Mini-Quiches

Barb James, Iola, Wisconsin

SERVES 4 TO 6

2 cups shredded Swiss cheese

½ cup half-and-half

½ cup mayonnaise

2 eggs

2 tablespoons all-purpose flour

1 cup diced ham, cooked bacon, crab, or
   shrimp

¼ cup diced mushrooms

¼ cup finely chopped onion

½ teaspoon seasoned salt

⅛ teaspoon black pepper

TIPS FROM OUR TEST KITCHEN

The cups will be puffy when removed from the oven, but deflate rapidly, giving each a "personality" of its own.

"On New Year's Eve, I was looking in my cookbooks for something different to serve for brunch the next day. I combined a couple of quiche recipes and got out my blender for an easy way to use up dinner leftovers."

1. Preheat the oven to 350°F. Grease 12 mini-quiche cups or a nonstick muffin tin.

2. Combine the Swiss cheese, half-and-half, mayonnaise, eggs, and flour in a blender. Process until well blended.

3. Mix the ham, mushrooms, onion, seasoned salt, and black pepper in a medium bowl.

4. Fill each quiche cup with about 2 tablespoons of the ham mixture and pour equal amounts of the egg mixture over each. Cups will be about half full. Bake for 22 minutes, or until the quiches are lightly golden and a knife inserted in the center comes out clean.

Green Eggs and Ham Cups

Gay Martin, Albertsville, Alabama

SERVES 4 TO 8

3 eggs

1 tablespoon all-purpose flour

2 tablespoons butter, melted

1 cup cottage cheese

2 cups shredded sharp Cheddar

⅛ teaspoon hot pepper sauce, or to taste

1 cup spinach leaves, loosely packed

8 thin slices ham

TIPS FROM OUR TEST KITCHEN

If using a blender, you may have to turn it off frequently in order to use a spatula or a long-handled spoon to press down the spinach.

"I first served these miniature quiches at a family Christmas brunch and chose the name of the recipe with a nod to Dr. Seuss because it describes the dish and appeals to kids."

1. Preheat the oven to 350°F. Grease 8 cups of a muffin tin or eight 4-ounce ramekins.

2. Combine the eggs, flour, butter, cottage cheese, Cheddar, and hot sauce in a food processor or blender. Process until well blended. Add the spinach and pulse briefly. Do not overprocess; green flecks should be visible.

3. Line the muffin tins with the ham slices, pressing down with your fingertips. Pour equal amounts of the egg mixture, a scant ⅓ cup, into each tin.

4. Bake for 25 minutes, or until a wooden pick inserted in the center comes out clean. Do not overcook.

Grandma's Christmas Casserole

Debra Amunrud, Glencoe, Arkansas

SERVES 12

1 pound bacon slices

2 cups diced potatoes

2 cups diced ham or cooked ground sausage

2 red bell peppers, chopped

2 green bell peppers, chopped

1½ cups chopped onions

Two 2-ounce cans sliced ripe olives, drained

1 cup sliced mushrooms

12 eggs

3 cups milk

1 cup biscuit mix

1½ teaspoons salt

1 teaspoon black pepper

1 teaspoon garlic pepper

½ teaspoon dried parsley

2 cups shredded mild Cheddar

2 cups shredded mozzarella

One 16-ounce container salsa

One 16-ounce carton sour cream

"Our children and grandchildren come to our home Christmas Eve, and we open one gift each—our Christmas pajamas. The next morning, after we see what Santa left in our stockings, we enjoy breakfast. I created this one-dish casserole so I wouldn't have to spend all my time in the kitchen."

1. Preheat the oven to 375°F. Grease a 13 x 9-inch glass baking dish.

2. Heat a large skillet over medium-high heat. Add half of the bacon and cook until crisp, stirring frequently. Drain on paper towels; discard the drippings. Repeat with the remaining bacon. Crumble and set aside.

3. Layer the potatoes, ham, red bell peppers, green bell peppers, onions, olives, mushrooms, and bacon in the order listed in the prepared pan.

4. Whisk the eggs in a medium bowl until well beaten. Add the milk, biscuit mix, salt, black pepper, garlic pepper, and parsley and stir until well blended. Pour evenly over the potato mixture; cover the casserole with foil. Line the oven rack with foil to catch any drippings.

5. Bake for 1 hour, uncover, and bake for 20 minutes longer, or until a knife inserted in the center comes out clean. Sprinkle the Cheddar and mozzarella evenly over the top and return to the oven for 10 to 15 minutes until the cheese melts and begins to brown.

TIPS FROM OUR TEST KITCHEN

Even though the list is lengthy, most of the ingredients, such as the ham, cheese, olives, and mushrooms, may be purchased already chopped. You can even purchase cooked bacon.

6. Remove from the oven and let stand for 15 minutes. Top each serving with a dollop of salsa and sour cream.

Italian Easter Pies

Nancy Disciascio, New Alexandria, Pennsylvania

SERVES 24

16 eggs

1½ cups grated Asiago

1 cup shredded provolone

One 15-ounce carton ricotta

2 tablespoons grated Romano

2 cups diced ham

1 cup chopped pepperoni

1 cup milk

1½ teaspoons baking powder

1 teaspoon dried parsley

Four 9-inch frozen pie shells, thawed

TIPS FROM OUR TEST KITCHEN

This recipe may be halved easily.

"This recipe was handed down from my mom. Many years ago, she decided to throw this together and see what happened. Every Easter season after that, our family would ask if she was going to make her pies. She called them ricotta pies, but I've added a little more Italian."

1. Preheat the oven to 350°F.

2. Whisk the eggs in a large bowl until well beaten. Add the cheeses, ham, pepperoni, milk, baking powder, and parsley; mix well. Divide the mixture evenly among the pie shells. Place the pies on baking sheets.

3. Bake for 45 to 50 minutes until a knife inserted in the center comes out clean.

Sonoran Sunrise Bake

Mary Shivers, Ada, Oklahoma

SERVES 8 TO 12

1 pound bacon

¼ cup (½ stick) butter

½ cup chopped onions

3 tablespoons chopped roasted red peppers

One 4-ounce can chopped green chiles

7 thick bread slices, cut into 1-inch pieces

1½ cups shredded Cheddar

1½ cups shredded Monterey Jack or Pepper Jack

8 eggs

2 cups milk

½ teaspoon chili powder

TIPS FROM OUR TEST KITCHEN

This is ideal when serving buffet style. It holds its heat and flavor for a long time.

"This is what our sons have requested most often for breakfast or brunch for more than twenty years, especially during the Thanksgiving or Christmas holiday. I like it because I can prepare it at night and bake it early in the morning."

1. Heat a large skillet over medium-high heat. Add half of the bacon and cook until crisp, stirring frequently. Drain on paper towels and discard the drippings. Cook the remaining bacon, drain, and crumble.

2. Heat the butter in a medium skillet over medium heat until melted. Add the onions and cook, stirring frequently, until translucent, about 4 minutes. Stir in the roasted peppers and chiles. Remove from the heat and set aside.

3. Grease a 13 × 9-inch glass baking pan. Arrange the bread cubes in the bottom of the pan. Sprinkle the crumbled bacon and cheeses over the bread cubes.

4. Whisk the eggs in a large bowl until well beaten. Add the milk and chili powder; mix well. Stir in the onion mixture. Pour evenly over the top of the casserole. Cover with plastic wrap and refrigerate for at least 3 hours or overnight.

5. Remove the casserole from the refrigerator and let stand for 30 minutes.

6. Preheat the oven to 300°F. Remove the plastic wrap and bake for 60 to 70 minutes until the center is set. Let stand for 10 minutes before serving.

Wake-Up Casserole

Marsha Baker, Pioneer, Ohio

SERVES 8 TO 12

8 frozen hash brown patties

4 cups shredded Colby-Jack or Cheddar

2 cups cubed ham

7 eggs

1 cup whole milk

¼ to ½ teaspoon salt

½ teaspoon dry mustard

TIPS FROM OUR TEST KITCHEN

You may substitute sausage or bacon for the ham, if desired.

"For our family Easter brunch, I substituted frozen hash brown patties for bread slices and we all just loved it. It's very simple and can be made the night before."

1. Preheat the oven to 350°F. Grease a 13 x 9-inch nonstick metal cake pan.

2. Arrange the hash brown patties over the bottom of the prepared pan. Sprinkle the cheese and ham evenly over the patties.

3. Whisk the eggs in a medium bowl until well blended. Stir in the milk, salt, and mustard; mix well. Pour the egg mixture evenly over the cheese and ham.

4. Cover with foil and bake for 1 hour. Remove the foil and bake for 15 minutes longer, or until the edges are golden and a knife inserted near the center comes out clean.

Apple Pecan French Toast

Barbara Schindler, Napoleon, Ohio

SERVES 4 TO 6

4 eggs

1 cup milk

¼ cup sugar

¼ teaspoon ground cinnamon

1 medium Jonathan or McIntosh apple,
    peeled and shredded

½ teaspoon vanilla extract

Nonstick cooking spray or melted butter

1 loaf French bread, cut into twelve
    1-inch slices

½ cup chopped pecans

2 tablespoons melted butter

Maple syrup

"Because this recipe is made the night before serving, it's great for busy people."

1. Combine the eggs, milk, sugar, cinnamon, apple, and vanilla in a medium mixing bowl; stir to combine.

2. Coat the bottom of a 12 x 8-inch glass baking dish with nonstick cooking spray or brush with melted butter. Arrange the bread slices in a single layer in the pan. Pour the egg mixture over the bread. Turn the bread slices over to coat the other side. Cover the pan with plastic wrap and refrigerate overnight.

3. When ready to serve, preheat the oven to 425°F. Remove the pan from the refrigerator and remove the plastic wrap. Sprinkle the pecans over the top and drizzle with the melted butter. Bake for 20 to 25 minutes until the bread slices puff. Serve with maple syrup.

Apricot- and Blueberry-Stuffed French Toast
Trisha Kruse, Eagle, Idaho

SERVES 6

1 cup sliced fresh or canned apricots

1 cup fresh or frozen blueberries, thawed and drained on paper towels

2 tablespoons sugar

One 8-ounce package cream cheese

1/2 cup apricot preserves

3 eggs

2/3 cup half-and-half

2 tablespoons honey

2 teaspoons vanilla extract

12 slices thick white bread

1/4 cup (1/2 stick) butter

3/4 cup vanilla yogurt, optional

"I grew up eating this special breakfast on Christmas morning. We filled plates with this wonderful French toast and opened our presents while we ate. I recall the warmth and excitement of those occasions much more than the gifts. Now I make this every Christmas morning at my house."

1. Preheat the oven to 300°F.

2. Combine the apricots, blueberries, and sugar in a small bowl. Combine the cream cheese and preserves in a medium microwave-safe bowl and heat on high for 30 to 40 seconds to soften the cream cheese and slightly melt the preserves. Whisk until well blended.

3. Whisk the eggs in a shallow dish until well blended. Add the half-and-half, honey, and vanilla; mix well. Spread the cream cheese mixture evenly over 6 of the bread slices and top with the remaining slices. Dip each "sandwich" into the egg mixture, turning to coat well.

4. Melt 2 tablespoons of the butter in a large skillet over medium heat. Cook three of the "sandwiches" until golden, about 2 minutes on each side. Place on an ovenproof platter and keep warm in the oven. Repeat with the remaining "sandwiches." Top each serving with the sweetened fruit and yogurt, if desired.

Crunchy Crust French Toast

Marsha Baker, Pioneer, Ohio

SERVES 4 TO 8

2 eggs

⅔ cup milk

4 teaspoons sugar

¼ to ½ teaspoon ground cinnamon

1 cup flaked coconut

⅔ cup crushed cornflakes

6 tablespoons margarine or butter

2 tablespoons vegetable oil

8 bread slices

Maple syrup, warmed

TIPS FROM OUR TEST KITCHEN

Work quickly when dipping the bread slices into the egg mixture or they will absorb too much egg mixture and fall apart. This dish tastes like a "cousin" to the macaroon.

"My kids are all grown, but they loved this recipe growing up. Now we often have brunch for our family get-togethers and this is always a hit. It's a little different from regular French toast and can be kept warm while other dishes are being prepared."

1. Preheat the oven to 300°F.

2. Whisk the eggs in a medium bowl until well beaten. Add the milk, sugar, and cinnamon; mix well.

3. Combine the coconut and cornflakes in a shallow pan.

4. Heat the margarine and oil in a large skillet over medium heat until bubbly. Dip 4 bread slices into the egg mixture, then coat with the coconut mixture. Place the bread slices in the pan and cook until golden brown, 2 to 3 minutes on each side. Keep warm in the oven on an ovenproof platter. Repeat with the remaining bread. Serve with maple syrup.

Holiday French Toast

Connie Brooks, Hayti, Missouri

SERVES 4 TO 8

4 eggs

4 cups eggnog

⅛ teaspoon salt

2 tablespoons vegetable oil

8 bread slices

Butter, optional

Confectioners' sugar, optional

Maple syrup, warmed, optional

TIPS FROM OUR TEST KITCHEN

For a variation, use cinnamon-raisin, sourdough, wheat, or French bread slices. This recipe is a great way to use leftover eggnog during the holidays.

"I came up with this recipe several years ago when I had some leftover eggnog. Now it's a family favorite. I start making it around Thanksgiving when eggnog appears on grocery shelves. My children are grown, and the grandchildren are enjoying the tradition."

1. Preheat the oven to 300°F.

2. Whisk the eggs in a medium bowl until well blended. Add the eggnog and salt; mix well.

3. Heat 1 tablespoon of the oil in a large skillet over medium heat. Tilt the skillet to coat the bottom. Dip 4 of the bread slices in the eggnog mixture and turn to coat evenly.

4. Place the bread in the skillet and cook until golden, 2 to 3 minutes on each side. Keep warm in the oven on an ovenproof platter. Repeat with the remaining bread slices.

5. Serve warm topped with butter, confectioners' sugar, or maple syrup, if desired.

Oven French Toast

Martha Wolf, Brighton, Michigan

TOAST

¼ cup (½ stick) butter, melted

8 thick slices French or Italian bread

4 eggs

⅔ cup orange juice

¼ cup sugar

½ teaspoon vanilla extract

¼ teaspoon ground nutmeg

½ cup chopped pecans

SYRUP

½ cup (1 stick) butter

1 cup orange juice

½ cup sugar

TIPS FROM OUR TEST KITCHEN

For additional orange flavor, add ¼ teaspoon grated orange zest to the syrup.

"I like to serve this on Christmas morning since I can make it ahead of time. I usually invite some neighbors so we can relax a bit before we start opening gifts and getting ready for our holiday dinner."

1. To prepare the toast, pour the melted butter into a 13 × 9-inch glass baking pan. Tilt the pan to coat the bottom evenly. Arrange the bread slices in a single layer in the pan.

2. Whisk the eggs in a medium bowl until well beaten. Add the orange juice, sugar, vanilla, and nutmeg. Whisk until well blended. Pour the egg mixture evenly over the bread, cover with plastic wrap, and refrigerate for 2 hours or overnight.

3. Preheat the oven to 350°F.

4. Remove the plastic wrap from the pan and bake, uncovered, for 20 minutes. Sprinkle the pecans over the top and bake for 10 minutes longer.

5. To prepare the syrup, melt the butter in a small saucepan over medium heat. Add the orange juice and sugar. Cook until thoroughly heated and the sugar has dissolved. Do not boil. Serve with the French toast.

Stuffed French Toast

Laura Frerich, Napoleon, Ohio

SERVES 8 TO 12

24 raisin-bread slices, crusts trimmed
8 eggs
3 cups low-fat or whole milk
1 cup half-and-half
1 cup granulated sugar
1 tablespoon vanilla extract
⅛ teaspoon ground nutmeg
Two 8-ounce packages Neufchâtel or
    regular cream cheese, softened
Cinnamon sugar, optional

TIPS FROM OUR TEST KITCHEN

To make cinnamon sugar, mix together ½ cup sugar and 1 tablespoon cinnamon. Store in a shaker jar or bottle for sprinkling on buttered toast.

"As a new bride five years ago, I was nervous about preparing something special that my mother-in-law would enjoy. This proved to be a winner and has since become part of our yearly brunch tradition after church on Christmas morning."

1. Grease a 13 × 9-inch glass baking pan. Arrange 12 of the bread slices in the bottom of the pan, overlapping slightly.

2. Whisk 6 eggs in a large bowl until well beaten. Add the milk, half-and-half, and ½ cup of the granulated sugar; mix well. Pour half of the milk mixture evenly over the bread slices.

3. Combine the remaining 2 eggs, the remaining ½ cup granulated sugar, the vanilla, nutmeg, and cream cheese in a blender. Cover and blend until smooth. Pour the cheese mixture over the bread in the pan. Arrange the remaining 12 bread slices on top of the cheese mixture, overlapping slightly, and pour the remaining milk mixture evenly over all. Cover with plastic wrap and refrigerate overnight.

4. Preheat the oven to 350°F.

5. Remove the plastic wrap from the baking pan. Bake for 55 minutes, or until a knife inserted in the center comes out clean. Remove from the oven and let stand for 10 minutes. Sprinkle with cinnamon sugar, if desired.

Lotta Lemon Pancake Roll-Ups

Margee Berry, Trout Lake, Washington

SYRUP

2 cups fresh or thawed frozen blueberries

1 cup light corn syrup

2 teaspoons lemon juice

PANCAKES

One 8-ounce package light cream cheese

2 tablespoons lemon juice

1 teaspoon finely grated lemon zest

2 tablespoons honey

1½ cups all-purpose flour

1 teaspoon baking soda

¼ cup sugar

½ teaspoon salt

3 eggs

1¼ cups buttermilk

1 cup milk

2 tablespoons unsalted butter

½ cup chopped pecans, toasted

"This is a weekend-favorite breakfast recipe I created last summer. The syrup can be made from any type of berry."

1. To prepare the syrup, combine the blueberries, corn syrup, and lemon juice in a small saucepan. Simmer for 10 minutes. Pour into a sieve and strain into a small bowl.

2. To prepare the pancakes, beat the cream cheese in a bowl using a mixer for 1 minute. Add the lemon juice, zest, and honey; beat for 1 minute longer.

3. Combine the flour, baking soda, sugar, and salt in a large bowl. In a separate bowl, whisk the eggs, buttermilk, and milk. Fold into the flour mixture.

4. Heat a large nonstick griddle or skillet over medium heat. Melt 1 tablespoon of the butter. Using a ½-cup measure, pour the batter onto the griddle. Cook until bubbles form on the surface, 2 to 3 minutes. Turn and cook for 1½ minutes longer. Keep warm in the oven. Repeat with the remaining batter, adding additional butter as needed.

5. Spread each pancake with 2 tablespoons of the cream cheese mixture; roll up. Place 2 roll-ups on each plate and sprinkle with pecans. Drizzle with the syrup.

Oatmeal and Applesauce Pancakes

Mrs. Billy Cheshire, Luling, Texas

SERVES 4

SYRUP

1½ cups orange juice

½ cup sugar

1 tablespoon cornstarch

2 cups fresh cranberries

PANCAKES

1 egg

½ cup old-fashioned oats

½ cup all-purpose flour

½ cup milk

½ cup applesauce

1 tablespoon sugar

3 tablespoons vegetable oil

2 teaspoons baking powder

½ cup chopped pecans

"Trying to cook healthy for my husband, I came up with this pancake recipe. The cranberry syrup is for Christmas morning. Other times of the year, I use maple syrup."

1. To prepare the syrup, combine the orange juice, sugar, and cornstarch in a medium saucepan. Stir until the cornstarch dissolves. Add the cranberries and bring to a boil, stirring frequently. Reduce the heat and simmer, uncovered, for 30 minutes, stirring occasionally. Whisk the sauce after 30 minutes for a smoother consistency.

2. To prepare the pancakes, whisk the egg in a medium bowl until well beaten. Add the oats, flour, milk, applesauce, sugar, 2 tablespoons of the oil, the baking powder, and pecans; mix well.

3. Heat a large skillet over medium heat. Add the remaining 1 tablespoon oil and tilt the skillet to coat the bottom; pour off excess oil. Using a ¼-cup measure, pour the batter into the skillet. Cook until golden, about 2 minutes on each side. Remove to a platter and repeat with the remaining batter. Serve with the cranberry syrup.

Oatmeal Pancake Mix

Theresa Slemp, Afton, Tennessee

MAKES 10 CUPS

MIX

4 cups old-fashioned oats

2 cups all-purpose flour

2 cups whole wheat flour

1 cup packed brown sugar

1 cup instant nonfat dry milk

3 tablespoons baking powder

2 tablespoons ground cinnamon

5 teaspoons salt

½ teaspoon cream of tartar

PANCAKES

2 eggs

⅓ cup canola oil

TIPS FROM OUR TEST KITCHEN

This mix is great to have on hand for weekend guests and to give as gifts along with a card printed with the recipe.

"These pancakes are so wonderful, easy, and healthful."

1. To prepare the mix, combine all of the ingredients in a large bowl; blend well. Store in a sealed gallon-sized plastic storage bag or airtight container.

2. To prepare the pancakes, beat the eggs in a large bowl. Gradually beat in the canola oil. Alternately add 2 cups pancake mix and 1 cup water to the mixture. Blend well.

3. Preheat and oil a griddle. Using a ⅓-cup measure, pour the batter onto the griddle. Cook until bubbles form around the edges; turn and continue to cook until done. Repeat with the remaining batter.

Christina's Pumpkin Pie Pancakes

Christina Wood, Martinsburg, Missouri

SERVES 5 TO 10

2 cups all-purpose flour

¾ cup sugar

1 tablespoon baking powder

½ teaspoon salt

2 eggs

One 15-ounce can pumpkin

One 12-ounce can evaporated milk

2 teaspoons ground cinnamon

1 teaspoon ground ginger

½ teaspoon ground cloves

Whipped topping, optional

TIPS FROM OUR TEST KITCHEN

You may allow the pancakes to cool, cover with plastic wrap, and refrigerate until needed.

"Pumpkin pie is one of my favorite Thanksgiving dishes. One day, I decided to experiment a little and see if I could get the taste of pumpkin pie into a pancake. To remind people of pumpkin pie, I serve these pancakes cold, with whipped topping to dip them in."

1. Combine the flour, sugar, baking powder, and salt in a large bowl.

2. Whisk the eggs in a medium bowl until well beaten. Add the pumpkin, evaporated milk, cinnamon, ginger, and cloves; whisk until well blended. Pour the pumpkin mixture into the flour mixture; mix well. The batter will be thick.

3. Preheat an electric griddle to 375°F, or place a large skillet over medium heat. Coat with nonstick cooking spray. Using a ¼-cup measure, pour the batter on the griddle or skillet. Using the back of a spoon, spread the mixture to create 4-inch circles. Cook until golden, about 2½ minutes on each side. Turn the pancakes more than once, if necessary. Repeat with the remaining batter.

4. Serve warm or cool with whipped topping, if desired.

Blueberry Brunch Casserole

Robin Decker, Kalispell, Montana

SERVES 8 TO 12

6 eggs

2 cups milk

1 cup lemon yogurt

1/4 cup sugar

8 day-old white bread slices or 8 ounces
French bread, cut into 1/2-inch cubes

One 8-ounce package cream cheese, cut
into 1/2-inch cubes

3 cups fresh or thawed frozen
blueberries, preferably fresh

1 cup strawberries

One 8-ounce container frozen whipped
topping, optional

TIPS FROM OUR TEST KITCHEN

If the bread is fresh, place the bread on a large cookie sheet in a single layer and let stand for at least 30 minutes to dry out slightly. If you are using frozen blueberries, rinse and drain them well on paper towels before adding to the egg mixture.

"I grew up in a family of eight kids, so our holiday gatherings are a time to get caught up with each other. This means talking into the wee hours of the morning and then sleeping late. We make this casserole the night before, and the first person up pops it into the oven. It's a perfect way to start July 4 with summer's sweet berries."

1. Whisk the eggs in a large bowl until well beaten. Add the milk, yogurt, and sugar; mix well. Add the bread cubes and toss gently to coat completely. Add the cubed cream cheese and 2 cups of the blueberries and toss gently to blend.

2. Grease a 13 × 9-inch glass baking pan with vegetable oil. Pour the egg mixture into the pan, cover with plastic wrap, and refrigerate for at least 1 hour or overnight.

3. Preheat the oven to 350°F.

4. Remove the plastic wrap and bake for 50 to 55 minutes until a knife inserted in the center comes out clean. Remove from the oven and let stand for 15 minutes. Garnish with the strawberries, the remaining blueberries, and whipped topping, if desired.

Danish Puff

Lois Bradshaw, Kingsville, Texas

PASTRY
1 cup all-purpose flour
½ cup (1 stick) butter or margarine

FILLING
½ cup (1 stick) butter or margarine
1 cup all-purpose flour
3 eggs
½ teaspoon almond extract

FROSTING
1 cup confectioners' sugar
1 tablespoon butter or margarine,
    softened
½ teaspoon almond extract
1 to 2 tablespoons milk

TIPS FROM OUR TEST KITCHEN

Sprinkle ½ cup toasted almond slices
on top for added flavor.

"This recipe has been handed down for generations. It reminds me of a cream puff. It's always a hit at coffee time."

1. Preheat the oven to 350°F.

2. To prepare the pastry, combine the flour, butter, and 1 tablespoon water in a bowl, cutting in with two knives to form a dough similar to a piecrust. Spread in a 13 × 9-inch baking pan.

3. To prepare the filling, combine 1 cup water and the butter in a medium saucepan and bring to a boil. Remove from the heat. Add the flour. Stir until smooth. Stir in the eggs, 1 at a time, beating well after each addition. Add the almond extract. Pour over the crust. Bake for 55 to 60 minutes.

4. To prepare the frosting, combine the confectioners' sugar, butter, and almond extract. Add the milk, a little at a time, until the frosting reaches a spreading consistency. Spread over the baked puff.

Raspberry Cream Cheese Coffee Cake

Ruth Fuller Lature, Hopkinsville, Kentucky   SERVES 5 TO 10

2 cups biscuit mix
One 3-ounce package cream cheese,
    cut into ½-inch cubes
¼ cup (½ stick) butter or margarine,
    cut into ½-inch cubes
⅓ cup plus 1 to 2 tablespoons milk
⅔ cup raspberry or cherry preserves
1 cup confectioners' sugar
½ teaspoon vanilla extract

"The red filling makes a colorful, special Valentine breakfast treat. This recipe comes from a former elementary school principal. Once a month, different faculty members would bring potluck breakfast as a way of celebrating everyone's birthday."

1. Preheat the oven to 425°F.

2. Place the biscuit mix in a medium bowl. Using two knives or a pastry blender, cut in the cream cheese and butter until the mixture resembles coarse crumbs. Add ⅓ cup of the milk and stir until blended.

3. Turn the mixture onto a floured work surface and knead 8 to 10 strokes. Place the dough on a large sheet of wax paper and roll it out to 12 × 18 inches. Turn the dough onto a large, greased baking sheet and remove the wax paper.

4. Place the preserves in a microwave-safe bowl and heat for 15 seconds to melt slightly; stir to blend. Spread the preserves evenly lengthwise down the center of the dough, about 3 inches wide.

5. Make 2½-inch cuts at 1-inch intervals on each side and fold the strips over the filling. Do not overlap the strips. Bake for 12 minutes, just until golden; do not overcook. Place the baking sheet on a wire rack.

6. Combine the confectioners' sugar, the remaining 1 to 2 tablespoons milk, and the vanilla in a small bowl; mix well. Drizzle evenly over the warm coffee cake. Cool completely before serving.

Appetizers and Beverages

When guests arrive to celebrate a holiday, make-ahead appetizers can be a cook's best friend. Family and friends eagerly await the meal, while the cook puts the final touches on the main course. Holidays are a time to pull out all the stops and serve an appetizer that not only tides over your guests until mealtime, but also evokes memories of cherished relatives and holidays.

Family members and friends who join Gwen Swanson of Pukwana, South Dakota, for Easter dinner whet their appetites with her Smoky Salmon Spread with crackers. Swanson particularly likes this recipe because she can make it ahead, leaving her time to prepare the big meal of the day. Her recipe was the winner in the appetizer category in *American Profile*'s Hometown Holiday Recipe Contest.

In Karnes City, Texas, Christmas Eve wouldn't be the same without tamales, beans, and enchiladas, and Mary Louise Jonas offers the perfect opener for the meal. Her Sombrero Spread is a good choice for other holidays as well.

Rosemond Creech, called "Grandma Great" by her great-grandchildren, created Christmas Cheese Balls for her family long ago, and today her granddaughter-in-law, DeeDee Yantz of Smithfield, Kentucky, keeps her memory alive by serving the colorful appetizer to her family.

Preparing Water Chestnut Bites is a family affair, say Cora and Kandi David of Cassville, Pennsylvania, and guests arrive early to be sure they get one of these tasty morsels straight from the oven.

Sue Thomas of Canyon, Texas, has a special holiday tradition. She and her husband enjoy her tasty Shrimp Dip by candlelight before sitting down to a rich lobster dinner each New Year's Eve. And when the rest of the family comes by on January 1, there's enough of the dip to share.

Beer Cheese

Juanita Jones, Kingsville, Texas

SERVES 6

One 8-ounce package shredded sharp
   Cheddar
One 3-ounce package cream cheese,
   softened
1 tablespoon Worcestershire sauce
1 garlic clove, minced
½ teaspoon dry mustard
¼ teaspoon cayenne pepper
¼ cup beer
2 tablespoons finely chopped green
   onions or parsley, optional

"Beer Cheese is a traditional Kentucky hors d'oeuvre, served with celery, crackers, or bread, everywhere from elegant parties to sports bars. I was given this recipe in Berea, Kentucky, many years ago."

1. Combine the Cheddar, cream cheese, Worcestershire, garlic, dry mustard, cayenne, and beer in a medium bowl; mix well.

2. Cover with plastic wrap and refrigerate for 2 hours or overnight to allow the flavors to blend. Shape into a log or ball and sprinkle with green onions, if desired.

TIPS FROM OUR TEST KITCHEN

To soften cream cheese quickly, unwrap the cheese and place it on a microwave-safe plate. Heat in the microwave on high for 15 seconds. Keep the ingredients for Beer Cheese on hand in the refrigerator. It can be prepared up to a week in advance.

Blue Cheese- and Cranberry-Stuffed Endive

Margee Berry, Trout Lake, Washington

SERVES 12

4 ounces cream cheese, softened

2 tablespoons apple jelly

1/3 cup crumbled blue cheese

1/4 cup dried sweetened cranberries

2 heads Belgian endive

1/4 cup pecan pieces, toasted and finely chopped

TIPS FROM OUR TEST KITCHEN

Don't confuse the leafy green variety of endive with Belgian endive. Belgian endive resembles a pointed, closed tulip, is creamy in color, and has large leaves. Goat cheese may be substituted for the blue cheese.

"I created this recipe at Christmas and found the nice thing about using the endive was it stayed crisp for several hours, so I was able to make the appetizer in advance. With the green in the endive and the red in the cranberries, it's perfect for the season."

1. Combine the cream cheese and apple jelly in a medium bowl. Using a mixer, beat until smooth. Fold in the blue cheese and cranberries.

2. Carefully peel the leaves from the endive, discarding any bruised leaves. Trim the ends. Fill the center of each leaf with 2 teaspoons of the cheese mixture and arrange on a serving platter. Sprinkle evenly with the pecans.

Christmas Cheese Balls

DeeDee Yantz, Smithfield, Kentucky

SERVES 16

Two 8-ounce packages cream cheese, softened
1 cup shredded mild or sharp Cheddar
2 tablespoons diced pimiento, drained
2 tablespoons finely chopped green onions (white and green parts)
1 tablespoon finely chopped green bell pepper
2 teaspoons Worcestershire sauce
⅛ teaspoon garlic salt
1 teaspoon lemon juice, optional
¼ teaspoon cayenne pepper, optional
1 cup chopped pecans
Crackers

TIPS FROM OUR TEST KITCHEN

Toast the pecans for added flavor. Place a large skillet over medium-high heat. Add the pecans and cook until they are fragrant and light brown, about 2 minutes, stirring constantly. Cool before using. For peak flavor, let the cheese balls stand for 30 minutes at room temperature before serving.

"My husband's late grandmother, Rosemond Creech, called 'Grandma Great' by my children instead of 'Great-Grandmother,' created this recipe long ago to serve to her holiday guests. It is still a staple on our table, with its red pimiento and green onions and peppers carrying out the Christmas theme."

1. Combine the cream cheese, Cheddar, pimiento, green onions, bell pepper, Worcestershire, garlic salt, lemon juice, and cayenne, if using; mix well.

2. Form the cheese mixture into 2 balls and roll in the pecans to cover completely. Cover with plastic wrap and refrigerate for 1 to 2 hours or overnight. Serve with crackers.

Delicious Deviled Eggs

Sheila Babin, Orange, Texas

12 hard-cooked eggs
¾ cup Kraft Sandwich Spread
Paprika
¼ cup chopped precooked bacon bits

"My mother always made the best deviled eggs, adding pickle relish to her recipe. When I married thirty-two years ago, I carried on the tradition. One day, I was out of pickle relish and substituted the sandwich spread I had on hand. The result was delicious! These eggs are always a hit."

1. Peel and cut the eggs in half lengthwise. Scoop the yolks into a medium bowl and mash with a rubber spatula. Add the sandwich spread to the yolks; mix well.

2. Spoon equal amounts of the mixture into each egg white half, sprinkle lightly with paprika, and top with about ½ teaspoon bacon bits per egg half.

Fresh Tomato Salsa

Anna Victoria Reich, Stafford, Virginia

3 medium tomatoes

1 medium green bell pepper, finely chopped

6 medium green onions, finely chopped (white and green parts)

1 medium jalapeño chile, seeded and finely chopped

2 tablespoons chopped cilantro, or to taste

3 garlic cloves, minced

2 tablespoons lime juice, or to taste

½ teaspoon salt

Tortilla chips

"I grow tomatoes in a pot, and I have enough fully grown tomatoes to make a fresh tomato salsa."

1. Cut the tomatoes in half crosswise. Squeeze to remove any excess liquid and seeds, and chop.

2. Combine the tomatoes, bell pepper, green onions, jalapeño, cilantro, garlic, lime juice, and salt in a medium bowl. Toss gently to blend, cover with plastic wrap, and refrigerate for at least 1 hour to allow the flavors to blend. Serve with tortilla chips.

Tasty Toasty Turkey Day Pecans

Chris Warren, Cedar Rapids, Iowa

SERVES 28

1 egg white
1 pound pecan halves
1 cup sugar
1 teaspoon ground cinnamon
¾ teaspoon salt

"I created this recipe for Thanksgiving. My relatives all wanted the recipe, so I have made dozens of copies and bring these munchies to every family get-together. This will be a prefeast snack at Thanksgiving in my family for good."

1. Preheat the oven to 250°F. Coat a large baking sheet with butter-flavored nonstick cooking spray.

2. Pour the egg white into a large bowl. Beat with a mixer at high speed until soft peaks form. Add the pecans and toss gently to coat completely.

3. Combine the sugar, cinnamon, and salt in a small bowl and sprinkle over the pecans; toss to coat. Using a large slotted spoon, transfer the pecans to a baking sheet, shaking off the excess sugar. Arrange in a single layer.

4. Bake for 1 hour, stirring after 30 minutes. Turn off the oven and allow the pecans to cool in the oven. Store any leftovers in an airtight container.

Artichoke Dip

Vicky Navarrete, Hesperia, California

One 15-ounce can quartered artichoke
  hearts, drained
One 3-ounce can diced mild green chiles
  or diced jalapeño chiles
1 cup grated Parmesan
1 cup mayonnaise
3 to 4 green onions, chopped
One 8-ounce package cream cheese,
  softened
French bread or toast

TIPS FROM OUR TEST KITCHEN

This creamy, spicy dip is also
excellent served with vegetable
sticks.

"I got this recipe from my aunt in San Francisco. Every time I make the dip, I am asked for the recipe. It's very good, but addicting."

1. Preheat the oven to 350°F.

2. Combine the artichoke hearts, chiles, Parmesan, mayonnaise, and green onions in a large bowl. Stir in the cream cheese and mix well.

3. Spoon the mixture into a 9-inch square baking dish. Bake for 45 minutes, or until golden brown. Serve with slices of French bread or toast.

Nutty Caramel Apple Dip

Gwen Swanson, Pukwana, South Dakota

One 8-ounce package cream cheese,
softened

1/2 cup applesauce

1/4 cup packed brown sugar

1/2 teaspoon vanilla extract

1/2 cup chopped salted peanuts

3 apples, cored and sliced

"This recipe makes a quick and healthful appetizer. It's a fun change of pace, and great for adults and my grandchildren."

Combine the cream cheese, applesauce, brown sugar, and vanilla in a large bowl and beat well using a mixer. Stir in the peanuts. Serve with the apple slices. Refrigerate any leftovers.

Hot and Crabby Dip

Eva Seibert, Allentown, Pennsylvania

1 cup mayonnaise

½ cup shredded mild Cheddar

½ cup shredded sharp Cheddar

½ cup grated Parmesan

2 tablespoons finely chopped onion

1 garlic clove, minced

2 tablespoons minced jarred roasted red peppers

One 6-ounce can lump crabmeat, picked over for shells and cartilage

Bagel chips

TIPS FROM OUR TEST KITCHEN

As this rich dip cools, stir it a few times to help keep it creamy.

"This appetizer is a favorite among my Bunco buddies. Every month, eleven friends and I get together to play a dice game, gossip, and, of course, eat. This rich dip is a winner every time."

1. Preheat the oven to 350°F.

2. Combine the mayonnaise, cheeses, onion, garlic, and red peppers in a bowl; mix well. Gently fold in the crabmeat.

3. Spread the mixture in a 9-inch pie plate. Bake for 20 minutes, or until lightly browned and bubbly. Serve with bagel chips.

Pumpkin Dip

Marcia Emig, Goodland, Kansas

Two 8-ounce packages cream cheese,
    softened
One 16-ounce package confectioners'
    sugar, sifted
One 15-ounce can pumpkin
2 teaspoons ground cinnamon
½ teaspoon ground nutmeg
Gingersnaps

TIPS FROM OUR TEST KITCHEN

You may use a small, fresh pumpkin
to serve this dip. Cut the top off the
pumpkin, remove the seeds and mem-
brane, and fill with Pumpkin Dip.

"This can be used at Halloween and Thanksgiving. It
makes a very cute centerpiece as well as a great, easy
snack."

1. Place the cream cheese in a medium bowl. Beat with a
mixer at medium speed until creamy.

2. Add the confectioners' sugar gradually and beat until
blended. Add the pumpkin, cinnamon, and nutmeg; beat
until well blended.

3. Cover with plastic wrap and refrigerate for 2 hours to allow the flavors to blend. Serve with gingersnaps.

Rancho Dip

Ann Senter, Graeagle, California

1 cup sour cream

2 tablespoons mayonnaise

2 to 3 tablespoons lemon juice

2 green onions, chopped

½ cup crumbled blue cheese

Salt and pepper

TIPS FROM OUR TEST KITCHEN

Stir in ⅓ cup milk to thin the dip for use as a salad dressing.

"This is always a favorite dip to serve with potato chips for all our family get-togethers or to use as a salad dressing."

Combine the sour cream, mayonnaise, and lemon juice in a small bowl; mix well. Stir in the green onions and blue cheese. Season with salt and pepper. Refrigerate for several hours before serving.

Shrimp Dip

Sue Thomas, Canyon, Texas

1 pound shrimp, peeled, deveined, and
    cooked
¼ cup minced onion
¼ cup minced celery
¼ cup minced green bell pepper
½ teaspoon grated lemon zest, or to
    taste
2 teaspoons lemon juice, or to taste
¾ cup mayonnaise
4 to 5 drops hot pepper sauce, or to taste
¼ teaspoon black pepper
Assorted crackers

TIPS FROM OUR TEST KITCHEN

This is a great "add-to" recipe: Add a
bit of cilantro, parsley, or finely
chopped red bell pepper to make
this new every time you serve it. Add
1 teaspoon grated lemon zest and
1 to 2 teaspoons lemon juice for a
splash of freshness.

"My husband started a New Year's Eve tradition when
we married. We often enjoy Shrimp Dip with crackers by candlelight, and, much later, we have a broiled
lobster dinner. We always have enough dip left for
New Year's Day."

Combine the shrimp, onion, celery, bell pepper, lemon
zest, lemon juice, mayonnaise, hot pepper sauce, and black
pepper in a large bowl; mix well. Cover the bowl with plastic
wrap and refrigerate for 3 to 4 hours to allow the flavors to
blend. Serve with crackers.

Touchdown Taco Dip

Pamela Shank, Parkersburg, West Virginia

SERVES 12

2 pounds ground beef
One 15-ounce can refried beans
One 1¼-ounce package taco
    seasoning mix
2 cups shredded Cheddar
One 16-ounce container sour cream
One 16-ounce jar salsa
2 cups shredded lettuce
1 large tomato, diced
4 green onions, chopped
2 cups shredded Mexican-style cheese
Corn chips

"I started making this dip for parties and get-togethers about thirty years ago. As my children were growing up, their friends always requested it. Now my grandchildren love it."

1. Brown the ground beef in a large skillet; drain. Add the refried beans, taco seasoning mix, and ¼ cup water. Mix well and cook over low heat until thoroughly heated, about 10 minutes.

2. Spread the taco mixture in a 13 × 9-inch baking dish. Sprinkle the Cheddar over the top. Cover with the sour cream and pour the salsa over the top. Sprinkle the shredded lettuce, diced tomato, green onions, and Mexican-style cheese over the salsa layer. Serve with corn chips.

42   Hometown Recipes for the Holidays

Autumn's Harvest Spread

Donna Wilson, Washington, Missouri

SERVES 8

½ cup chopped pecans

1 cup mayonnaise

4 ounces cream cheese, softened

1 cup shredded mozzarella

1 cup shredded Cheddar

¼ cup chopped green onions

½ cup seedless blackberry jam

Assorted crackers

"Our river town is in the heart of wine country. I spent summers in the field picking grapes and autumns working as a tour guide at the wineries. This is where and when my love for autumn, food, and social gatherings began. This simple appetizer is a wonderful complement to wine."

1. Preheat the oven to 350°F. Spread the pecans on a baking sheet and toast for 10 to 15 minutes. Watch carefully to prevent burning. Set aside to cool.

2. Combine the mayonnaise, cream cheese, mozzarella, Cheddar, and green onions in a bowl; mix well. Spread the mixture in a shallow dish or pie plate. Refrigerate for 1 hour to set slightly.

3. Remove the spread from the refrigerator, sprinkle with the toasted pecans, and spread the jam evenly over the top. Serve with crackers.

Smoky Salmon Spread

Gwen Swanson, Pukwana, South Dakota

SERVES 8 TO 10

One 8-ounce package cream cheese,
    softened
2 teaspoons finely chopped onion
1 teaspoon prepared horseradish
1 tablespoon lemon juice
1 teaspoon liquid smoke
$\frac{1}{2}$ teaspoon salt
One 16-ounce can salmon, drained,
    bones removed, and flaked
$\frac{1}{2}$ cup chopped pecans, preferably
    toasted
$\frac{1}{4}$ cup finely chopped parsley
Assorted crackers

"I have family home for Easter, so morning is a busy food preparation time. While they wait for the big meal of the day, they nibble on this Smoky Salmon Spread and crackers instead of sweets that would interfere with the meal. This is a healthier treat for all ages."

1. Place the cream cheese in a medium bowl. Beat until fluffy using a mixer at medium speed.

2. Add the onion, horseradish, lemon juice, liquid smoke, and salt; beat until well blended. Stir in the salmon.

3. Cover with plastic wrap and refrigerate for at least 1 hour to firm slightly. Place in a serving bowl and sprinkle the pecans and parsley on top. Serve with crackers.

Sombrero Spread

Mary Louise Jonas, Karnes City, Texas

SERVES 12

2 pounds ground beef or turkey

1½ cups chopped onions

One 10-ounce can diced tomatoes and chiles

4 to 5 teaspoons chili powder

1 teaspoon cumin seeds

½ teaspoon garlic salt

1 pound cooked pinto beans, mashed, or two 15-ounce cans refried beans

5 cups shredded Cheddar

1 cup chopped stuffed green olives

Corn chips, tortilla chips, or flour tortillas

"This recipe is now a holiday tradition for our family's Christmas Eve meal of tamales, beans, and enchiladas."

1. Add the ground beef to a large skillet and cook over medium-high heat, breaking the meat up with a fork. When the beef starts to change color, about 5 minutes, add 1 cup of the chopped onions and sauté until slightly browned, about 5 minutes. Stir in the tomatoes and chiles, chili powder, cumin seeds, and garlic salt. Simmer until the liquid is slightly reduced, about 10 minutes.

2. Add the beans and cook until thoroughly heated. Add 4 cups of the shredded Cheddar. Serve immediately, refrigerate, or freeze.

3. When ready to serve, pour the mixture into a large chafing dish or crockpot. Arrange the chopped olives in a mound in the center. Circle with a ring of the remaining ½ cup chopped onions and 1 cup Cheddar. Serve with corn chips or tortilla chips, or spread on flour tortillas.

Anchovy Tomato Toasts

Chris Makalinao, Dallas, Texas

SERVES 8

¼ cup (½ stick) unsalted butter

¼ cup extra virgin olive oil

2 tablespoons minced garlic (about
    1 head or 12 garlic cloves total)

1 to 2 teaspoons anchovy paste

1 tablespoon chopped parsley or
    1 teaspoon dried parsley

1 loaf French bread, cut on the diagonal
    into eight ¾-inch-thick slices

8 medium spinach or basil leaves

4 slices provolone, quartered

2 Roma tomatoes, cut into 8 slices total

TIPS FROM OUR TEST KITCHEN

Don't underestimate the power of fresh garlic. Use it, not the bottled or dried varieties, for the best flavor.

"This has always been one of our family 'must-have' starters at our get-togethers. Because it is topped with bright red tomatoes, it's ideal for Christmas or Valentine's Day. It may be served warm or at room temperature, and is quick and easy to prepare."

1. Heat the butter in a small skillet over medium heat. Stir frequently until the butter melts and begins to darken slightly. Add the olive oil and stir until well blended. Add the garlic and cook for 15 seconds, stirring constantly. Stir in the anchovy paste. Remove from the heat and add the parsley.

2. Preheat the oven to 350°F. Arrange the bread slices on a baking sheet and bake for 5 to 6 minutes on each side until golden. Set aside to cool.

3. Spoon an equal amount of the anchovy mixture, about 1 tablespoon, on each bread slice and spread evenly. Place a spinach leaf on each bread slice and top with provolone. Top with a tomato slice. Serve warm or at room temperature.

Water Chestnut Bites

Cora and Kandi David, Cassville, Pennsylvania

SERVES 14

1 pound bacon slices, cut into 3-inch
  pieces
Three 8-ounce cans whole water
  chestnuts, drained
1 cup packed dark brown sugar
1 cup chili sauce
½ cup mayonnaise

"These Water Chestnut Bites were first served at a family wedding reception. Since then, they have been a staple in our home for all occasions—especially New Year's Day. Family members come early with the expectation of getting one hot out of the oven. The whole family gets involved—my father, husband, oldest son, and I wrap the chestnuts while my mother prepares the sauce."

1. Preheat the oven to 350° F. Line a baking sheet with foil.

2. Wrap a piece of bacon around each water chestnut and secure with a wooden pick. Arrange the water chestnuts on the baking sheet. Bake for 40 minutes, or until golden brown; drain.

3. Combine the remaining ingredients in a medium bowl; mix well. Pour evenly over the water chestnuts and bake for 30 minutes longer, or until glazed.

4. Remove the water chestnuts to a serving platter, reserving the sauce. Pour the sauce into a bowl and pass with the water chestnuts.

Baked Cream Cheese in Puff Pastry

Terry Ramirez-McCarty, Helendale, California

SERVES 16

½ pound bacon slices

¼ teaspoon black pepper

1 medium sweet onion, such as Vidalia, finely chopped

¼ teaspoon salt

12 ounces cream cheese, softened

½ cup shredded sharp Cheddar

3 tablespoons grated Parmesan

1 teaspoon dried dill weed

1 teaspoon garlic powder

¼ teaspoon paprika

1 puff pastry sheet, thawed

1 egg

Crackers, mini toasts, or fresh vegetables

"A wonderful alternative to baked Brie, this dish packs lots of flavor. It's easy to make, yummy, and looks like a million bucks."

1. Place a large skillet over medium-high heat. Add the bacon and black pepper; cook until the slices are translucent. Remove the bacon to a paper towel–lined plate, reserving ¼ cup of the drippings in the skillet.

2. Place the skillet over medium heat; add the onion and salt. Cook, stirring frequently, until the onion is translucent, about 3 minutes. Return the bacon to the skillet and cook, stirring frequently, until the onion is richly browned and the bacon is crispy, about 8 minutes. Remove the bacon and onion from the skillet.

3. Beat the cream cheese in a large bowl using a mixer at medium speed. Add the Cheddar, Parmesan, dill weed, garlic powder, paprika, and bacon mixture; beat until well blended. Form into a ball, cover with plastic wrap, and refrigerate for 20 to 30 minutes.

4. Preheat the oven to 400°F. Line a baking sheet with parchment paper; spray with nonstick cooking spray.

5. Roll out the puff pastry on a clean work surface, reserving a ¼-inch strip to use for decoration, if desired. Place the cheese ball in the center of the pastry sheet and fold the edges over, pressing down lightly to flatten the cheese ball. Arrange, seam side down, on the baking sheet. Shape the

reserved pastry strip into leaves, if desired, and arrange on top.

6. Combine the egg and 1 tablespoon water in a small bowl; whisk until well blended. Brush the top and sides of the pastry with the egg wash, taking care not to let it drip on the parchment paper. Bake for 25 minutes, or until the pastry is golden brown and puffed. Remove from the oven and let stand for 5 minutes. Serve with crackers, mini toasts, or fresh vegetables.

Heavenly Ham Balls

Pearl Anna Bertsch, Ypsilanti, South Dakota

SERVES 20

HAM BALLS

1½ pounds cubed ham

1 pound ground pork

2 eggs

1 cup saltine cracker crumbs

1 cup finely chopped onions, optional

1 cup all-purpose flour

¾ cup vegetable oil

GLAZE

1¼ cups packed dark brown sugar

¾ cup orange juice

¼ cup rice vinegar

¼ cup prepared mustard

1 tablespoon dry mustard

GARNISH

Cilantro leaves, optional

Orange slices, optional

TIPS FROM OUR TEST KITCHEN

For easy handling, use a fork and spoon when turning the ham balls.

"This is my own recipe, which has become a family favorite for any occasion. It can be made ahead of time and frozen, or made into a loaf and served with the glaze."

1. To prepare the ham balls, place the ham in a food processor container and pulse to a coarse texture. Combine the ham, pork, eggs, cracker crumbs, and onions, if using, in a large bowl; mix well.

2. Form into 60 balls about the size of a walnut. The mixture will be very sticky and soft.

3. Pour the flour into a shallow pan and coat the meatballs with the flour. Cover with plastic wrap and refrigerate for 2 hours to overnight.

4. To prepare the glaze, combine all of the ingredients in a medium saucepan. Bring to a boil. Reduce the heat and simmer until slightly thickened, about 10 minutes.

5. Heat ¼ cup of the oil in a large skillet over medium-high heat. Add 20 ham balls and cook until golden brown, about 4 minutes. Repeat twice with the remaining ham balls.

6. Preheat the oven to 350°F. Arrange the browned ham balls in a 13 × 9-inch glass baking dish. Pour the glaze mixture evenly over the ham balls and bake, uncovered, for 1½ hours, or until richly glazed, turning every 30 minutes. Garnish with cilantro leaves and orange slices, if desired.

Ham and Cheese Party Rolls

Judy Taylor, Kenna, West Virginia

SERVES 20

Two 20-count packages small party rolls
1 pound shaved deli ham
1 pound thinly sliced Swiss cheese
½ cup (1 stick) butter or margarine
1½ teaspoons Worcestershire sauce
1 teaspoon dried onion flakes
1 teaspoon poppy seeds
½ teaspoon dry mustard

TIPS FROM OUR TEST KITCHEN

To give a boost of extra flavor to the rolls, double all of the sauce ingredients except the butter.

"My family fell in love with this recipe after a co-worker shared it with me. I use it often at Christmas and New Year's for family gatherings and church parties. It always seems to go over well."

1. Preheat the oven to 350°F.

2. Leaving the rolls intact, slice them in half horizontally. Remove the top portion and set aside. Arrange the ham evenly over the bottom portion of the rolls and top with the Swiss cheese.

3. Place the top portion of the rolls over the cheese. Lightly coat a large baking sheet with nonstick cooking spray and arrange the rolls on the baking sheet.

4. Combine the butter, Worcestershire, onion flakes, poppy seeds, and dry mustard in a small saucepan. Cook over medium-high heat until the butter melts. Drizzle the sauce evenly over the rolls.

5. Bake for 15 minutes, or until the cheese melts and the rolls are golden. Let stand for 15 minutes; cut into individual portions. Serve warm or at room temperature.

Wrapped Jalapeños

Lisa Barlett, Sapello, New Mexico

SERVES 8

4 ounces each Monterey Jack and Colby,
   cut into ¼-inch × 3-inch strips
8 large jalapeño chiles, cut in half
   lengthwise, seeded, and patted dry
16 bacon slices

"In New Mexico, chile peppers are one of the most popular 'vegetables.' A family member showed me how to put these together for a barbecue. They're quick, easy, and great for lots of occasions."

1. Preheat the broiler. Place a cheese strip on top of each jalapeño half and wrap tightly with 1 bacon slice. Secure with wooden picks, if desired.

2. Arrange the peppers on a foil-lined pan. Broil 4 inches from the heat source for 8 to 10 minutes until the bacon is cooked, turning occasionally.

Christmas Eve Meatballs

Betty Fortschneider, Brussels, Illinois

MEATBALLS

3 pounds ground beef

¾ cup dried bread crumbs

One 1-ounce package dried onion soup
   mix

3 eggs, beaten

½ teaspoon garlic powder

½ teaspoon salt

½ teaspoon black pepper

SAUCE

One 15-ounce jar grape jelly

One 24-ounce bottle ketchup

One 14-ounce jar pizza sauce

3 tablespoons lemon juice

TIPS FROM OUR TEST KITCHEN

For a sweeter heat, add the grated
zest of 1 medium orange and ¼ to
½ teaspoon dried red pepper flakes
to the sauce.

"My family refers to this recipe as Christmas Eve
Meatballs because it's the only time I make them. It
can't be skipped—they are popular!"

1. Preheat the oven to 350°F.

2. To prepare the meatballs, combine all of the ingredients
in a large bowl; mix well. Form the mixture into 64 meatballs.

3. Line two large baking sheets with foil and spray with nonstick cooking spray. Arrange 32 meatballs on each baking
sheet.

4. Bake for 25 to 30 minutes until the meatballs are no longer pink in the center, stirring occasionally.

5. To prepare the sauce, combine all of the ingredients in a
Dutch oven. Add the cooked meatballs and bring to a simmer over medium heat. Simmer, uncovered, for 10 minutes, stirring frequently. Remove from the heat and let stand
for 30 minutes.

Mushroom Mini-Muffin Cups

Julie Wesson, Wilton, Wisconsin

SERVES 8

7 tablespoons butter

1 cup finely chopped sweet or Vidalia onions

1 pound portobello mushroom caps, finely chopped

¾ cup shredded mozzarella

¼ cup shredded Swiss cheese

½ cup finely chopped flat-leaf parsley

2 egg yolks, beaten

1 teaspoon sea salt

2 teaspoons Italian seasoning

8 slices whole wheat bread

"Our family loves cheese and mushrooms. This rustic recipe is a favorite easy snack. The muffin cups can be frozen and reheated, which makes them handy."

1. Preheat the oven to 350°F.

2. Melt 3 tablespoons of the butter in a large skillet over medium heat. Add the onions and mushrooms and sauté until softened, 6 to 7 minutes. Remove from the heat. Stir in the cheeses, parsley, egg yolks, salt, and Italian seasoning.

3. Melt the remaining 4 tablespoons butter in a small saucepan. With a rolling pin, flatten each slice of bread and cut into 4 squares. Dip each square into the melted butter and place in a mini-muffin cup. Top each with a scoop of the mushroom mixture.

4. Bake for 20 to 25 minutes until lightly browned. Cool slightly and serve warm.

Sausage Mushrooms

Bobbie E. Bankston, Midland, Texas

SERVES 16 TO 24

1 pound bulk pork sausage

2 eggs, slightly beaten

1 cup shredded Swiss cheese

¼ cup mayonnaise

3 tablespoons butter, melted

2 tablespoons finely chopped onions

2 teaspoons spicy brown or horseradish mustard

1 teaspoon garlic powder

1 teaspoon Cajun seasoning

1 teaspoon Worcestershire sauce

48 large mushrooms, stems removed

"Try one—you will like it. I serve lots of appetizers for New Year's Eve, and these are different. Even the children will eat them."

1. Preheat the oven to 350°F. Place a large skillet over medium-high heat. Add the sausage and cook until browned, stirring frequently to break up large pieces. Drain on paper towels.

2. Remove the skillet from the heat, return the sausage to the skillet, and add the remaining ingredients, except the mushrooms. Stir until well blended.

3. Fill the mushrooms with equal amounts of the sausage mixture. Grease two 13 × 9-inch glass baking dishes; arrange the mushrooms in the pans. Bake for 20 minutes, or until thoroughly heated.

Mini-Pizza Jack-o'-Lanterns

Joni Hilton, Rocklin, California

SERVES 12

6 English muffins, split

4 cups shredded Cheddar

1 cup mayonnaise

2 green onions, minced (white and
green parts)

One 15-ounce can pitted ripe olives,
drained

TIPS FROM OUR TEST KITCHEN

These may be assembled as directed,
but simply place a few halved olives
on top instead of making faces, if
desired. Use for a fun snack,
breakfast, or lunch as well.

"I've always loved to play with food, and with four kids I have plenty of opportunities. This snack started out as a variation on a grilled cheese sandwich and evolved into a Halloween treat that everyone loves."

1. Preheat the broiler. Arrange the muffin halves, cut side up, in a single layer on a large baking sheet.

2. Combine the Cheddar, mayonnaise, and green onions in a medium bowl; mix well. Spread equal amounts of the mixture on each muffin half.

3. Broil 4 inches from the heat source for 2 minutes, or until bubbly. Remove from the oven. Cut the olives into shapes for the eyes, nose, and mouth, and arrange on each muffin half.

Pizza Rolls

Heather Stine, Catawissa, Pennsylvania

SERVES 16

1 pound bulk mild Italian sausage

4 cups shredded pizza-cheese blend or mozzarella

6 ounces sliced pepperoni, chopped

1 medium green bell pepper, finely chopped

1 medium red bell pepper, finely chopped

1 medium onion, finely chopped

Two 14-ounce jars pizza sauce

32 egg roll wrappers

Vegetable oil for frying

TIPS FROM OUR TEST KITCHEN

A large, deep skillet may be used instead of an electric skillet. Heat 1 inch of oil in the skillet over medium-high heat. To reheat frozen rolls, place on a baking sheet in a 350°F oven for 10 to 15 minutes.

"My children liked store-bought pizza rolls, but there were only a few in the box. I decided to find a way to make them to get more for my money. Even though they take a little bit of time, these are delicious and freeze very well."

1. Place a large skillet over medium-high heat. Add the sausage and cook until browned, stirring frequently and breaking up large pieces. Drain on paper towels.

2. Combine the sausage, cheese, pepperoni, bell peppers, onion, and pizza sauce in a large bowl; mix well. Arrange the egg roll wrappers on a work surface.

3. Spoon ¼ cup of the mixture in the center of each egg roll wrapper. Fold the bottom edge toward the center over the filling. Moisten the top edge with a small amount of water and fold over, sealing tightly.

4. Heat 1 inch of oil to 375°F in an electric skillet. Fry the rolls in batches until golden brown, 1 to 2 minutes per side. Drain on paper towels.

Savory Three-Cheese Italian Pockets

Dawn Onuffer, Crestview, Florida

SERVES 12

½ cup finely chopped pepperoni

One 4-ounce jar mushrooms, drained and finely chopped

2 tablespoons finely chopped black olives

4 ounces cream cheese, softened

1½ teaspoons dried oregano

½ teaspoon garlic powder

4 tablespoons grated Parmesan

⅛ teaspoon salt

⅛ teaspoon pepper

Four .83-ounce packages mozzarella string cheese

One 14-ounce can refrigerated pizza crust

3 tablespoons bottled Italian salad dressing

Pizza sauce or marinara sauce

"I like to experiment in the kitchen and came up with this recipe in order to use a variety of ingredients left in my refrigerator. This recipe quickly became one of my favorites."

1. Preheat the oven to 375°F.

2. Combine the pepperoni, mushrooms, olives, cream cheese, 1 teaspoon of the oregano, the garlic powder, 2 tablespoons of the Parmesan, the salt, and pepper in a medium bowl; mix well.

3. Cut each mozzarella stick into six ½-inch slices.

4. On a lightly floured surface, roll out the pizza dough to a 12 × 18-inch rectangle. Brush the dough with 2 tablespoons of the Italian dressing. Cut the dough into 24 equal pieces. Place 1 piece of the mozzarella and a scant tablespoon of the pepperoni mixture on each square.

5. Bring all four corners together above the filling and pinch to seal. Brush with the remaining 1 tablespoon Italian dressing and sprinkle with the remaining 2 tablespoons Parmesan and ½ teaspoon oregano.

6. Arrange the bundles on a 15 × 10-inch baking sheet about 1 inch apart. Bake for 15 to 20 minutes. Serve with pizza sauce or marinara sauce.

Hot Cranberry Punch

Cindy Sickbert, Rushville, Indiana

2 quarts cranberry-apple juice

2 quarts cranberry juice

1 cup orange juice

1½ cups sugar

1 cup lemonade

4 cinnamon sticks

20 whole cloves

30 red-hot candies

¾ to 1 cup rum, optional

TIPS FROM OUR TEST KITCHEN

For easy removal of the spices, place the cinnamon sticks and cloves in a piece of cheesecloth and secure with string before adding to the juice mixture.

"Hot Cranberry Punch is easy to make and handy to have in the refrigerator when guests come calling at holiday time. It's also wonderful to drink at night on a cold winter day."

1. Combine the juices, sugar, lemonade, spices, candies, and rum, if using, in a 5-quart stockpot. Bring the mixture to a boil. Reduce the heat and simmer, uncovered, for 1 hour. Remove the spices.

2. Cool and refrigerate until serving time. Reheat in a microwave-safe container.

Cranberry Slush

Laura Frerich, Napoleon, Ohio

Two 3-ounce boxes cherry-flavored
gelatin
One 12-ounce can frozen lemonade
concentrate
One 12-ounce can frozen orange juice
concentrate
2 cups cranberry juice
2 cups vodka
4 cups lemon-lime soda

"Cranberry Slush has been part of our yearly Christmas Eve open house for our neighborhood. We always have to be sure the recipe is doubled—and even then, it's sure to disappear quickly."

1. Combine 1 cup boiling water with the cherry gelatin in a large bowl; stir until the gelatin dissolves completely.

2. Add 3 cups cold water, the juice concentrates, cranberry juice, and vodka to the bowl; mix well. Cover the bowl with plastic wrap or transfer the juice mixture to a gallon-sized resealable plastic bag. Seal tightly and store in the freezer overnight or for up to 2 months. The mixture will not freeze solid because of the vodka.

3. To serve, spoon the juice mixture into cups or glasses; top each with an equal part of soda.

St. Valentine's Irish Crème Mists

Mary J. Lewis, Eatonton, Georgia

SERVES 2

1½ cups strawberry swirl ice cream or ¾ cup each vanilla ice cream and strawberry ice cream

2 teaspoons Irish crèam liquid coffee creamer

¼ cup chocolate liqueur or Irish crème liqueur

1 tablespoon Irish whiskey

¼ cup whipped cream

2 tablespoons shaved chocolate

2 strawberries

"On Valentine's Day, imagine a white linen tablecloth and tall, slender glasses filled with this wonderful dessert drink. This was developed over time for adults to enjoy at the end of their meal. It is light and sweet— a cross between a cocktail and an ice cream sundae."

1. Combine the ice cream, creamer, liqueur, whiskey, and whipped cream in a blender container and puree until smooth.

2. Pour the mixture into two tall glasses and refrigerate for 1 to 3 hours until well chilled.

3. Sprinkle shaved chocolate over the top of each glass and top with a strawberry. Serve with a long straw and a tall spoon, if desired.

Pitcher Punch

J. B. Robert, Murphy, North Carolina

SERVES 16

3 tea bags
4 lemons
1½ cups sugar
1 teaspoon vanilla extract
½ teaspoon almond extract
Dash of salt

"At the end of a hot day, there's nothing better than Aunt Alice's Pitcher Punch to cool you down and slake your thirst. I guarantee when you are hot and thirsty, there's nothing quite like it."

1. Pour 2 cups boiling water over the tea bags in a glass container. Steep for 20 minutes. Squeeze the juice from the lemons, reserving the juice and rinds.

2. Bring 2 cups water to a boil in a large pot. Add the lemon rinds and sugar. Simmer until the mixture is slightly thickened, about 10 minutes. Remove from the heat and discard the lemon rinds. Let cool.

3. Squeeze the tea bags and remove them from the glass container. Combine the lemon-sugar syrup and the tea in a large bowl. Strain the reserved lemon juice and add to the tea mixture along with the vanilla, almond extract, and salt. Mix well and refrigerate.

4. To serve, pour ⅓ to ½ cup of the mixture over ice in a glass and top with about ½ cup water.

Breads

Homemade yeast bread is possibly the most personal part of a family menu, drawing the baker into its touch, sight, and aroma. Muffins and quick breads, such as banana, poppy seed, blueberry, or apple, are also a key part of holidays throughout the year. Homemade bread represents an investment of time and care—and lets the baker slow down the pace of life for a while.

Breads also allow the creativity of bakers to emerge. Starting with a basic recipe for crescent rolls, Loyd Patton of Spokane, Washington, experimented with ingredients and proportions until he created his Garlic Parmesan Rolls, the winner in *American Profile* magazine's Holiday Recipe Contest bread category.

Sometimes breads become the most memorable and cherished recipes of a cook's repertoire. Connie Lahey's Christmas Cinnamon Rolls were legendary in her Illinois community. Her grown children missed them so much when they left home that they asked their mother to give them a tray of buns, in lieu of traditional gifts, at Christmas.

Baking often becomes a lifelong pursuit, and decades of experience only add to a signature recipe—just ask Elizabeth Rau of Westphalia, Iowa. Every week, Rau pulls out her seventy-year-old recipe for Melt-in-Your-Mouth German Buns and heats up her oven. In her century of life, she's baked thousands of the buns.

And sometimes breads can pose a challenge to the beginning and expert cook alike. Nancy Burlinson, of Horseshoe Bend, Arkansas, tinkered with her recipe for British Scones for years until she found a combination reminiscent of those her English husband's mother made when he was a child. He was so proud of her achievement, Burlinson says, that he wrote "Mom learned to make scones" on a garage wall and dated it.

Fresh Apple Muffins

Mrs. Ivor Stephenson, Winnsboro, South Carolina

1 cup vegetable oil

2 cups sugar

3 cups all-purpose flour

3 eggs

1 cup chopped nuts

2 teaspoons vanilla extract

1 teaspoon salt

1 teaspoon baking soda

2 cups chopped unpeeled apples

Cream cheese, softened

"These muffins are delicious for breakfast or for afternoon tea. Fresh apples in the fall make the best."

1. Preheat the oven to 350°F. Lightly grease muffin cups.

2. Combine the oil, sugar, flour, and eggs in a large bowl; mix well. Stir in the nuts, vanilla, salt, and baking soda. Gently fold in the apples. Fill muffin cups two-thirds full. Bake for 20 to 25 minutes. Serve warm with cream cheese.

Cheese Garlic Bread Sticks

Gwen Swanson, Pukwana, South Dakota

SERVES 10

1³/₄ to 2¹/₂ cups all-purpose flour

¹/₄ cup sesame seeds

One ¹/₄-ounce package active dry yeast

¹/₂ teaspoon salt

2 tablespoons olive oil

1 tablespoon honey

2 tablespoons parsley flakes

1 tablespoon dried crushed basil

3 garlic cloves, minced

¹/₂ cup shredded mozzarella

¹/₂ cup grated Parmesan

TIPS FROM OUR TEST KITCHEN

These bread sticks are great served with a garlicky marinara dipping sauce.

"These slightly chewy bread sticks have a great cheesy flavor. My eight grandkids always want me to double the recipe. It's a delight to see them enjoy them."

1. Combine 1¹/₂ cups of the flour, the sesame seeds, yeast, and salt in a large bowl; mix well.

2. Heat 1 cup water, 1 tablespoon of the olive oil, and the honey in a small saucepan to 120°F. Add the olive oil mixture to the dry ingredients and beat until just moistened. Stir in enough of the remaining flour to form a soft dough.

3. Turn onto a lightly floured surface and knead until smooth and elastic. Cover and let rest for 15 minutes.

4. Grease a 15 × 10-inch baking pan. Roll the dough into a rectangle. Transfer to the baking pan. Press the dough to the edges of the pan. Brush with the remaining 1 tablespoon olive oil. Sprinkle the parsley, basil, and garlic over the dough. Cover and let rise in a warm place for 40 minutes.

5. Preheat the oven to 400°F. Bake for 10 minutes. Sprinkle the dough with the cheeses. Bake for 3 to 5 minutes longer to melt the cheeses. Cut into 20 strips.

British Scones

Nancy Burlinson, Horseshoe Bend, Arkansas

SERVES 12

2½ to 3 cups all-purpose flour

⅓ cup sugar

1 teaspoon cream of tartar

1 teaspoon baking soda

½ teaspoon baking powder

½ cup (1 stick) butter, softened

¾ cup raisins

½ cup currants or candied fruit

1 cup sour milk

TIPS FROM OUR TEST KITCHEN

To sour milk, add 1 tablespoon lemon juice to 1 cup milk. Let stand for 15 minutes. For a sweeter scone, use Craisins instead of raisins or currants and sprinkle raw sugar on top.

"My husband, who is British, kept asking for scones like his mom's. American recipes just weren't the same. I just kept experimenting until one day I found the right combination. My husband was so excited he wrote 'Mom learned to make scones' on the inside wall of the garage and dated it."

1. Preheat the oven to 425°F.

2. Combine 2½ cups of the flour, the sugar, cream of tartar, baking soda, and baking powder in a medium bowl. Cut in the softened butter until the mixture resembles fine crumbs. Add the raisins and currants, mixing until the fruit is coated with the flour mixture.

3. Add the sour milk and mix well.

4. Turn the mixture onto a floured board and knead, adding enough extra flour to make a slightly stiff dough. Pat to about ¾-inch thickness and cut with a 2-inch round cutter. Place the scones on a baking sheet and bake for 12 to 15 minutes until lightly browned. Serve warm or cold.

Mamma's Banana Nut Bread

Amber Sheriff, Cumming, Georgia

5 tablespoons butter

½ cup granulated sugar

½ cup packed light brown sugar

1 egg

2 egg whites

1 teaspoon vanilla extract

1½ cups mashed, very ripe bananas

1¾ cups all-purpose flour

1 teaspoon baking soda

¼ teaspoon baking powder

½ teaspoon salt

½ cup heavy cream

⅓ cup chopped walnuts

"Ever since I can remember, my mother has enjoyed making banana nut bread. She loves to make it just as much as she does sitting down and eating some. Try a slice with butter or jam."

1. Preheat the oven to 350°F. Spray the bottom of a 9 × 5-inch loaf pan with nonstick cooking spray.

2. Beat the butter in a large bowl with a mixer until light and fluffy. Add the sugars and beat well. Add the egg, egg whites, and vanilla and beat until blended. Add the bananas and beat at high speed for 30 seconds.

3. Combine the flour, baking soda, baking powder, and salt in a medium bowl; mix well. Add the flour mixture to the butter mixture alternately with the cream, ending with the flour mixture; mix well. Stir in the walnuts.

4. Pour the batter into the prepared pan. Bake for about 1 hour and 15 minutes until browned and a wooden pick inserted near the center comes out clean.

5. Cool in the pan on a wire rack for 10 minutes. Remove the bread from the pan and cool completely on the wire rack.

Boston Brown Bread

Barbara Mulvaney, Billings, Montana

1 pound chopped dates

2 teaspoons baking soda

2 cups sugar

½ cup shortening

2 eggs

4 cups sifted all-purpose flour

1 cup walnut pieces

1 cup raisins

Six 14- to 16-ounce empty, clean
    vegetable or fruit cans

TIPS FROM OUR TEST KITCHEN

To grease the cans, use a paper towel dipped in a small amount of vegetable oil. To remove the bread from the cans, turn the cans upside down and gently shake or tap to loosen the bread. Gently tug the top of the bread to remove.

"My grandmother, mother, daughter, and I make Boston Brown Bread every Christmas. It's unique, because you bake the loaves in vegetable or fruit cans."

1. Preheat the oven to 325°F.

2. Combine the dates and baking soda in a bowl. Pour 2 cups boiling water over the mixture and let stand for 5 minutes.

3. Combine the sugar, shortening, and eggs in a large bowl. Using a mixer, beat at medium-high speed until creamy. Add the date mixture and flour and stir until well blended. Add the nuts and raisins; mix well.

4. Fill the cans about two-thirds full with batter. Bake for 1¼ hours until a wooden pick inserted in the center comes out clean. Cool in the cans on a wire rack for 15 minutes before removing the bread from the cans and returning to the rack to cool completely.

Carrot Pear Bread

Norma Frandson, Grand Forks, North Dakota

SERVES 24

½ cup sugar

2 eggs, beaten

½ cup vegetable oil

1½ cups all-purpose flour

½ teaspoon salt

1 teaspoon baking soda

1 teaspoon cinnamon

1 cup grated carrots

1 cup sliced pears

½ cup chopped walnuts

"This is a great recipe I received about fifteen years ago. It's easy to make, and the pears add a tasty flavor."

1. Preheat the oven to 350°F. Grease two 9 × 5-inch loaf pans.

2. Combine the sugar and eggs in a mixing bowl. Beat well using a mixer. Add the oil; mix well.

3. Combine the flour, salt, baking soda, and cinnamon in a separate bowl; mix well. Add to the egg mixture; mix well. Stir in the carrots, pears, and walnuts.

4. Pour the batter into the prepared pans and bake for 45 minutes to 1 hour until a wooden pick inserted in the center comes out clean.

Tex-Mex Corn Bread

Gloria Payette, Friendswood, Texas

1½ cups cornmeal, preferably stone ground

¾ cup all-purpose flour

3 tablespoons sugar

1 teaspoon salt

2 teaspoons baking powder

1 teaspoon baking soda

2 extra-large eggs, beaten

¼ cup canola or olive oil

1 to 1½ cups whole buttermilk

¾ cup chopped onions

1 cup frozen whole-kernel corn, thawed

2 tablespoons finely chopped jalapeño chiles, or to taste

2 cups shredded mild Cheddar

"Tex-Mex Corn Bread is delicious with just about anything—gumbo, chili, soup, or a big pot of beans. I've been making it for more than forty years."

1. Preheat the oven to 375°F. Grease a jelly-roll pan.

2. Combine the cornmeal, flour, sugar, salt, baking powder, and baking soda in a large bowl; mix well. Add the remaining ingredients and stir just until blended. Pour the mixture into the prepared pan and bake for 15 minutes, or until golden.

70   **Hometown Recipes for the Holidays**

Mexican Spoon Bread

Jo K. Feazell, Worthham, Texas

SERVES 8

½ teaspoon baking soda

¾ cup milk

1 cup cornmeal

⅓ cup vegetable oil

2 eggs, beaten

One 15-ounce can cream-style corn

1 teaspoon salt

1 cup chopped green onions

1 to 2 ounces chopped pimientos

4 jalapeño chiles, seeded and chopped

1½ cups shredded Cheddar

2 tablespoons bacon drippings or
    vegetable oil

TIPS FROM OUR TEST KITCHEN

This is a very moist, soft bread.

"I have had this recipe several years. My whole family loves it, and I make it for them often."

1. Preheat the oven to 400°F.

2. Dissolve the baking soda in the milk in a small bowl. Combine the cornmeal, oil, and eggs in a large mixing bowl. Stir in the corn, milk mixture, and salt. Add the green onions, pimientos, jalapeños, and Cheddar; mix well.

3. Heat the bacon drippings in a large cast-iron skillet. Pour in the batter. Bake for 45 minutes to 1 hour until golden brown.

Passover Mandel Bread

Marion E. Hankin, Boynton Beach, Florida

SERVES 18

2 cups plus 3 tablespoons sugar

1 cup (2 sticks) margarine, softened

6 eggs

2¾ cups cake meal

¾ cup potato starch

1 cup chopped walnuts

6 ounces semisweet chocolate chips

¼ to ½ teaspoon ground cinnamon

TIPS FROM OUR TEST KITCHEN

Potato starch is gluten-free flour made from cooked, dried, and ground potatoes. It is available in health food stores. Cake meal is matzoh bread that has been ground to a fine powder. It is available in health food stores or in the baking section of major grocery stores.

"My children really like Passover Mandel Bread year-round. Now I can't make enough for my family and friends. My daughter has adopted it for her children, who love it."

1. Preheat the oven to 350°F.

2. Combine 2 cups of the sugar and the margarine in a large bowl. Beat with a mixer at medium-high speed until creamy. Add the eggs, 1 at a time, and beat until well blended.

3. Sift the cake meal and potato starch into the egg mixture. Beat until well blended. Fold in the walnuts and chocolate chips.

4. Shape the mixture into 3 loaves, about 3 × 6 inches each, on a wax paper–lined baking sheet. Arrange the loaves about 2 inches apart on the baking sheet. The dough will be sticky.

5. Combine the remaining 3 tablespoons sugar and the cinnamon in a small bowl; mix well. Sprinkle the mixture evenly over the loaves.

6. Bake for 45 minutes, or until golden brown. Remove from the oven and slice immediately or let stand for 10 minutes, then slice and cool completely.

Sweet Pistachio Bread

Oggie St. Martin, Menominee, Michigan

1 teaspoon ground nutmeg

2 teaspoons ground cinnamon

6 tablespoons sugar

One 18-ounce package yellow cake mix

One 3-ounce box instant pistachio
   pudding mix

½ cup vegetable oil

4 eggs

1 cup sour cream

"When I married my husband thirty years ago, I asked his mother for some of his favorite recipes so that I'd have guaranteed successes from my kitchen. This pretty, simple bread is very versatile—wonderful for breakfast, dessert, or snacks."

1. Preheat the oven to 350°F. Grease two 8 × 4-inch loaf pans.

2. Combine the nutmeg, cinnamon, and 2 tablespoons of the sugar in a small bowl.

3. Combine the remaining 4 tablespoons sugar, the cake mix, pudding mix, oil, eggs, ½ cup water, and the sour cream in a large bowl; mix well.

4. Pour half the batter into the prepared pans. Sprinkle the cinnamon mixture on top. Pour in the remaining batter. Bake for 45 minutes.

Poppy Seed Bread

Marsha Baker, Pioneer, Ohio

SERVES 20 TO 24

BREAD

1 cup plus 2 tablespoons vegetable oil

3 eggs

1¾ cups sugar

1½ cups milk

1½ teaspoons almond extract

1½ teaspoons vanilla extract

3 cups all-purpose flour

1½ teaspoons poppy seeds

1½ teaspoons baking powder

1½ teaspoons salt

GLAZE

2 teaspoons butter or margarine

¾ cup sugar

¼ cup orange juice

½ teaspoon vanilla extract

½ teaspoon almond extract

"This recipe came from a dear aunt years ago. It's so well received in my family, a brother-in-law doesn't think his holidays are complete until he has his own loaf!"

1. Preheat the oven to 350°F. Grease two 9 × 5-inch loaf pans or four 4 × 2-inch mini-loaf pans.

2. To prepare the bread, combine the oil and eggs in a large bowl and whisk until well blended and fluffy. Add the sugar; mix well. Stir in the remaining bread ingredients until just blended. The batter will be very thin.

3. Pour the batter into the prepared pans. Bake the large loaves for 45 minutes, or until a wooden pick inserted in the center comes out clean. Bake the small loaves for 30 minutes.

4. To prepare the glaze, combine all of the ingredients in a small saucepan over low heat. Heat until the sugar dissolves, stirring frequently.

5. Remove the bread from the oven and immediately poke holes in the top with a wooden pick or fork. Pour the glaze evenly over each loaf. Let stand for 15 to 20 minutes before removing the bread from the pans to a wire rack to cool completely.

74 **Hometown Recipes for the Holidays**

Chocolate Chip Pumpkin Bread

Marsha Baker, Pioneer, Ohio

SERVES 24

1 cup packed dark brown sugar

1 cup granulated sugar

2/3 cup butter or margarine, softened

3 eggs

One 15-ounce can pumpkin

1/2 cup milk or water

2 teaspoons baking soda

1 teaspoon salt

1 teaspoon ground cinnamon

1/2 teaspoon ground cloves

2 1/3 cups all-purpose flour

2 cups semisweet chocolate chips

"I've baked this fragrant bread for years. The combination of cloves and chocolate makes it different, and it's a perfect choice for holiday gift giving—when I can get the loaves away from my family."

1. Preheat the oven to 350°F. Grease four 6 × 3-inch mini-loaf pans.

2. Combine the brown sugar, granulated sugar, butter, and eggs in a large bowl. Using a mixer at medium-high speed, beat until creamy.

3. Add the pumpkin, milk, baking soda, salt, cinnamon, and cloves and beat at low speed until smooth.

4. Stir in the flour until just blended. Fold in the chips. Pour the batter into the prepared pans.

5. Bake for 35 to 40 minutes until a wooden pick inserted in the center of the loaf comes out clean. Cool completely on wire racks.

Gramma Tillie's Pumpkin Bread

Tillie B. Vaughan, Victorville, California

1 cup olive oil or vegetable oil

3 cups sugar

4 eggs

1 2/3 cups pumpkin

3 1/3 cups all-purpose flour

1 1/4 teaspoons salt

2 teaspoons baking soda

2 teaspoons ground cinnamon

2 teaspoons ground nutmeg

2 teaspoons ground ginger

1 cup chopped walnuts, optional

TIPS FROM OUR TEST KITCHEN

If you prefer to make cupcakes, pour the batter into muffin tins and bake for 50 to 55 minutes.

"Back in the 1960s, I became hostess for our family's Thanksgiving dinners. This recipe has been a mainstay. I'm now seventy-seven and have baked as many as thirty-six loaves for gifts."

1. Preheat the oven to 350°F. Lightly grease three 9 × 5-inch loaf pans.

2. Combine the olive oil, sugar, eggs, and pumpkin in a large bowl. Using a mixer, beat well.

3. Mix the flour, salt, baking soda, cinnamon, nutmeg, and ginger in a separate bowl. Add the flour mixture to the pumpkin mixture gradually, beating at low speed. Stir in the walnuts, if using.

4. Fill the prepared pans half full. Bake for 1 hour, or until a wooden pick inserted near the center comes out clean.

Irish Soda Bread

Judy Lynn, Huntley, Illinois

5 cups all-purpose flour

1 cup sugar

1 tablespoon baking powder

1 teaspoon baking soda

1½ teaspoons salt

½ cup (1 stick) cold unsalted butter, cut into ¼-inch cubes

2½ cups raisins

3 tablespoons caraway seeds

2½ cups whole buttermilk

1 egg, beaten

"Soda bread is popular in Ireland, especially with afternoon tea. As with any oft-made recipe, everyone makes it a little differently and is sure theirs is the best. My mother-in-law always baked it for St. Patrick's Day, and now I carry on the tradition."

1. Preheat the oven to 350°F. Grease two 9 × 5-inch loaf pans.

2. Combine the flour, sugar, baking powder, baking soda, and salt in a large bowl. Cut in the butter, using two knives or a pastry blender, until the mixture is the texture of cornmeal.

3. Add the raisins and caraway seeds; mix well. Add the buttermilk and egg and stir until just blended.

4. Divide the batter evenly between the prepared pans. Bake for 50 minutes, or until golden. Cool on a wire rack for 10 minutes before removing from the pans to cool completely.

Whole Wheat Soda Bread

Theresa Slemp, Afton, Tennessee

SERVES 10 TO 12

1 cup all-purpose flour
2 tablespoons brown sugar
1 teaspoon baking soda
1/2 teaspoon salt
2 tablespoons cold butter
2 cups whole wheat flour
1/2 cup old-fashioned oats
1 1/2 cups buttermilk

"This hearty bread goes very nicely with soups. It is my most requested bread."

1. Preheat the oven to 375°F. Grease a baking sheet.

2. Combine the all-purpose flour, brown sugar, baking soda, and salt in a large bowl; mix well. Cut in the butter using a pastry cutter or two knives. Stir in the whole wheat flour and oats.

3. Make a well in the center of the mixture and pour in the buttermilk all at once. Mix with a fork until well blended.

4. Turn the dough onto a floured board and knead for 1 minute. Shape into a ball and set on the baking sheet. Press into a 6-inch circle. Cut a cross in the top.

5. Bake for 40 minutes, or until well browned and the loaf sounds hollow when tapped on the bottom.

Melt-in-Your-Mouth German Buns

Elizabeth Rau, Westphalia, Iowa

SERVES 28

1 teaspoon salt
1 cup plus 1½ teaspoons sugar
⅓ cup vegetable shortening
Two ¼-ounce packages active dry yeast
10 to 11 cups all-purpose flour

"This is a seventy-year-old recipe handed down from my mother-in-law. I've baked thousands of rolls for grateful recipients through the years and still bake weekly."

1. Combine 4 cups warm water (105° to 115°F) and salt in a large bowl; mix well. Add 1 cup of the sugar, the shortening, and yeast and stir gently to dissolve the yeast.

2. When the yeast starts to foam, add the flour, 2 cups at a time, until the dough is elastic.

3. Turn the dough onto a lightly floured work surface and knead until smooth and satiny, about 5 minutes.

4. Place the dough in a large greased bowl. Set in a warm place and let rise, covered, until doubled in size, 1 to 2 hours. Punch down the dough, cover with a cloth, and let rise again until doubled, ½ to 1 hour.

5. Preheat the oven to 350°F. Pinch off pieces of dough about the size of walnuts and roll into 56 balls. Place on two 17 × 11-inch cookie sheets and flatten slightly. Do not crowd the buns. Bake for 12 to 15 minutes until golden brown. Do not overbake.

6. Combine the remaining 1½ teaspoons sugar and ½ cup warm water in a small bowl; stir until the sugar dissolves. Brush the glaze on the hot rolls.

Christmas Cinnamon Rolls

Connie Lahey, Bethalto, Illinois

SERVES 30

ROLLS

2 cups milk

Two ¼-ounce packages active dry yeast

½ cup shortening

½ cup granulated sugar

2 eggs

1 tablespoon salt

7 to 8 cups all-purpose flour

SYRUP

One 16-ounce package light brown sugar

½ cup white corn syrup

½ cup milk

¼ cup (½ stick) butter

1½ cups chopped pecans, or to taste, optional

FILLING

¼ cup (½ stick) butter, softened

½ cup (1 stick) margarine, softened

1⅓ cups packed light brown sugar

2 tablespoons plus 2 teaspoons ground cinnamon

"Our mother, Dorothy Lahey, always made a big impression with her famous cinnamon rolls. She loved her kitchen, and the cinnamon rolls were top priority in our family, especially at the holidays. When we were all adults, we thought, 'Forget the presents under the tree.' When it was time to leave, we each got a package of cinnamon rolls to take home. The day she passed away, there were two dozen in the freezer. Today, there are four surviving children, all with memories of our mother that will live on as we carry on the tradition of making her cinnamon rolls."

1. To prepare the rolls, heat the milk in a small saucepan until scalded and set aside to cool to 110°F. Dissolve the yeast in ¼ cup warm water (105° to 115°F) in a small bowl.

2. Cream the shortening and granulated sugar in a large bowl, using a mixer at medium-high speed, until light and fluffy. Beat in the eggs and salt. Add the yeast mixture and warm milk. Reduce the mixer to medium speed and gradually add 3 cups of the flour, 1 cup at a time, blending well after each addition. Stir in the remaining flour, 1 cup at a time, until a stiff dough forms.

3. Turn the dough onto a floured work surface and knead for about 5 minutes until smooth and elastic. Place the dough in a large greased bowl, turning once to coat both sides. Cover and place in a warm area until doubled in size, 1 to 2 hours.

4. To prepare the syrup, combine the light brown sugar, corn syrup, milk, and butter in a medium saucepan. Cook over medium heat, stirring constantly, just until the sugar is dissolved. Do not boil. Set aside to cool.

5. Lightly coat five 8-inch round or square pans with non-stick cooking spray. Pour 5 tablespoons of the syrup into each pan; sprinkle the pecans, if using, over each pan. Punch down the dough and knead two or three times. Divide the dough into 4 pieces, keeping each piece covered until used.

6. To prepare the filling, combine the softened butter and margarine in a small bowl; mix well. Combine the brown sugar and cinnamon in a bowl.

7. Working with one-quarter of the dough at a time, roll it out into a 19 × 24-inch rectangle. Spread one-quarter of the butter mixture evenly over the dough. Sprinkle one-quarter of the sugar mixture over the dough. Using a rolling pin, roll the topping mixture into the dough. Drizzle with 3 to 4 tablespoons of the syrup.

8. Roll up the dough jelly-roll style, starting at the small end and pinching the seam to seal. Slice into 15 pieces each and place 12 in each prepared pan, cut side down. Repeat with the remaining dough and filling. Cover and let rise in a warm place for about 1 hour until doubled in size.

9. Preheat the oven to 350°F. Bake for 18 minutes, or until golden brown. Do not overbake. Remove from the oven, let stand for 5 minutes, and invert onto plates.

Garlic Parmesan Rolls

Loyd Patton, Spokane, Washington

SERVES 16 TO 24

Two ¼-ounce packages active dry yeast

1 cup sugar

2 eggs, beaten

1 cup (2 sticks) butter or margarine, melted

2 teaspoons salt

10 cups all-purpose flour

5 medium garlic cloves, minced

1 cup grated Parmesan

"I went to work in the kitchen, experimenting with different kinds of breads. These savory rolls started out as a recipe for crescent rolls. I played with it a while and decided to add garlic butter and Parmesan to give it a kick."

1. Combine the yeast with 1½ cups warm water (105° to 115°F) in a large bowl. Cover and let stand for 5 minutes.

2. Add 1½ cups warm water (110° to 115°F), the sugar, eggs, ½ cup of the melted butter, the salt, and 5 cups of the flour; mix well. Add the remaining flour, 1 cup at a time, to form a soft dough.

3. Turn the dough onto a lightly floured work surface and knead until elastic. Place in a greased bowl, turning the dough to grease the entire surface. Cover with plastic wrap and let rise 1 hour, or until doubled in size.

4. Preheat the oven to 375°F. Combine the remaining ½ cup melted butter with the garlic in a small bowl and set aside.

5. Punch the dough down and turn onto a floured work surface. Cut the dough into 3 or 4 equal sections. Three sections will make 24 large rolls that can be used for sandwiches. Four sections will make 32 smaller dinner rolls. Roll each section into a circle 12 to 15 inches in diameter, depending on the size of the rolls desired.

Refrigerate any leftover rolls in an airtight container.

6. Baste the sections with ¼ cup of the garlic butter and sprinkle with ½ cup of the Parmesan. Using a pizza cutter or a sharp knife, cut each circle into 8 wedges and roll up from the smaller end. Baste the rolls with the remaining garlic butter and sprinkle with the remaining Parmesan.

7. Arrange the rolls on two baking sheets, 12 to a sheet. Place them close but not touching, seam side down.

8. Bake one sheet of rolls at a time for 15 minutes, or until golden brown. Cover the other baking sheet while the first is in the oven.

Kolac

Robert Shranko, Prescott, Arizona

DOUGH

Two ¼-ounce packages active dry yeast

1 cup vegetable shortening

1 cup sugar

1 teaspoon salt

2 eggs

6 to 6½ cups all-purpose flour

FILLING

1 pound walnuts, ground

1½ to 2 cups sugar, or to taste

1½ to 2 teaspoons ground nutmeg, or to taste

ASSEMBLY

2 cups (4 sticks) butter, melted

"These walnut-filled sweet rolls came from Slovakia when my mother emigrated to the United States about 1920. The ground-walnut filling is my favorite, but my mother also made it with ground poppy seeds. She liked to give away loaves because it made her feel good. My brother, my son, and I carry on the family legacy of baking this old-world pastry."

1. To prepare the dough, combine the yeast with 1 cup warm water (105° to 115°F) in a small bowl; stir to dissolve the yeast. Combine 1 cup warm water (105° to 115°F) and the shortening in a separate bowl and stir until the shortening dissolves.

2. Mix the sugar, salt, eggs, yeast mixture, and shortening mixture in a large bowl.

3. Add 6 cups of the flour, 2 cups at a time. Turn the dough out onto a floured board and knead until smooth, adding another ½ cup flour if needed. Cover and let rise in a warm place until doubled, ½ to 1 hour.

4. To prepare the filling, combine all of the ingredients in a medium bowl; mix well.

5. To assemble, separate the dough into 5 pieces. On a floured surface, roll out each piece of dough into a 10 × 15-inch rectangle. Brush each piece with about ⅓ cup of the melted butter and sprinkle 1½ cups of the filling mixture evenly over the dough. Roll up the dough jelly-roll style to form a 15-inch roll and place on a cookie sheet. Repeat with the remain-

ing dough pieces. Place the rolls on the cookie sheets about 2 inches apart. Cover and let rise in a warm place for 1 hour.

6. Preheat the oven to 350°F. Bake for 20 to 25 minutes until golden. Brush lightly with melted butter, if desired. Place on wire racks to cool completely before slicing each roll into 15 pieces.

Sour Cream Buns

Heather Stine, Catawissa, Pennsylvania

One ¼-ounce package active dry yeast

One 8-ounce container sour cream

3 tablespoons granulated sugar

2 tablespoons vegetable shortening

1 teaspoon salt

⅛ teaspoon baking soda

1 egg

3¼ cups all-purpose flour

2 tablespoons butter, softened

⅓ cup packed dark brown sugar

1 to 1½ teaspoons ground cinnamon, or
   to taste

¾ cup confectioners' sugar

"My grandmother was a woman after my own heart. She loved making people happy with the food that she prepared. That's where my love of cooking began. I enjoy making people smile by cooking for them and have even thought about opening my own restaurant. I got this recipe from her years before she passed away."

1. Dissolve the yeast in ¼ cup warm water (105° to 115°F) in a large bowl. Combine the sour cream, granulated sugar, shortening, and salt in a small saucepan. Heat until the mixture reaches a temperature of 120° to 130°F and the shortening is almost melted.

2. Add the baking soda to the sour cream mixture and remove from the heat. Add the sour cream mixture and the egg to the yeast mixture. Stir in 3 cups of the flour.

3. Place the dough on a lightly floured surface and knead in enough of the remaining flour to make a moderately soft dough. Let stand, covered, for 5 minutes.

4. Grease a muffin tin and set aside. Roll the dough into a 12 × 18-inch rectangle. Spread the butter evenly over the dough.

5. Combine the brown sugar and cinnamon in a small bowl and sprinkle evenly over the dough. Starting from the long side, roll up, seal the seam, and slice into 12 pieces, about 1½ inches wide.

6. Place each bun, cut side down, in a muffin tin cup. Cover and let rise in a warm place until the buns are ¼ to ½ inch above the tops of the cups, 1 to 1½ hours.

7. Preheat the oven to 400°F. Bake the buns for 15 minutes, or until golden brown. Remove from the pan and arrange on a serving platter.

8. Combine the confectioners' sugar with 2 to 4 teaspoons water in a small bowl to make an icing thin enough to drizzle. Drizzle evenly over the buns.

Sour Cream Nut Rolls

Margaret Kopach, Charleroi, Pennsylvania

SERVES 30

PASTRY

Two ¼-ounce packages active dry yeast

½ cup lukewarm milk

5 cups all-purpose flour

5 tablespoons sugar

1 teaspoon salt

1 cup (2 sticks) butter

3 egg yolks

1 cup sour cream

FILLING

½ cup (1 stick) butter

¼ cup milk

1½ to 2 pounds walnuts, ground

2 cups sugar

1 tablespoon vanilla extract

TIPS FROM OUR TEST KITCHEN

Pour icing made from 2 cups confectioners' sugar and 2 to 4 tablespoons milk over the top when the rolls are cool.

"I make this nut-roll recipe for Easter and Christmas. A longtime friend, who got the recipe from her mother, gave it to me."

1. To prepare the pastry, dissolve the yeast in the warm milk (105° to 115°F) in a small bowl. Combine the flour, sugar, and salt in a large bowl.

2. Cut the butter into the flour mixture using a pastry cutter or two knives. Add the yeast mixture, egg yolks, and sour cream. Knead slightly until smooth. Form into a large ball, cover with plastic wrap, and refrigerate overnight.

3. To prepare the filling, combine the butter and milk in a small saucepan. Heat until the butter melts. Combine the ground walnuts and sugar in a large bowl. Stir in the butter mixture and vanilla; mix well.

4. Divide the dough into 5 equal balls. Lightly sprinkle flour over a large, flat surface. With a rolling pin, roll out each ball into a large rectangle, about 10 × 12 inches.

5. Preheat the oven to 350°F. Spread the filling down the middle of each rectangle. Roll the dough and pinch the seams and ends. Transfer the rolls to a baking sheet and bake for 30 to 35 minutes until golden brown. Cut into 2-inch slices to serve.

Soups

Tradition often has a hand in planning the soup course for a special menu. What is New Year's Day—at least in the South—without black-eyed peas? The peas are the star of the Black-Eyed Pea Soup that Joyce Gates of Clovis, New Mexico, cooks each January. If her son can't be at home, Gates makes sure to freeze some for him.

For Joni Hilton of Rocklin, California, and Dee Shanklin of New Smyrna Beach, Florida, St. Patrick's Day provides an irresistible opportunity to salute the holiday's signature color—green—or potatoes, one of Ireland's most famous crops. Hilton's Leprechaun Soup is a favorite of her four children with its "golden" corn nuggets and peas. Shanklin, a native of St. Louis, Missouri, now lives in the Sunshine State. She prepares Cream of Potato Soup each March because, as she says, "If you are Irish, you have potatoes in your bones."

A trip to the North Carolina state farmers' market in Raleigh, North Carolina, inspired Sam McDaniel to create Spiced Sweet Potato Soup with Maple Crème Fraîche. With sweet potatoes plentiful and inexpensive, McDaniel says the soup is a good choice for Thanksgiving or Christmas dinner—or any evening meal.

Other recipes that take advantage of seasonal produce are Fantastic Fennel Pumpkin Soup, by Margee Berry of Trout Lake, Washington, and Carolina Chicken and Collard Greens Stew, by Candace McMenamin of Lexington, South Carolina.

Julia M. Wall of Rushville, Illinois, reports her widely scattered extended family has come up with a creative solution to gathering everyone together for Christmas. With weather and travel constraints, Wall's relatives congregate at her home in midsummer to celebrate Christmas in July—starring Christmas in July Soup, a tomato soup featuring the red, ripe fruit at its peak. Their innovative celebration and the garden-fresh soup meet with everyone's approval.

Black Bean Soup

Virgie Griffith, Washington, Texas

SERVES 4 TO 6

1 tablespoon vegetable oil

⅔ cup chopped onions

1 tablespoon ground cumin

Three 15-ounce cans black beans

One 15-ounce can chicken broth

3 cups medium-chunky salsa

Juice and zest of 1 lime

¼ cup chopped cilantro, optional

Sour cream, optional

"When I came across this recipe, it sounded interesting, so I tried it. I'm glad I did—my husband and I could hardly put down our spoons."

1. Heat the vegetable oil in a large saucepan. Add the onions and cumin and cook over medium heat until the onions are tender.

2. Puree 2 cans of beans with their liquid and the chicken broth in a blender. Add to the saucepan.

3. Stir in the remaining can of beans, the salsa, lime juice and zest, and cilantro, if using. Bring to a boil. Reduce the heat to low and simmer, uncovered, for 30 minutes. Top each serving with a dollop of sour cream, if using.

Black-Eyed Pea Soup

Joyce Gates, Clovis, New Mexico

1 pound ground beef

1 cup finely chopped onions

1 pound Polish sausage, cut into bite-sized pieces

Two 15-ounce cans black-eyed peas with jalapeños

One 14-ounce can beef broth

One 14-ounce can diced tomatoes

One 10-ounce can mild diced tomatoes and green chiles

One 4-ounce can chopped mild green chiles

1 to 2 medium jalapeño chiles, seeded and chopped, optional

⅛ teaspoon salt

TIPS FROM OUR TEST KITCHEN

Browning the sausage before adding it to the pot adds flavor.

"This soup is a must when family is home at New Year's. If my son can't be here, I freeze it for him. It's also always on the stove during deer season to provide hungry hunters with a filling, warm lunch. Serve it with corn bread, salad, and dessert."

1. Place a Dutch oven over medium-high heat. Add the ground beef and onions and cook until the beef is browned, stirring frequently.

2. Add the sausage, black-eyed peas, broth, diced tomatoes, tomatoes with chiles, green chiles, jalapeños, if using, and salt; mix well.

3. Bring the mixture to a boil, reduce the heat, and cover tightly. Simmer for 45 minutes.

4. Refrigerate overnight to allow the flavors to blend. Reheat before serving.

Broccoli Soup

Cindy Sickbert, Rushville, Indiana

1 cup (2 sticks) butter or margarine

1 cup all-purpose flour

4 cups chicken broth

1 pound broccoli, cut into bite-sized
   pieces

8 ounces sliced mushrooms

4 cups half-and-half

¼ teaspoon dried tarragon leaves,
   crushed

2 teaspoons salt

¼ teaspoon white or black pepper

TIPS FROM OUR TEST KITCHEN

Be careful not to allow the soup to come to a full boil after the cream mixture is added. It will boil over and the cream may curdle.

"When I was a child, we always had soup on Christmas Eve. My siblings and I have continued the tradition when we get together for the holidays now. As our taste buds have changed, so have the soup choices. This is one of our favorites."

1. Place a Dutch oven over medium heat. Add the butter and when it is melted, whisk in the flour until well blended. Add the broth, whisking constantly, and increase the heat to medium-high. Bring the mixture to a boil, stirring frequently.

2. Add the remaining ingredients and return the mixture just to a boil. Reduce the heat and simmer, uncovered, stirring occasionally, until the broccoli is very tender, about 25 minutes.

Cauliflower Soup

Bryon Klapal, Castle Rock, Colorado

¼ cup (½ stick) plus 2 tablespoons butter

½ cup finely chopped onions

1 large head cauliflower, cut into florets

3 medium baking potatoes, peeled and
   sliced

1 cup thinly sliced celery

1 small carrot, grated

4 cups chicken broth

1 bay leaf

⅛ teaspoon dried tarragon

¼ cup all-purpose flour

1 cup milk

1½ cups half-and-half

1 teaspoon salt, or to taste

¼ teaspoon white pepper, or to taste

2 cups shredded Cheddar

¾ cup chopped green onions, optional

"Often an overlooked vegetable, cauliflower is the star in this soup. Don't let the long list of ingredients intimidate you. The recipe is not complicated, and the resulting taste is worth the effort."

1. Place a Dutch oven over medium heat. Add 2 tablespoons butter. When the butter is melted, add the onions and cook for 2 to 3 minutes, stirring frequently.

2. Add the cauliflower, potatoes, celery, carrot, and broth. Bring the mixture to a boil over high heat. Reduce the heat and simmer, covered tightly, for 15 minutes, or until the cauliflower and potatoes are just tender. Add the bay leaf and tarragon.

3. Melt the remaining ¼ cup butter in a heavy saucepan over medium-low heat. Whisk in the flour and add the milk gradually, stirring constantly. Cook until the sauce thickens, stirring frequently.

4. Add the milk mixture to the cauliflower mixture; mix well. Stir in the half-and-half, salt, and pepper.

5. Simmer, uncovered, for 15 minutes. Remove from the heat and discard the bay leaf. At this point, you may refrigerate the soup until serving time. Reheat the soup and add the Cheddar, just before serving, stirring until melted. Top with green onions, if desired.

Carolina Chicken and Collard Greens Stew

Candace McMenamin, Lexington, South Carolina

SERVES 4

3 cups chicken broth

1 pound boneless, skinless chicken thighs

1 medium onion, diced

1 garlic clove, minced

1 celery stalk, sliced

1 medium carrot, sliced

1 large potato, diced

1 tablespoon chopped thyme or
 ½ teaspoon dried thyme

1 tablespoon chopped basil or
 ½ teaspoon dried basil

1 tablespoon chopped oregano or
 ½ teaspoon dried oregano

1 tablespoon sugar

2 tablespoons white vinegar

4 cups loosely packed chopped collard
 greens

1 teaspoon salt

½ teaspoon black pepper

4 crisply cooked bacon slices

½ cup chopped pecans, toasted

"This is one of my family's favorite recipes. Collard greens are plentiful here in the South, and I developed this recipe to showcase them in a stew. Some folks say they don't like the taste of collards, but I believe that is because they have not had them fixed correctly. Trust me, anyone who tries this stew with a chunk of homemade corn bread will be begging for the recipe."

1. Heat the chicken broth and 3 cups water in a large Dutch oven over medium-high heat. Bring the mixture to a boil. Add the chicken thighs. Reduce the heat and simmer, covered, until thoroughly cooked, about 15 minutes. Remove the chicken to a plate with a slotted spoon; keep warm.

2. Add the onion, garlic, celery, carrot, potato, thyme, basil, and oregano to the broth. Stir and bring to a boil. Reduce the heat and simmer, covered, until the potatoes are tender, about 10 minutes.

3. Stir in the sugar, vinegar, collard greens, salt, and pepper. Return to a boil, reduce the heat, and simmer, covered, for 10 minutes.

4. Shred the chicken into 1-inch strips and add to the stew; mix well. Simmer over medium heat until the chicken is thoroughly heated, about 2 minutes.

5. Ladle the stew into 4 shallow soup bowls. Crumble 1 bacon slice over each serving. Sprinkle pecans over the top. Serve immediately.

Cheesy Chicken Chowder

Marsha Baker, Pioneer, Ohio

3 cups chicken broth

2 cups diced, peeled potatoes

1 cup diced carrots

1 cup diced celery

½ cup diced onions

1½ teaspoons salt

¼ teaspoon pepper

¼ cup (½ stick) butter or margarine

⅓ cup all-purpose flour

2 cups milk

2 cups shredded Cheddar

2 cups diced, cooked chicken

"All three of my grown children have requested this dish after I served it to them one time. I make it to give to folks who aren't feeling well. It's simple to make and doesn't require any fancy ingredients. This is great comfort food."

1. Bring the chicken broth to a boil in a large pan. Reduce the heat and add the potatoes, carrots, celery, onions, salt, and pepper. Simmer, covered, until the vegetables are tender, about 15 minutes.

2. Melt the butter in a medium saucepan. Add the flour and mix well. Stir in the milk gradually and cook over low heat until slightly thickened, about 3 minutes. Stir in the Cheddar and heat until melted, about 2 minutes. Add the Cheddar mixture to the broth and vegetables along with the chicken. Cook and stir over low heat until thoroughly heated, about 3 minutes.

Spicy Chicken Soup

Sonya Barron, Hamilton, Texas

SERVES 6 TO 8

1 skinless, bone-in chicken breast

¼ teaspoon dried basil

1 tablespoon salt

1 garlic clove, minced

One 10-ounce can tomatoes and green chiles

1 medium carrot, sliced

3 celery stalks, chopped

1½ cups small shell pasta

Shredded Colby-Jack

Flour tortillas

Tortilla chips

"We have lived miles from any grocery store most of my life. I would want to fix a recipe only to discover that my pantry lacked some of the essential ingredients. I created this soup on a frosty winter evening from what I had in the pantry and refrigerator."

1. Combine the chicken, basil, salt, garlic, and 4 cups water in a large saucepan. Bring to a boil, reduce the heat, and simmer, covered, until the chicken is done, about 45 minutes. Remove the chicken to cool, reserving the broth in the pan.

2. Add the tomatoes and chiles, carrot, celery, pasta, and 2 to 4 more cups of water to the pan. Simmer, uncovered, until the vegetables are tender, about 20 minutes.

3. Remove the chicken from the bone and chop into ½-inch chunks. Return the chicken to the soup and heat thoroughly. Serve with shredded Colby-Jack cheese and warmed flour tortillas or tortilla chips.

Leprechaun Soup

Joni Hilton, Rocklin, California

3 tablespoons butter

One 10-ounce package frozen green
    peas, thawed

1 medium head Boston lettuce, chopped

4 medium green onions, chopped
    (green and white parts)

5 cups chicken broth

One 15-ounce can corn kernels, drained

Salt and pepper

½ cup sour cream

"This festive soup with bits of Leprechaun gold in it is always fun to serve on St. Patrick's Day. You don't have to be Irish to enjoy it! My four kids and husband love it, and the children enjoy finding the gold nuggets—the corn—in their bowls."

1. Melt the butter in a Dutch oven over medium-high heat. Add the peas, lettuce, and green onions to the melted butter. Cook until the onions are translucent, stirring frequently.

2. Add the broth and bring the mixture to a boil. Reduce the heat and simmer, uncovered, until the peas are tender, about 8 minutes.

3. Working in 1-cup batches, puree the broth mixture in the blender. Return the pureed mixture to the Dutch oven. Add the corn and cook over medium-high heat for 2 to 3 minutes, or until thoroughly heated. Season with salt and pepper.

4. To serve, ladle the soup into individual serving bowls and top each serving with 1 to 2 tablespoons sour cream. If desired, spoon sour cream into a plastic bag and snip one corner to pipe it onto the soup in a decorative manner.

Savory Mushroom and Barley Soup

Laura Frerich, Napoleon, Ohio

1 tablespoon olive oil

2 cups chopped onions

1 cup chopped celery

1½ pounds sliced mushrooms

6 cups beef broth

½ cup quick-cooking barley

2 cups sliced carrots

One 6-ounce can tomato paste

½ teaspoon salt, or to taste

½ cup finely chopped parsley

TIPS FROM OUR TEST KITCHEN

To substitute pearl barley for the quick-cooking variety, combine ¾ cup pearl barley and 4 cups water in a saucepan. Simmer, covered, until partially cooked, about 30 minutes. Do not drain. Add this mixture when the beef broth is added.

"This flavorful soup reminds me of a mushroom-Swiss hamburger. I like to have it on hand for Thanksgiving weekend meals when we have company. It's easy to make ahead of time and reheat when guests arrive."

1. Heat the olive oil in a Dutch oven over medium heat. Add the onions and celery and cook, stirring frequently, until tender, about 8 minutes Add the mushrooms and cook for 5 minutes, stirring frequently. Stir in the broth.

2. Bring the mixture to a boil. Add the barley, carrots, and tomato paste. Reduce the heat and simmer, covered, for 30 minutes, stirring occasionally.

3. Remove from the heat. Stir in the salt and parsley and let stand for 30 minutes to thicken slightly and allow the flavors to blend.

Cream of Potato Soup

Dee Shanklin, New Smyrna Beach, Florida

SERVES 7

3 pounds baking potatoes (about
    8 medium), peeled and diced

1½ cups chopped onions

1 medium jalapeño chile or ¼ teaspoon
    dried red pepper flakes

1½ tablespoons salt

½ teaspoon black pepper

½ cup (1 stick) butter

½ cup heavy cream

1 cup milk

Salt and pepper

Chopped parsley

TIPS FROM OUR TEST KITCHEN

For a thinner consistency, add more milk or cream.

"I am of Irish descent and I love to celebrate St. Patrick's Day. I've prepared this soup for many occasions and always find it a pure delight. If you are Irish, you have potatoes in your bones."

1. Bring 8 cups water to a boil in a Dutch oven. Add the potatoes, onions, jalapeño, salt, and black pepper. Return to a boil.

2. Reduce the heat and simmer, uncovered, until the potatoes are tender when pierced with a fork, about 18 minutes.

3. Remove from the heat. Mash the potato mixture using a potato masher. For a creamier consistency, purée about 4 cups of the potato mixture in a blender, working in batches and holding the lid down securely. Return the puréed potatoes to the Dutch oven.

4. Add the butter, cream, and milk; mix well. Season with salt and pepper. Top each serving with a small amount of parsley.

Spiced Sweet Potato Soup With Maple Crème Fraîche

Sam McDaniel, Cary, North Carolina   SERVES 4 TO 6

CRÈME FRAÎCHE

1/2 cup sour cream

1/2 cup heavy cream

1/4 cup pure maple syrup

SOUP

2 tablespoons extra virgin olive oil

1 medium yellow onion, diced

2 pounds sweet potatoes, peeled and cut into 1/2-inch cubes

4 cinnamon sticks

10 whole cloves

1/4 teaspoon ground nutmeg

4 cups chicken broth

Salt and coarsely ground black pepper

1/4 cup toasted walnuts

"I came up with this recipe after an autumn trip to the North Carolina state farmers' market, where sweet potatoes were available for pennies a pound. The flavors are simple enough for everyday, but the soup is also elegant enough to serve for Thanksgiving or Christmas dinner."

1. To prepare the crème fraîche, whisk together the sour cream, heavy cream, and maple syrup in a small bowl. Let stand at room temperature.

2. To prepare the soup, heat the olive oil in a large pot; add the onion. Sauté, stirring frequently, until the onion is translucent, about 5 minutes. Add the sweet potatoes, cinnamon sticks, cloves, nutmeg, and broth. Bring to a boil. Reduce the heat and simmer, covered, until the potatoes are very tender, about 25 minutes. Remove 1 cup of the cooking liquid and set aside. Discard the cinnamon sticks and cloves.

3. Purée the sweet potatoes and stock using an immersion blender or a stand blender until very smooth. Add the reserved liquid as needed to achieve the desired consistency. Return to the pan and cook until thoroughly heated. Season with salt and pepper.

4. Ladle into large soup bowls. Garnish with a swirl of crème fraîche and a sprinkle of toasted walnuts.

Fantastic Fennel Pumpkin Soup

Margee Berry, Trout Lake, Washington

1 tablespoon olive oil

1 large fennel bulb, trimmed and chopped

1 cup chopped onions

4 medium garlic cloves, minced

3 cups chicken or vegetable broth

One 16-ounce can pumpkin

2 teaspoons chopped thyme leaves

Salt

2 cups chopped fresh shiitake mushroom caps

2 ounces Parmesan

TIPS FROM OUR TEST KITCHEN

You'll need about 5 ounces fresh shiitake mushrooms to yield 2 cups chopped mushroom caps.

"I created this recipe for Thanksgiving. It is fast and easy—a blessing in itself for holiday meal preparations—and it tastes like a gourmet soup from a nice restaurant."

1. Heat 2 teaspoons of the olive oil in a Dutch oven over medium heat. Add the fennel and onions and cook, stirring frequently, until the vegetables are tender, about 15 minutes. Add the garlic and cook for 15 seconds, stirring constantly. Remove from the heat.

2. Combine the fennel mixture, 1 cup of the chicken broth, and the pumpkin in a blender. Purée, tightly covered, until smooth, scraping down the sides occasionally with a rubber spatula.

3. Return the fennel mixture to the pan and add the remaining 2 cups broth and the thyme. Cook over medium-low heat for 10 minutes, stirring frequently. Season with salt.

4. Heat a skillet over medium heat. Add the remaining 1 teaspoon olive oil and tilt the skillet to lightly coat the bottom. Add the mushroom caps and cook for 5 minutes, stirring frequently.

5. To serve, spoon the soup into individual bowls and sprinkle with the chopped mushrooms. Using a vegetable peeler, shave the Parmesan over each serving.

Christmas in July Soup

Julia M. Wall, Rushville, Illinois

SERVES 4

3 tablespoons vegetable oil

½ cup finely chopped white onions

½ cup thinly sliced celery, cut on the
diagonal

1 medium garlic clove, minced

8 sage leaves, chopped

8 basil leaves, chopped

1 teaspoon chicken bouillon granules
(or 1 bouillon cube)

6 to 8 Roma tomatoes, peeled

2 cups chicken broth

TIPS FROM OUR TEST KITCHEN

Roma tomatoes are less watery than
regular tomatoes. If using regular
tomatoes, remove the seeds first. For a
thicker consistency, mix 1 tablespoon
flour with 1 tablespoon softened butter,
add to the soup, and cook for a few more
minutes. To peel tomatoes, cut a cross on
the top of each tomato. Bring water to
boil in a Dutch oven, add the tomatoes,
and simmer until the tomatoes begin to
split slightly, about 1 minute. Drain in a
colander and run under cold water to
stop the cooking process. Using a paring
knife, remove the peels easily.

"Our family is widely scattered across the United
States—including Hawaii—and winter weather
makes Christmas family reunions almost impossi-
ble. So we celebrate Christmas in July in Rushville,
Illinois. Mom's fresh tomato soup, made from Roma
tomatoes grown in my garden, is always in demand."

1. Heat the oil in a Dutch oven over medium heat. Add the
onions, celery, garlic, sage, basil, and bouillon granules.
Cook, stirring frequently, until the onions are soft, 2 to 3
minutes.

2. Add the tomatoes; reduce the heat to medium-low. Cook,
uncovered, for 15 minutes, stirring occasionally.

3. Add the chicken broth and bring the mixture to a boil. Reduce the heat and simmer, uncovered, for 15 minutes. Break
up any large pieces of tomato with a fork or potato masher.
Serve immediately.

Snow Day Vegetable Soup

Joann Simon, Wilkes-Barre, Pennsylvania

SERVES 8

½ cup (1 stick) unsalted butter

3 celery stalks, chopped

1 large white onion, chopped

2 green onions, chopped

½ garlic clove, minced

3 large white potatoes, diced

3 large carrots, diced

1½ teaspoons parsley, fresh or dried

1½ teaspoons thyme, fresh or dried

1½ teaspoons basil, fresh or dried

1 or 2 bay leaves

Garlic salt

3½ quarts chicken broth or water

15 ounces tomato paste

1 cup green peas, fresh or frozen

1 cup corn, fresh or frozen

1 cup green beans, fresh or frozen

Grated Parmesan

"This recipe has been in the family for years. My husband and I have always believed in a good hearty soup for a cold, snowy day."

1. Melt the butter in a large Dutch oven. Add the celery, onion, green onions, garlic, potatoes, and carrots; sauté until slightly tender. Add the parsley, thyme, basil, and bay leaves; mix well. Season with garlic salt to taste.

2. Add the chicken broth and tomato paste. Bring to a boil. Add the peas, corn, and green beans. Reduce the heat and simmer, covered, for 45 minutes to 1 hour. Discard the bay leaves. Garnish with Parmesan.

Winter-Busting White Chili

Mike and Melinda Rhodes, Capron, Illinois

SERVES 7

One 16-ounce package dried navy or Great Northern beans, rinsed

1 pound mild Italian sausage, casings removed

1 cup chopped onions

1 cup chopped celery

1½ tablespoons chicken bouillon granules (or 4 bouillon cubes)

2 to 3 medium garlic cloves, minced

1½ teaspoons ground cumin

1 teaspoon dried oregano

¼ teaspoon hot pepper sauce, or to taste

2 to 3 cups cooked, diced chicken or turkey

One 4-ounce can chopped green chiles, drained

Salt and black pepper

1 cup freshly grated Parmesan

"We took a great chili recipe and elaborated on it to suit our tastes. It is awesome when topped with freshly grated Parmesan."

1. Bring 8 cups water to a boil in a Dutch oven. Add the beans and return to a boil. Reduce the heat and simmer, uncovered, for 2 minutes. Remove from the heat and let stand, covered, for 1 hour. Drain the beans.

2. Return the Dutch oven to medium heat, add the sausage, and cook until browned, breaking up large pieces while cooking. Remove the sausage to a bowl and refrigerate until needed.

3. Add 4 cups water to the Dutch oven; bring to a boil. Add the beans, onions, celery, bouillon, garlic, cumin, oregano, and hot pepper sauce. Return just to a boil. Reduce the heat and simmer, covered, until the beans are tender, 1½ to 1¾ hours.

4. Add the sausage, chicken, and green chiles to the pot. Cook for 3 minutes longer to thoroughly heat. Season with salt and pepper. Ladle into soup bowls and sprinkle Parmesan on top of each serving.

TIPS FROM OUR TEST KITCHEN

Flavors improve if the chili is refrigerated overnight. Reheat to serve.

FEBRUARY
[2]

Salads

The salad course is an important part of a holiday meal—not just an afterthought. Fresh produce at its peak is featured in many summertime salads that have become favorites at annual Memorial Day and July 4 celebrations around the country.

Diane Montagano of Plymouth, Michigan, is up with the birds to begin the festivities marking the nation's birthday, since her town's annual parade begins at 7:30 a.m. Sure to be on the red-white-and-blue menu is her Super Summer Salad, which showcases red, ripe tomatoes and cucumbers.

The cool, refreshing colors of Doris Ann Rose's Summertime Bean and Corn Salad make it a popular choice for the season's table. Rose, of Eddy, Texas, was the winner in the soup and salad category of the *American Profile* Holiday Recipe Contest.

Helen Heino of Dunlevy, Pennsylvania, grew up during the Depression and inherited her mother's love of gardening. Her Freezer Pickles make use of the season's bounty and provide a tasty addition to a meal long after summer is gone.

American Profile readers know how to add their own touch to potato salad, another staple of holiday gatherings. Michaela Rosenthal of Woodland Hills, California, uses applewood-smoked bacon and sun-dried tomatoes to give a distinctive flair to her Tangy Warm Potato Salad. And Grace Schroeder of Livonia, Michigan, prepares her mother's recipe for German Potato Salad for all of her family's gatherings.

Susan McFarland continues a family legacy with her great-grandmother's coleslaw recipe. The name says it all: The Best Coleslaw. McFarland, of Racine, Wisconsin, says it's the only coleslaw her family will eat.

Salad is far from forgotten in fall and winter. Rita Heitkamp of New Bremen, Ohio, always finds a spot at her crowded Thanksgiving table for Cranberry Freeze. It's a dish she has prepared for years for her six children, twenty-three grandchildren, and five great-grandchildren. For Ellen Schirmer of Spokane, Washington, it wouldn't be Thanksgiving without Grandma Julia's Fresh Cranberry Relish, a specialty of her mother's.

Summertime Bean and Corn Salad

Doris Ann Rose, Eddy, Texas

SERVES 14

One 15-ounce can black beans, rinsed and drained

One 15-ounce can yellow corn, rinsed and drained

One 15-ounce can white corn, rinsed and drained

1 cup thinly sliced celery

½ medium green bell pepper, chopped

½ medium red bell pepper, chopped

½ medium orange bell pepper, chopped

⅓ cup thinly sliced red onions

⅓ cup sliced stuffed green olives

⅓ cup extra virgin olive oil

¼ cup dry red wine

2 tablespoons lime juice

3 garlic cloves, minced

¾ teaspoon salt, or to taste

¼ teaspoon black pepper, or to taste

½ cup chopped cilantro

Lettuce leaves, optional

TIPS FROM OUR TEST KITCHEN

You may use one whole red or orange pepper instead of half of each, but the salad is very colorful with the variety of peppers.

"Summertime is striking in its colors. That means fast, attractive dishes with nutritious value. This recipe is cool and refreshing at summer luncheons and backyard cookouts."

1. Combine the beans, corns, celery, bell peppers, onions, and olives in a large bowl; toss gently to blend.

2. Combine the olive oil, wine, lime juice, garlic, salt, and pepper in a small bowl; mix lightly. Stir in the cilantro just until blended. Add to the bean mixture.

3. Cover the bowl with plastic wrap and refrigerate for 4 hours to allow the flavors to blend.

4. At serving time, line a platter with lettuce leaves, if desired, and spoon the salad on top.

Black-Eyed Pea Salad

Frances Barnwell, Marion, North Carolina

SERVES 8

Two 15-ounce cans black-eyed peas,
  rinsed and drained
½ cup thinly sliced red onion rings
½ cup finely chopped green bell pepper
½ teaspoon minced garlic
One 4-ounce jar diced pimientos,
  drained
¼ cup cider vinegar
¼ cup vegetable oil
1 teaspoon sugar
½ teaspoon salt, or to taste
⅛ teaspoon black pepper, or to taste
Hot pepper sauce

TIPS FROM OUR TEST KITCHEN

If canned black-eyed peas are not available, use one 16-ounce package frozen peas and cook according to the package directions. Pour the cooked peas into a colander and rinse under cold running water. Shake off excess liquid and season with salt.

"This is a delicious way to enjoy the traditional 'good luck' black-eyed peas on New Year's Day. I prepare most of the traditional foods for January 1 ahead of time, which allows me to watch the parades and football games."

1. Combine the peas, onion rings, bell pepper, garlic, pimientos, vinegar, oil, sugar, salt, pepper, and hot pepper sauce to taste in a medium bowl; mix well.

2. Cover the bowl with plastic wrap and refrigerate for at least 12 hours or overnight before serving.

Broccoli Bacon Salad

June Stoos, St. Cloud, Florida

SERVES 12 TO 16

1 bunch broccoli, broken into small
    florets (about 3 cups total)
1 bunch cauliflower, broken into small
    florets (about 3 cups total)
½ red onion, chopped
10 bacon slices, cooked and crumbled
1 cup raisins
½ cup shelled sunflower seeds
1 cup mayonnaise
½ cup sugar
2 tablespoons red wine vinegar

TIPS FROM OUR TEST KITCHEN

For variety, try toasted pecan pieces
in place of the sunflower seeds.

"I started serving this salad at showers and parties, but I found it was most appreciated on New Year's Day. It's very easy to prepare ahead of time. Just add the dressing before serving."

1. Combine the broccoli, cauliflower, onion, bacon, raisins, and sunflower seeds in a large bowl; mix gently.

2. Whisk together the mayonnaise, sugar, and vinegar in a small bowl. Refrigerate the salad and dressing separately until serving time.

3. To serve, pour the dressing over the broccoli mixture; toss to mix.

Cucumber Salad

Barb Jones, Panama, Illinois

SERVES 12

3 large cucumbers, thinly sliced

1 large green bell pepper, thinly sliced

1 cup thinly sliced onions

1 tablespoon celery seeds

1 tablespoon salt

½ cup cider vinegar

¾ cup sugar

TIPS FROM OUR TEST KITCHEN

The longer you store this salad in the refrigerator, the more reminiscent it is of crunchy, crisp bread-and-butter pickles. You may peel the cucumbers, if desired. For a festive look, cut thin strips from the cucumber, leaving alternate strips of green peel.

"Cucumber Salad is great for July 4 picnics—it stays crisp in a cooler. To make it more colorful, use ½ green bell pepper and ½ red bell pepper."

1. Combine the cucumbers, bell pepper, onions, celery seeds, and salt in a large bowl.

2. Cover with plastic wrap and let stand for 1 hour at room temperature.

3. Drain the cucumber mixture in a colander, shaking off the excess liquid. Return the mixture to the bowl.

4. Add the vinegar and sugar; toss gently. Cover with plastic wrap and refrigerate for 6 hours to overnight. The salad may be stored in the refrigerator for up to 3 weeks.

Freezer Pickles

Helen Heino, Dunlevy, Pennsylvania

SERVES 20

7 cups sliced cucumbers (about
   3 medium), peeled, if desired

1 cup sliced onions

1 medium green bell pepper, thinly sliced

1 medium red bell pepper, thinly sliced

1 cup white vinegar

2 cups sugar

1½ teaspoons salt

1 teaspoon celery seeds

1 teaspoon mustard seeds

TIPS FROM OUR TEST KITCHEN

The longer the pickles stand after thawing, the more blended the flavors become.

"I am eighty-five years old and grew up during the Depression. Mom took care of four children, and Dad worked in the coal mines. Mom had a big garden and she canned everything—now I do the same. I love gardening."

1. Combine the cucumbers, onions, bell peppers, vinegar, sugar, salt, celery seeds, and mustard seeds in a large bowl; stir gently to blend well.

2. Cover with plastic wrap and let stand at room temperature for 2 hours, stirring frequently.

3. Divide the mixture evenly between two quart-sized freezer bags. Seal tightly and freeze overnight or for up to 6 months. Thaw completely before serving. Store any leftovers in the refrigerator.

German Potato Salad

Grace Schroeder, Livonia, Michigan

SERVES 8

3 pounds baking potatoes

6 bacon slices

¾ cup chopped onions

⅓ to ½ cup cider vinegar

2 tablespoons sugar

½ teaspoon celery seeds

1 teaspoon salt

⅛ teaspoon black pepper

2 tablespoons all-purpose flour

TIPS FROM OUR TEST KITCHEN

You may need to gently turn the potato slices so the flavors become absorbed more evenly.

"Whenever we have a family get-together, I'm asked to bring the German Potato Salad. I like it much better than American potato salad. My mother made this recipe, and I inherited the job."

1. Place the potatoes in a Dutch oven with water to cover. Bring to a boil, reduce the heat, and simmer, uncovered, until the potatoes are just tender, 30 to 35 minutes. Do not overcook.

2. Drain the potatoes well and let stand for 15 to 20 minutes to cool slightly. Slice the potatoes and arrange in a shallow pasta bowl or a 13 × 9-inch glass baking dish.

3. Heat a large skillet over medium-high heat. Add the bacon and cook until crisp. Remove from the skillet and drain on paper towels.

4. Add the onions to the pan drippings and cook until translucent, about 3 minutes, stirring frequently. Stir in ¾ cup water, the vinegar, sugar, celery seeds, salt, and pepper. Whisk in the flour until well blended.

5. Bring the mixture to a boil and boil for 1 minute, stirring constantly. Remove from the heat and spoon evenly over the potatoes. Crumble the bacon and sprinkle on top. Let stand for 10 minutes to absorb the flavors.

Southwest Potato Salad

Phyllis Wong, Laughlin, Nevada

SERVES 6 TO 8

3 medium baking potatoes (about
    1 pound total), peeled if desired
¾ teaspoon salt
¾ cup light mayonnaise
1½ teaspoons Dijon mustard
⅛ to ¼ teaspoon cayenne pepper
6 jalapeño chile-stuffed olives, thinly
    sliced
½ cup finely chopped celery
¼ cup finely chopped onions
2 hard-cooked eggs, chopped

TIPS FROM OUR TEST KITCHEN

To speed the cooling process, cut the hot potatoes in half and refrigerate for 15 minutes. Cut into cubes.

"My favorite holiday is July 4. I love celebrating it with my friends with a barbecue, fresh corn, iced tea, and a cool potato salad on a hot summer day and then watching fireworks light up the night sky."

1. Combine the potatoes, 2 quarts water, and ½ teaspoon of the salt in a stockpot. Bring to a boil, reduce the heat, and simmer, covered, until the potatoes are tender when pierced with a fork, 30 to 35 minutes.

2. Drain well and cool completely, about 1 hour. Cut the cooled potatoes into cubes.

3. Combine the mayonnaise, mustard, the remaining ¼ teaspoon salt, and cayenne in a large bowl; mix well. Stir in the olives, celery, and onions. Add the potatoes and eggs; stir gently to blend. Serve immediately, or cover with plastic wrap and refrigerate until needed.

112 **Hometown Recipes for the Holidays**

Breakfast Granola (page 4)

*A*pple Pecan French Toast *(page 15)*

Lotta Lemon Pancake Roll-Ups (page 21)

Danish Puff (page 26)

Apricot- and Blueberry-Stuffed French Toast (page 16)

Hot and Crabby Dip (page 38)

Savory Three-Cheese Italian Pockets (page 58)

Artichoke Dip (page 36)

Sombrero Spread (page 45)

Mushroom Mini-Muffin Cups (page 54)

Smoky Salmon Spread (page 44)

Pitcher Punch (page 62)

Whole Wheat Soda Bread (page 78)

Cheese Garlic Bread Sticks (page 65)

Sour Cream Nut Rolls (page 88)

Gramma Tillie's Pumpkin Bread (page 76)

Garlic Parmesan Rolls (page 82)

Spicy Chicken Soup (page 96)

*Spiced Sweet Potato Soup with Maple
Crème Fraîche (page 100)*

*S*now Day Vegetable Soup (page 103)

Nature's Perfect Salad (page 123)   *Blueberry Jell-O Salad (page 120)*

Summertime Bean and Corn Salad (page 106)

Tangy Warm Potato Salad with Bacon and Sun-Dried Tomatoes

Michaela Rosenthal, Woodland Hills, California

SERVES 12

3 pounds baby new potatoes (2-inch diameter), scrubbed

1 teaspoon sea salt

½ pound applewood-smoked bacon, diced

1½ cups finely chopped red onions

⅓ cup minced, oil-packed, sun-dried tomatoes, drained

1 tablespoon whole-grain mustard

2 medium garlic cloves, minced

¼ cup chopped parsley

⅓ cup cider vinegar

Salt and pepper

TIPS FROM OUR TEST KITCHEN

Use a rubber spatula or "spoonula" to toss the potatoes to help prevent them from breaking.

"Applewood-smoked bacon, sun-dried tomatoes, and chopped red onions give this salad a distinctive flair."

1. Combine the potatoes and salt in a Dutch oven with water to cover. Bring to a boil; reduce the heat and simmer, uncovered, until the potatoes are just tender, 30 to 35 minutes. Do not overcook.

2. Drain well and slice each potato into 3 pieces (about ½ inch thick). Place in a large bowl.

3. Heat a large skillet over medium-high heat. Add the bacon and cook until almost crisp. Remove the skillet from the heat and stir in the onions, tomatoes, mustard, and garlic.

4. Pour the mixture over the potatoes while they are still hot; add the parsley and vinegar. Toss gently to coat. Season with salt and pepper.

5. Let stand for 15 minutes to absorb the flavors. Serve warm or at room temperature.

Super Summer Salad

Diane Montagano, Plymouth, Michigan   SERVES 12

6 medium tomatoes (1½ pounds), seeded
    and diced
1 English cucumber, seeded and diced
    (do not peel)
1 cup diced red onions
Two 7-ounce fresh mozzarella balls, cut
    into ½-inch cubes
1 tablespoon minced garlic
½ cup chopped basil
½ cup chopped parsley
1 tablespoon dried fines herbes or
    2 teaspoons dried oregano and
    ½ teaspoon dried tarragon
1 cup Italian salad dressing
Salt and pepper

"Our July 4 celebration starts at 7:30 a.m. when our town has a great parade. Dinner is an all-American picnic, including this refreshing salad, which uses the bounty of the season."

1. Combine the tomatoes, cucumber, onions, mozzarella, garlic, basil, parsley, fines herbes, and salad dressing in a large bowl; mix well.

2. Cover with plastic wrap and refrigerate for 2 hours, or until chilled. Season with salt and pepper before serving.

TIPS FROM OUR TEST KITCHEN

It's important to seed the tomatoes and cucumber so they won't water down the flavors of the other ingredients. To seed tomatoes easily, cut in half crosswise and remove the seeds. Squeeze the tomatoes over a bowl to release the seeds and juices. To seed a cucumber, cut in half lengthwise and run the tip of a teaspoon down the center.

The Best Coleslaw

Susan McFarland, Racine, Wisconsin

1 small head cabbage (about 1 pound),
   shredded

1 medium carrot, grated

½ cup sugar

½ cup mayonnaise

⅓ cup olive oil

¼ cup cider vinegar

1 teaspoon prepared mustard

1 teaspoon celery seeds

1 tablespoon prepared horseradish

TIPS FROM OUR TEST KITCHEN

For variety and more heat, use
1 teaspoon dry mustard instead of
the prepared mustard.

"This coleslaw has been in the family for years—my great-grandmother used to make it. It's the only coleslaw my family will eat."

1. Combine the cabbage and carrot in a large bowl.

2. Mix the sugar, mayonnaise, olive oil, vinegar, mustard, celery seeds, and horseradish in a small bowl; whisk to blend. Toss the mayonnaise mixture with the cabbage mixture.

Dandelion Salad

Barbara Eakin, Utica, Pennsylvania

SERVES 4

2 quarts dandelion greens or endive
¼ cup chopped onion
6 bacon slices, cut into small pieces
3 tablespoons all-purpose flour
¼ cup vinegar
1 egg, beaten
1½ to 2 cups milk

"Every spring, my mother would make Dandelion Salad as soon as the tender dandelion greens popped through the ground. I've been making this salad for my family ever since."

1. Wash the greens thoroughly. Drain and spin dry. Place in a large bowl. Add the onion.

2. Fry the bacon in a skillet. Drain, reserving ¼ cup of the drippings in the skillet. Add the bacon to the greens. Add the flour to the drippings and cook until bubbly. Whisk in ¼ cup water, the vinegar, and egg. Add the milk gradually and stir until thickened.

3. Pour the mixture over the greens; mix well. Cover until ready to serve.

Layered Lettuce Salad

Lucille Cathelyn, Geneseo, Illinois

SERVES 8 TO 12

1 small head iceberg lettuce (about
    1 pound), torn into bite-sized pieces
¼ to ½ cup chopped celery
½ cup chopped green bell pepper
¼ cup finely chopped onion
1½ cups frozen green peas
1 cup shredded Cheddar
6 bacon slices, cooked and crumbled
2 cups mayonnaise
2 tablespoons sugar

TIPS FROM OUR TEST KITCHEN

There is no need to thaw the peas.
They will thaw in the refrigerator.

"This is very good at holiday times or on hot days."

1. Layer the lettuce, celery, bell pepper, onion, peas, Cheddar, and bacon in the order listed in a shallow pasta bowl or a 13 × 9-inch casserole dish.

2. Combine the mayonnaise and sugar in a small bowl. Spoon over the casserole, using the back of a spoon to spread evenly. Cover with plastic wrap and refrigerate for 4 hours or overnight.

Colorful Pasta Salad

Claudia Stubblefield, Lebanon, Missouri

One 12-ounce package tricolor spiral pasta

One 16-ounce can pitted ripe olives, drained and cut in half

One 14-ounce can cut green beans, drained

One 14-ounce can wax beans, drained

One 15-ounce can dark kidney beans, rinsed and drained

1¼ cups finely chopped red onions

1¾ cups chopped Roma tomatoes (about 4 medium)

½ cup chopped red bell pepper

⅔ cup sugar

¾ cup red wine vinegar

½ cup canola oil

1 teaspoon salt

½ teaspoon black pepper

"When we entertain our large family—four children, their spouses, fourteen grandchildren, and two great-grandsons—they request this favorite pasta salad. It goes well with any type of meat dish. Leftovers keep well."

1. Cook the pasta according to the package directions. Drain in a colander and run under cold water to stop the cooking process and cool quickly. Shake to drain excess liquid. Place in a very large bowl.

2. Add the olives, beans, onions, tomatoes, and bell pepper to the pasta; mix well.

3. Combine the sugar, vinegar, oil, salt, and black pepper in a jar with a lid. Close tightly and shake vigorously to blend. Pour over the salad and toss gently. Cover with plastic wrap and refrigerate for 1 hour to allow the flavors to blend.

TIPS FROM OUR TEST KITCHEN

If wax beans are unavailable, use a second can of cut green beans. It will still be very colorful.

Taffy Apple Salad

Duaine Heart, Hartselle, Alabama

SERVES 16 TO 24

One 20-ounce can crushed pineapple in juice

½ cup sugar

1½ tablespoons cider vinegar

1 tablespoon all-purpose flour

1 egg, beaten

2 pounds Granny Smith apples (about 6 apples), sliced

2 cups miniature marshmallows

One 12-ounce container frozen whipped topping, thawed

1½ cups peanuts, optional

TIPS FROM OUR TEST KITCHEN

While the juice mixture is chilling, you may combine the cut apples with the pineapple in a bowl. Be sure to blend thoroughly. The acid from the pineapple will keep the apples from browning. Cover with plastic wrap and refrigerate until ready to assemble.

"My name is Heart, I was married on February 14, and I live in Hartselle—so Valentine's Day is my favorite holiday. I just love this recipe. It is refreshing without being too sweet."

1. Drain the pineapple, reserving the juice. Combine the reserved juice, the sugar, vinegar, flour, and egg in a small saucepan; whisk until well blended. Cook over medium heat until the mixture thickens, stirring constantly with a whisk. Remove from the heat and refrigerate for 2 hours.

2. Combine the apples, marshmallows, whipped topping, pineapple, and peanuts, if using, in a large bowl. Add the pineapple juice mixture and toss gently to blend thoroughly.

Blueberry Jell-O Salad

Michelle Fyfe, Mesa, Arizona

SERVES 10 TO 12

One 6-ounce box black cherry Jell-O

2 cups fresh blueberries

One 16-ounce can crushed pineapple, drained

½ cup sugar

One 16-ounce container sour cream

One 8-ounce package cream cheese, softened

1 cup chopped pecans, toasted

"This recipe was used by my mom every holiday meal. I can't remember a Thanksgiving without it. In fact, aside from the turkey, this is a must-have dish at our table."

1. Prepare the Jell-O according to the package directions in a large bowl. Add the blueberries and pineapple. Pour into a 13 × 9-inch glass dish. Refrigerate until set.

2. Combine the sugar, sour cream, cream cheese, and chopped pecans in a bowl; mix well to spreading consistency. Spread over the set Jell-O and refrigerate until ready to serve.

120 **Hometown Recipes for the Holidays**

Cranberry Freeze

Rita Heitkamp, New Bremen, Ohio

6 ounces cream cheese, softened

2 tablespoons mayonnaise

2 tablespoons sugar

One 16-ounce can whole cranberry sauce

One 8-ounce can crushed pineapple in juice

½ cup chopped walnuts

1 cup whipping cream

"My husband of forty-eight years and I have six children, twenty-three grandchildren, and five great-grandchildren. We enjoy getting together for the holidays. I've had this recipe for many years and always make it for Thanksgiving Day—as well as at other times throughout the year."

1. Combine the cream cheese, mayonnaise, and sugar in a bowl and mix well. Add the cranberry sauce, pineapple, and walnuts. Stir until well blended.

2. Pour the cream into a mixing bowl. Using a mixer, beat at high speed until stiff peaks form. Fold the whipped cream into the cranberry mixture.

3. Spoon the mixture into a 12 × 8-inch glass baking pan or a 9-inch deep-dish pie pan. Cover with plastic wrap and freeze for at least 6 hours, or until firm. To serve, remove from the freezer and let stand for at least 45 minutes.

Grandma Julia's Fresh Cranberry Relish

Ellen Schirmer, Spokane, Washington

SERVES 6

1 large navel orange

1 medium lemon

One 12-ounce package fresh cranberries, rinsed and drained

1 Golden Delicious apple, halved, cored, and cut into large pieces

2½ cups sugar

TIPS FROM OUR TEST KITCHEN

For additional flavor, before peeling the orange, grate 1 teaspoon zest. Add to the cranberry mixture after it has been strained.

"My mother always said she only ate the turkey and dressing at Thanksgiving so she could have the cranberry sauce. Our family has enjoyed her yummy cranberry relish for half a century. She had to chop the fruit by hand and then got a food grinder. Today's preparation is quite simple—in the food processor."

1. Peel the orange and lemon and place in a food processor with the cranberries and the apple. Pulse to a coarse texture.

2. Transfer the mixture to a medium bowl, add the sugar, and mix well. Cover with plastic wrap and refrigerate for 4 hours. Place the mixture in a fine-mesh strainer and let stand for 15 minutes before serving.

Nature's Perfect Salad

Dorothea Hartman, Decatur, Indiana

SALAD

1 cup baby spinach

1 cup shredded carrots

1 cup torn lettuce

½ cup diced celery

½ cup fresh or frozen blueberries

½ cup quartered fresh or frozen
strawberries

DRESSING

3 tablespoons apple cider vinegar

2 tablespoons honey

2 tablespoons minced onion

2 tablespoons vegetable oil

2 tablespoons prepared horseradish

½ teaspoon celery seeds

¼ teaspoon salt

"My husband and I enjoy eating healthy, so I created Nature's Perfect Salad. All the ingredients are rich in nutrition, and my husband loves it."

To prepare the salad, combine all of the ingredients in a glass bowl. To prepare the dressing, combine the ingredients in a small bowl and pour over the salad. Toss to coat.

Sides

Side dishes may not take center stage at a Christmas, Easter, or Thanksgiving dinner, but they can make the meal a star. No matter what the occasion, the vegetables, starches, and grains selected to complement the main course can tie the menu together. Many are favorites prepared each and every year. Others are developed out of a garden's abundance.

Mary J. Lewis's Autumn Rum-Glazed Carrots carry out a Halloween theme with a rich, orange color. Raisins, rum, and brown sugar give the dish a gourmet twist. Lewis, of Eatonton, Georgia, was the winner in the side dish category of the *American Profile* Holiday Recipe Contest with her carrot creation.

Country Cabbage with Buttery Crumb Topping reflects both a cook's creativity and a family's heritage. Joy Parker of Covington, Georgia, prepares this dish with thoughts of her late mother, who loved sharing it with friends in her beauty shop.

Not many of the crispy Holiday Dressing Patties that Barb Casola's mother cooked made it to the dinner table. Casola, of Venice, Florida, says she and her siblings would gobble them up as soon as they were out of the pan. The tradition continued with Casola's own four children, who now prepare them for their offspring.

When La Juan Thompson's husband planted eggplants in his garden for the first time, the couple, of Washington, Arkansas, was surprised by the prolific results. After sharing with others, the Thompsons still had more eggplants than they knew what to do with. Thompson's Eggplant Casserole, with cheese and a crumb topping, is the family's favorite, she says.

Kimberly Hammond of Kingwood, Texas, turned her Stuffed Pumpkins recipe into a learning experience for her children as well as a colorful, tasty accompaniment for a fall holiday meal. Hammond's two young sons helped pick out a pair of small pie pumpkins from the pumpkin patch. As the boys watched and helped, Hammond says they learned pumpkins can become more than jack-o'-lanterns.

Italian-Style Baked Beans

Gail Van Osdell, St. Charles, Illinois

1½ pounds Italian sausage, casings removed

Six 16-ounce cans beans (mixture of garbanzo, baked, kidney, and Great Northern)

2 large onions, minced

2 large green bell peppers, diced

Two 6-ounce cans tomato paste

2 bay leaves

2 tablespoons dry mustard

2 tablespoons brown sugar

2 teaspoons dried oregano

1 teaspoon garlic salt

"This recipe has been in our family for many years. It is a dish that can be served with almost any meat. We like it as a side dish when grilling outside."

1. Cut the sausage into bite-sized pieces. Fry it in a skillet and drain off the fat.

2. Drain the beans and pour them into a slow cooker. Add the onions, bell peppers, tomato paste, bay leaves, mustard, brown sugar, oregano, and garlic salt. Add the sausage to the bean mixture and mix well. Scrape the browned bits from the skillet into the slow cooker.

3. Cook on high until the mixture bubbles. Reduce the heat to low and cook for 6 to 8 hours. Drain any excess liquid. Remove the bay leaves before serving.

Grandmother Bunny's Baked Beans

Barbara Miller, New Bern, North Carolina

SERVES 12

½ to ¾ pound bacon slices, cut in half

Two 28-ounce cans baked beans

½ cup ketchup

½ cup cider vinegar

¾ cup pancake syrup

1 tablespoon dry mustard

2 cups diced apples, such as Gala or
   Jonathan

"My granddaughter, Morgan Haynes, and I were looking for the perfect bean recipe for our July 4 celebration. Morgan came up with this one, and we changed it to suit our tastes. It's delicious."

1. Preheat the broiler. Arrange the bacon on a pan and broil 6 inches from the heat source for 6 minutes, or until partially done.

2. Preheat the oven to 350°F. Combine the baked beans, ketchup, cider vinegar, syrup, dry mustard, and apples in a large bowl; mix well.

3. Pour the bean mixture into a greased 13 × 9-inch glass baking dish. Arrange the bacon slices on top.

4. Bake, uncovered, for 1 hour. Stir in the bacon before serving.

Butter Bean Medley

Ruth Jackson, Sturgis, Mississippi

SERVES 6 TO 8

2 smoked ham hocks

2 onion slices, preferably Vidalia, about
  ¼ inch thick, separated into rings

4 cups fresh or frozen butter beans

2 slices bacon or 2 tablespoons bacon
  drippings

4 to 6 drops hot pepper sauce

1 teaspoon sugar

Salt

"My husband won't eat anything with butter in it. As a youngster, he asked his mother if butter beans had butter in them. She had a vegetable garden and allowed him from start to finish to see the process and make the determination for himself."

1. Bring 8 cups water to a boil in a Dutch oven. Add the ham hocks, onion, beans, bacon, and hot sauce. Return to a boil and reduce the heat.

2. Simmer, covered, until the beans are tender, about 40 minutes. Add more water, if needed.

3. Drain the beans, if desired. Sprinkle with the sugar and season with salt; stir gently to blend. Spoon into a serving bowl.

Country Cabbage with Buttery Crumb Topping

Joy Parker, Covington, Georgia

SERVES 8

1 small cabbage or ½ large cabbage
    (about 1¼ pounds total), chopped
1 cup chopped onions
¾ cup (1½ sticks) butter or margarine,
    melted
¼ teaspoon pepper
One 10-ounce can cream of chicken
    soup
¼ cup mayonnaise
1 cup shredded Cheddar
1 sleeve butter crackers (about
    34 crackers), crushed

"My mother truly enjoyed cooking for her family, and this casserole was one of her favorites. She loved sharing it with friends in her beauty shop. I know she would be happy that others have the chance to sample it, too."

1. Preheat the oven to 350°F.

2. Place the cabbage in a greased 9-inch square baking dish and sprinkle evenly with the onions. Pour ¼ cup of the melted butter on top and sprinkle with the pepper.

3. Combine the soup and mayonnaise in a medium bowl; mix well. Spread evenly over the cabbage mixture.

4. Mix the remaining ½ cup melted butter, the Cheddar, and crushed crackers in the same bowl. Sprinkle the cracker mixture on top of the cabbage mixture.

5. Bake, uncovered, for 45 minutes, or until golden and bubbly.

German Red Cabbage and Beets

Mary J. Lewis, Eatonton, Georgia

SERVES 8 TO 12

3 medium beets, peeled

6 cups shredded red cabbage

¼ cup sweet red wine

½ cup red wine vinegar

½ teaspoon sugar, or to taste

½ teaspoon pepper

½ teaspoon salt, or to taste

TIPS FROM OUR TEST KITCHEN

Beet juice stains. To peel beets easily without staining your fingertips, peel them under slowly running water. The juice will rinse away before it has time to stain your fingertips.

"My mother was born in Germany, and her cooking reflected her heritage. I learned a lot from just watching her cook our meals. Cabbage and beets were inexpensive, so we had them often in many different dishes. I think everyone has a recipe that came from their mother or father—every time I cook one, I am reminded of her, and it makes things taste more like home."

1. Bring 8 cups water to a boil in a Dutch oven. Add the beets and return to a boil.

2. Reduce the heat and simmer, covered, until the beets are tender, about 15 minutes. Remove the beets from the Dutch oven using a slotted spoon. Reserve the cooking liquid in the pot.

3. Add the cabbage to the cooking liquid and stir until well coated. Let stand, covered, for 10 minutes. Drain the cabbage, reserving ¼ cup of the cooking liquid.

4. Whisk together the ¼ cup reserved cooking liquid with the wine, vinegar, sugar, pepper, and salt in a small bowl.

5. Arrange the cabbage in a 2-quart casserole and top with the beets. Pour the cooking liquid mixture evenly over the top. Cover the dish with plastic wrap and let stand for at least 15 minutes.

6. Serve hot or cold. The casserole keeps well in the refrigerator for 3 to 4 days.

Autumn Rum-Glazed Carrots

Mary J. Lewis, Eatonton, Georgia

½ cup (1 stick) butter or margarine

3 pounds whole medium carrots,
   trimmed (16 carrots)

½ cup packed dark brown sugar

½ cup dark rum

¼ cup raisins

½ teaspoon pepper

TIPS FROM OUR TEST KITCHEN

The carrots should remain whole while cooking for peak flavors, texture, and presentation. Use two utensils, such as a fork and spoon, and turn the carrots gently.

"If it's orange, it's made for the Halloween table. Between the cookies and the candies, dinner still needs to be served before the trick-or-treaters make their rounds. Simple is always best—and that's what this dish offers. The raisins and rum give it a special touch."

1. Melt the butter in a large skillet over medium heat. Add the carrots and toss to coat with the butter. Cook, turning every 10 minutes, until just tender and beginning to brown, about 30 minutes.

2. Combine the brown sugar, rum, raisins, and pepper in a bowl; mix well. Pour evenly over the carrots. Reduce the heat to low and cook for 10 minutes, stirring occasionally. Spoon into a bowl and serve hot.

Creamy Cauliflower Casserole

Terri Martin, Dublin, Virginia

1 medium head cauliflower, broken into
small florets
One 10-ounce can cream of chicken
soup
½ cup mayonnaise
1 cup shredded medium sharp Cheddar
1 sleeve butter crackers (about
34 crackers), crushed
2 tablespoons butter or margarine,
melted

TIPS FROM OUR TEST KITCHEN

The cauliflower is very subtle with a
creamy texture.

"I have been making this dish for a number of years.
It is always a favorite at family dinners. Even the kids
love it. And, best of all, it's so easy to make."

1. Preheat the oven to 400°F. Grease an 8-inch square baking dish.

2. Place the cauliflower in a vegetable steamer. Steam, covered, until tender, about 7 minutes.

3. Combine the soup and mayonnaise in a large bowl; mix well. Stir in the Cheddar. Add the cauliflower and mix gently until well coated.

4. Spoon the mixture into the prepared pan. Sprinkle the cracker crumbs over the top and drizzle evenly with the melted butter. Bake, uncovered, for 25 minutes, or until golden.

Baked Creamed Corn

Mrs. W. Hoff, Coldwater, Michigan

SERVES 4

2 eggs

One 8-ounce can cream-style corn

2/3 cup milk

1/2 cup crushed saltine crackers

2 to 3 tablespoons melted butter or
 margarine

1 tablespoon sugar

1/4 teaspoon salt

1/8 teaspoon pepper

"This recipe is out of this world. It can easily be doubled to feed a crowd."

1. Preheat the oven to 350°F.

2. Beat the eggs in a mixing bowl until frothy. Add the corn, milk, crackers, butter, sugar, salt, and pepper; mix well. Spoon into a deep casserole dish. Bake for 25 to 30 minutes.

Corn Scallop

Mickey Carlucci, Peralta, New Mexico

SERVES 6

2 eggs

One 15-ounce can whole kernel corn

One 15-ounce can cream-style corn

One 6-ounce can evaporated milk

¼ cup (½ stick) butter, cubed

2 tablespoons minced onions

½ teaspoon salt

¼ teaspoon black pepper

2 cups coarsely crushed crackers, about 50 crackers

One 12-ounce package diced Pepper Jack or Swiss cheese

"I live in a tiny rural New Mexico community. It is not unusual to see large cornfields in the fall, so this dish blends in with the season and our lifestyle."

1. Preheat the oven to 325°F. Grease a 13 × 9-inch baking dish.

2. Beat the eggs lightly in a large bowl. Stir in the undrained whole kernel corn and cream-style corn. Add the evaporated milk, cubed butter, onions, salt, and pepper. Fold in the cracker crumbs and diced cheese.

3. Spoon into the prepared dish. Bake for 1 hour, or until set. Let stand for 5 minutes. Cut into squares to serve.

Holiday Dressing Patties

Barb Casola, Venice, Florida

3 tablespoons butter

¼ cup bulk pork sausage

¼ cup minced onions

½ cup finely chopped celery

⅛ teaspoon salt

⅛ teaspoon pepper

½ cup chicken or turkey broth

1 to 1½ teaspoons poultry seasoning

⅛ teaspoon celery salt

10 slices white bread, cut into ½-inch cubes

TIPS FROM OUR TEST KITCHEN

This would also be good as an entrée with steamed vegetables and a green salad.

"When my sisters, brothers, and I were growing up, our mother would make these crispy dressing patties, and we would eat them as fast as she could cook them. My four children enjoyed them just as we did, and now they are making them, too. Aren't family traditions wonderful?"

1. Melt 1 tablespoon of the butter in a large skillet over medium heat. Add the sausage and cook until browned, breaking up large pieces with a spoon.

2. Add the onions, celery, salt, and pepper and cook for 2 minutes, stirring frequently. Stir in the broth, poultry seasoning, and celery salt. Remove from the heat.

3. Place the bread cubes in a large bowl. Pour the sausage mixture over the bread; mix well. Let stand for 10 to 15 minutes. Shape the mixture into 8 patties about 3½ inches in diameter.

4. Melt the remaining 2 tablespoons butter in the skillet over medium heat. When bubbly, add the patties, in batches if necessary, and cook until golden, about 2 minutes on each side.

Eggplant Casserole

La Juan Thompson, Washington, Arkansas

SERVES 6

1 pound eggplant, peeled and diced

3 medium onions, chopped

1 egg, beaten

2 teaspoons salt

Pepper

2 tablespoons butter

1 cup sour cream

1 cup grated cheese

1 cup butter cracker crumbs, about
    25 crackers

TIPS FROM OUR TEST KITCHEN

Try the mellow flavors of provolone or mozzarella or kick up the flavor with Pepper Jack cheese.

"When my husband planted eggplants for the first time several years ago, we had no idea how prolific they could be. We shared with neighbors but still had an abundance of the pretty purple vegetables. This eggplant recipe is the one my family likes the best."

1. Preheat the oven to 350°F. Grease a 1½-quart baking dish.

2. Cook the eggplant and onions in a small amount of water in a saucepan until tender; drain. Add the egg, salt, pepper, and butter; mix well.

3. Combine the sour cream and cheese in a small bowl; mix well.

4. Spoon half of the eggplant mixture into the prepared dish. Top with half of the cheese mixture. Repeat the layers and top the casserole with the cracker crumbs. Bake for 45 minutes.

Garlic Cheese Grits

Ruth Fuller Lature, Hopkinsville, Kentucky

1 cup quick-cooking grits

1 teaspoon salt

½ cup (1 stick) butter or margarine, cut into ½-inch cubes

1 cup milk

One 6-ounce roll garlic cheese, cut into ½-inch cubes

2 eggs, beaten

¼ cup shredded American cheese or mild Cheddar

TIPS FROM OUR TEST KITCHEN

This resembles a soft polenta. It is great for potlucks and family gatherings because it holds the heat well.

"This could be a breakfast casserole for brunch or a side dish for lunch or dinner. Grits are a Southern tradition. What a wonderful way to start a new year!"

1. Preheat the oven to 350°F. Grease a 13 × 9-inch glass baking dish.

2. Cook the grits with the salt and 4 cups water in a large saucepan, according to the package directions. Stir in the butter, milk, garlic cheese, and eggs; mix well.

3. Spoon into the prepared pan. Sprinkle the American cheese over the top. Bake for 45 minutes, or until set.

Hoppin' John

Betty Fulks, Onia, Arkansas

SERVES 6 TO 8

2 cups fresh or frozen black-eyed peas
1 slice bacon
1½ teaspoons salt, or to taste
2 tablespoons butter
1 small red bell pepper, seeded and
    chopped
1 small onion, chopped
2 cups cooked rice
¼ teaspoon garlic powder
¼ teaspoon black pepper
Parsley sprigs, optional

"This is an excellent side dish for New Year's Day. Tradition says if you eat Hoppin' John on January 1, you will have good luck."

1. Bring 2 cups water to a boil in a medium saucepan. Add the peas, bacon, and 1 teaspoon of the salt. Return to a boil, reduce the heat, and simmer, covered, until tender, 20 to 25 minutes; drain well.

2. Melt the butter in a large skillet over medium heat. Add the bell pepper and onion and cook, stirring frequently, until crisp-tender, about 3 minutes.

3. Add the drained peas and rice and cook until thoroughly heated, about 10 minutes, stirring occasionally. Be careful not to overcook. Add the garlic powder, the remaining ¼ teaspoon salt, and the pepper. Garnish with parsley sprigs, if using.

138   **Hometown Recipes for the Holidays**

Sugar Snap Peas with Wilted Mesclun Greens

Candace McMenamin, Lexington, South Carolina

SERVES 4

2 tablespoons butter

2 tablespoons pine nuts

1 shallot, finely chopped

1 pound sugar snap peas

½ cup dry white wine

Salt and pepper

2 cups loosely packed mesclun greens or spring mix

2 green onions, finely chopped

2 tablespoons shredded basil

"I created this recipe to serve at a spring dinner party. Sugar snap peas are plentiful here in the spring, and I actually grow the greens and green onions used in this recipe from late February to late April."

1. Melt the butter over medium-high heat in a large saucepan. Add the pine nuts and shallot. Cook, stirring frequently, until browned, about 2 minutes. Add the peas and wine. Season with salt and pepper. Heat until just simmering. Cook, covered, for 5 minutes, stirring occasionally.

2. Stir in the greens and simmer, uncovered, until the greens just wilt. Stir in the green onions and basil. Remove from the heat and serve immediately.

Roasted Green Bell Peppers

Carmela Porter, Holland, Michigan

SERVES 4

4 large green bell peppers, rinsed and
  patted dry
4 medium garlic cloves, minced
¼ cup olive oil
½ teaspoon salt, or to taste

TIPS FROM OUR TEST KITCHEN

To remove the seeds easily, pull the
stem of the pepper and all of the
seeds will come out in almost one
piece. Cut the roasted peppers into
smaller pieces and toss with cooked
white rice for an interesting side
dish.

"My Italian mother made Roasted Green Bell Peppers for special occasions as a side dish—or a salad—especially in the summer when peppers were cheap. I make them whenever I get the yearning for peppers. This recipe is easy and delicious."

1. Preheat the oven to 450°F.

2. Place a sheet of foil on a baking sheet and arrange the whole bell peppers on it. Place on the center oven rack. Roast the peppers for 30 to 40 minutes until the skins begin to split and the peppers are richly browned, turning every 10 minutes.

3. Remove the peppers from the oven, place in a bowl, and cover with plastic wrap. Let stand for 20 minutes to cool slightly and absorb the smoky flavors.

4. Remove the skins and seeds. Rinse fingertips frequently to allow for a better grip. Pull the peppers apart into thin strips and place in a medium bowl. Add the garlic, olive oil, and salt; mix gently.

Garlic Au Gratin Potatoes

Pamela Shank, Parkersburg, West Virginia

SERVES 10

5 pounds potatoes
2 cups whipping cream
2 garlic cloves, minced
½ teaspoon kosher salt
½ teaspoon pepper
6 eggs, slightly beaten
4 cups grated Parmesan
¼ cup Italian bread crumbs

"Scalloped potatoes of any kind is a favorite dish in our family. I am always trying a variety of cheese and ingredient combinations."

1. Spray a 13 × 9-inch baking dish with nonstick cooking spray.

2. Peel and wash the potatoes, cut into slices, and drain. Arrange in a large Dutch oven. Add the cream, garlic, salt, and pepper. Bring to a boil. Reduce the heat and simmer, covered, until the potatoes are tender, 20 to 25 minutes. Remove from the heat. Stir in the eggs and 3 cups of the Parmesan.

3. Preheat the oven to 350°F.

4. Spoon the potato mixture into the prepared baking dish. Combine the bread crumbs and remaining 1 cup Parmesan in a bowl; mix well. Sprinkle over the top of the potatoes. Bake for 25 to 30 minutes until the potatoes are tender.

Red, White, and Blue Potatoes

Rita Courson, Seneca, Pennsylvania

4 medium-to-large red potatoes, thinly
    sliced
1 small Vidalia onion, sliced
4 to 6 mushrooms, sliced
½ teaspoon salt
½ teaspoon pepper
2 tablespoons butter
¼ cup crumbled blue cheese or
    Gorgonzola

"These tasty potatoes suit July 4 to a T, but are appropriate for many occasions."

1. Preheat the oven to 375°F or preheat a grill.

2. Arrange the potatoes, onion slices, and mushrooms on a sheet of foil. Sprinkle with the salt and pepper and dot with the butter. Crumble the blue cheese on top. Fold the packet to seal and cook either in the oven or on a medium grill for 45 minutes, or until the potatoes are soft.

Gramma Tillie's Cheese Potatoes

Tillie B. Vaughan, Victorville, California

SERVES 6 TO 8

6 large russet potatoes
½ cup (1 stick) butter or margarine
2 large onions, sliced
½ cup all-purpose flour
4 cups cold milk
1 pound Velveeta cheese, cubed
Salt and pepper

"My mother-in-law used to bring our family dinner once a week in the 1970s when our children were growing up and we were both working. I loved the reprieve from cooking. This recipe of hers is still the family's favorite."

1. Boil the potatoes in water to cover in a large pot until they are easily pierced with a fork. Cool and peel. Cut into bite-sized chunks.

2. Preheat the oven to 350°F.

3. Melt the butter in a large saucepan over medium heat. Add the onions and cook until they are translucent. Sprinkle the flour over the onions and stir until the butter is absorbed; do not brown. Add the cold milk, stirring briskly with a whisk so the flour does not lump. Add the cheese and continue stirring until the cheese is melted and the sauce has thickened. Season with salt and pepper. Add the potatoes; mix well.

4. Spoon into a 13 × 9-inch casserole dish. Bake for 30 minutes.

Coconut-Crumble Sweet Potato Casserole

Kathleen Kechnie, Weatherford, Texas

SERVES 8 TO 10

2 eggs

3 cups cooked, mashed sweet potatoes or one 40-ounce can sweet potatoes, rinsed, drained, and mashed

½ cup granulated sugar

¼ cup sweetened condensed milk

⅔ cup butter or margarine, melted

1 teaspoon vanilla extract

1 cup flaked coconut

1 cup packed dark brown sugar

⅓ cup all-purpose flour

"This is a great side dish to serve with Easter ham. It's quick and easy, and my family likes the way it gives extra flavor to the already nutritious sweet potatoes I like to serve."

1. Preheat the oven to 375°F. Grease an 8-inch square baking dish.

2. Place the eggs in a large bowl; beat well. Add the sweet potatoes, granulated sugar, condensed milk, ⅓ cup of the butter, and the vanilla; mix well. Spoon the mixture into the prepared baking dish.

3. Combine the coconut, brown sugar, flour, and remaining ⅓ cup butter in a medium bowl. Stir with a fork until well blended. Sprinkle evenly over the sweet potato mixture.

4. Bake, uncovered, for 35 to 45 minutes until the top is golden brown and a knife inserted in the center comes out clean. Let stand for 15 minutes before serving.

Sweet Potato Bonbons

Janet Curtis, North Platte, Nebraska

3 pounds sweet potatoes, peeled and cut into ½-inch cubes

¼ cup (½ stick) plus ⅓ cup butter or margarine, melted

½ cup packed dark brown sugar

1 teaspoon salt

½ teaspoon grated orange zest

3 cups crushed cornflakes

16 large marshmallows

16 pecan halves, optional

"This is a good 'show-off' recipe. People are surprised by the look and the taste of Sweet Potato Bonbons. Whether Thanksgiving is at my house or a daughter's, I do the sweet potatoes. Time is involved here, but it's worth it."

1. Bring 8 cups water to a boil in a Dutch oven. Add the sweet potatoes and return to a boil. Reduce the heat and simmer, covered, until the potatoes are tender, 18 to 20 minutes. Drain well and remove to a large bowl.

2. Beat the potatoes using a mixer at high speed until light and fluffy. Add ¼ cup melted butter, the brown sugar, salt, and orange zest. Beat until well blended. Cover the bowl with plastic wrap and refrigerate for 2 to 3 hours.

3. Preheat the oven to 450°F. Line a baking sheet with foil and coat the foil with nonstick cooking spray.

4. Place the crushed cornflakes in a shallow pan. Divide the sweet potatoes into 16 portions and shape them around the marshmallows in ovals or rounds. Brush each ball with the remaining ⅓ cup butter and coat evenly with the cornflakes.

5. Place the bonbons on the prepared baking sheet and top each with a pecan half, if desired, pressing down slightly. Bake for 8 to 10 minutes until golden.

Stuffed Pumpkins

Kimberly Hammond, Kingwood, Texas

SERVES 8 TO 12

2 small pie pumpkins, about 7 inches in
    diameter each

1 tablespoon olive oil

3 medium onions, finely chopped

3 medium celery stalks, diced

3 medium carrots, diced

1 teaspoon salt

3 cups cooked brown rice

1 teaspoon dried rosemary

½ cup pumpkin seeds, pecans, slivered
    almonds, or pine nuts, toasted

TIPS FROM OUR TEST KITCHEN

To toast the nuts or seeds, heat a
large skillet over medium-high heat.
Add the nuts or seeds and cook,
stirring constantly, until they begin
to turn golden, 2 to 3 minutes.
Remove from the skillet
immediately.

"I wanted to cook something with a fresh pumpkin
that still resembled a pumpkin when it was finished.
My children helped me pick two of the smaller ones
from the pumpkin patch, and together we learned
how a fresh pumpkin can become so much more than
a jack-o'-lantern."

1. Preheat the oven to 350°F.

2. Rinse the outside of the pumpkins well and pat dry. Cut
the tops off the pumpkins, and scoop out the seeds and
membranes and discard.

3. Heat the olive oil in a large skillet over medium-high heat.
Add the onions and cook, stirring frequently, for 6 minutes,
or until lightly browned.

4. Add the celery and carrots and cook for 2 minutes. Add
½ cup water and the salt. Bring the mixture to a boil, reduce
the heat, and simmer for 10 minutes. Add the rice, rosemary, and seeds; mix well. Remove from the heat.

5. Fill the pumpkin cavities with the rice mixture. Place the
pumpkins in a 13 × 9-inch glass baking dish and cover the
dish with foil. Bake for 1½ hours, or until the pumpkin is
fragrant and tender when pierced with a fork.

Mom's Spanish Rice

Linda Fahrenkamp, New Prague, Minnesota

SERVES 8

¾ cup uncooked white rice

½ pound bacon

½ cup chopped onions

½ cup chopped green bell pepper

2 cups canned whole tomatoes, crushed

¼ teaspoon black pepper

½ teaspoon celery salt

¼ teaspoon garlic powder

"My mom used to make this when I was growing up. Then I started making it, and now my kids request it when they come by."

1. Cook the rice according to the package directions.

2. Dice the bacon and fry in a skillet until crisp. Remove from the pan, reserving 2 to 3 tablespoons of drippings in the pan.

3. Add the onions and bell pepper to the skillet. Cook over medium heat until the vegetables are tender. Add the tomatoes, black pepper, celery salt, and garlic powder. Bring to a boil. Stir in the cooked rice and bacon and cook until thoroughly heated, about 5 minutes.

Spinach and Oyster Dressing

Robin Spires, Tampa, Florida

12 cups French or Italian bread, cut into
   ½-inch cubes
½ pound pancetta or bacon, chopped
2 tablespoons olive oil
2 cups finely chopped onions
½ cup thinly sliced leeks
1½ cups thinly sliced celery
One 10-ounce package frozen chopped
   spinach, thawed and squeezed dry
½ cup (1 stick) butter, melted
1 tablespoon chopped sage or 1 teaspoon
   dried sage
1 tablespoon minced garlic (about
   6 medium cloves)
¼ teaspoon salt
½ teaspoon black pepper
2½ cups chicken or turkey broth
One 10-ounce container shucked oysters,
   drained

"Spinach and Oyster Dressing in its original form has been a part of every holiday gathering in my family for many, many years. Over the past few years, I have tweaked it just slightly. It is always the most popular dish, and whenever I make it, I never fail to have many requests for the recipe. It's definitely one of my most prized recipes."

1. Arrange the bread cubes on sheets of wax paper or foil in a single layer and let dry overnight. For a quicker method, place the cubes on foil-lined oven racks and bake in a 325°F oven for 25 minutes, or until golden.

2. Preheat the oven to 350°F. Grease a 13 × 9-inch glass baking dish.

3. Heat a large skillet over medium-high heat. Add the pancetta and cook until crisp. Remove from the skillet and drain on paper towels.

4. Add the olive oil to the pan drippings. Stir in the onions, leeks, and celery. Reduce the heat to medium and cook, stirring frequently, until the celery is just tender, about 7 minutes.

5. Combine the bread cubes, pancetta, onion mixture, spinach, butter, sage, garlic, salt, and pepper in a large bowl. Toss until well blended. Stir in the broth and fold in the oysters. Spoon the mixture into the prepared pan.

Be sure to rinse the leeks well before slicing. Sand gets trapped inside them.

6. Bake, covered with foil, for 30 minutes until thoroughly heated. Remove the foil and bake for 15 minutes longer, or until lightly golden.

Spinach Rice with Cheddar and Pimiento

Marie Pantalone, Fairfax, Virginia

SERVES 8 TO 12

3 tablespoons butter

3 cups cooked rice

½ cup chopped green onions (white parts only)

¼ cup sliced almonds

Two 10-ounce cans condensed chicken broth

½ teaspoon pepper

Two 10-ounce packages frozen chopped spinach, thawed, undrained

2 cups shredded Cheddar

½ cup chopped pimientos, drained

TIPS FROM OUR TEST KITCHEN

For a thicker consistency, drain the spinach before adding.

"This has been a regular on my Christmas table for more than thirty years. It is a particular favorite because it is not only delicious and a perfect accompaniment to turkey and other traditional dishes but it is also colorful, with its green spinach and red pimiento."

1. Melt the butter in a large skillet over medium heat. Add the rice, green onions, and almonds and cook, stirring constantly, until the onions are translucent, about 4 minutes.

2. Add the broth and pepper. Bring to a boil; reduce the heat and simmer, covered, for 15 minutes.

3. Add the spinach and simmer, covered, for 10 minutes. Remove from the heat and stir in the cheese and pimientos. Spoon into a serving dish.

Wild Rice with Snow Peas and Raisins

Marlene Jensen, Rochester, Minnesota

SERVES 8 TO 12

Two 14-ounce cans chicken or vegetable broth
¾ cup uncooked wild rice, rinsed and drained
½ cup quick-cooking barley
1 cup fresh snow peas, cut into thirds
1 cup golden raisins
¾ cup sliced green onions (about 6 medium)
2 teaspoons grated orange zest
½ cup orange juice
¼ cup chopped mint or cilantro
2 tablespoons olive oil
½ teaspoon curry powder
¼ teaspoon salt

"Minnesota is famous for its wild rice, and this recipe is an ideal way to honor that heritage. We sometimes have to travel for Thanksgiving, and this dish is very portable—and healthful, too."

1. Bring the broth to a boil in a Dutch oven. Add the rice and return the mixture to a boil. Reduce the heat and simmer, covered, for 20 minutes.

2. Add the barley and cook, covered, until the barley is tender, about 20 minutes; drain well.

3. Return the rice mixture to the Dutch oven and stir in the remaining ingredients. Cook for 2 minutes until thoroughly heated. Serve at room temperature.

Butternut Squash Bake

Marsha Baker, Pioneer, Ohio

SQUASH

1/3 cup butter or margarine, softened

3/4 cup granulated sugar

2 eggs

One 5-ounce can evaporated milk

1 teaspoon vanilla extract

2 cups mashed cooked butternut squash

TOPPING

1/2 cup Rice Chex cereal

1/4 cup packed brown sugar

1/4 cup chopped pecans

2 tablespoons melted butter or
    margarine

"I'm always asked to share this recipe when I serve it. It's different and always a hit at potlucks."

1. Preheat the oven to 350°F. Grease an 11 × 7-inch baking pan.

2. For the squash, cream the butter and granulated sugar in a bowl using a mixer. Beat in the eggs, evaporated milk, and vanilla. Stir in the squash. The mixture will be thin. Pour into the prepared pan. Bake for 45 minutes, or until almost set.

3. For the topping, combine the cereal, brown sugar, pecans, and melted butter in a bowl; mix well. Remove the casserole from oven and sprinkle on the topping. Return to the oven for 5 to 10 minutes until bubbly.

Squash and Corn Bread Dressing

Juanita Jones, Kingsville, Texas

SERVES 6 TO 8

One 6-ounce package Mexican corn
    bread mix

2/3 cup milk

3 eggs

2 cups (about 10 ounces) sliced yellow
    squash

1/2 cup (1 stick) butter or margarine

3/4 cup finely chopped onions

One 10-ounce can cream of chicken
    soup

1/4 teaspoon pepper

"This recipe was given to me by the dietitian for the North Louisiana Hospital in Vivian, Louisiana."

1. Combine the corn bread mix, milk, and 1 of the eggs in a small bowl; mix well. Bake according to the package directions. Remove to a wire rack to cool slightly. Adjust the oven temperature to 350°F, if necessary.

2. Bring 2 cups water to a boil in a large saucepan. Add the squash and return to a boil. Reduce the heat and simmer, covered, until tender, about 5 minutes. Drain well.

3. Melt the butter in the saucepan over medium heat. Add the onions and cook, stirring frequently, until translucent, about 4 minutes. Remove from the heat.

4. Add the drained squash and mash with a potato masher. Beat the remaining 2 eggs in a small bowl. Add to the squash mixture. Stir in the soup and pepper. Crumble the corn bread and add to the squash mixture. Mix well.

5. Grease a 12 × 8-inch glass baking dish and spoon the dressing into the pan. Bake for 30 to 35 minutes until the edges begin to turn golden.

Squash Fritters with Fresh Tomato Salsa

Sue E. McCoy, Lexington, Virginia   SERVES 4 AS AN ENTRÉE OR 8 AS A SIDE DISH

SALSA

1½ cups chopped Roma tomatoes

½ cup minced red onion

2 jalapeño chiles, seeded and minced, or
⅛ to ¼ teaspoon dried red pepper
flakes

2 tablespoons red wine vinegar

⅛ teaspoon salt

FRITTERS

3 tablespoons vegetable oil

1 egg, beaten

⅔ cup milk

½ cup self-rising cornmeal

1 cup packed grated yellow squash or
zucchini (about 1 medium)

2 tablespoons grated onion

2 tablespoons sour cream

2 tablespoons finely grated Parmesan

¼ teaspoon cayenne pepper

½ teaspoon salt

¼ teaspoon black pepper

"With an abundance of garden vegetables, I have experimented with creative uses for zucchini and yellow squash. The fritters have been enjoyed during our annual July family beach gathering. They're a favorite with young and old."

1. For the salsa, combine the tomatoes, red onion, jalapeños, vinegar, and salt in a bowl; mix well. Refrigerate, covered with plastic wrap, until serving time.

2. For the fritters, combine 2 tablespoons of the oil, the egg, milk, cornmeal, squash, onion, sour cream, Parmesan, cayenne, salt, and black pepper in a medium bowl; mix well. Add additional milk for a thinner consistency.

3. Heat the remaining 1 tablespoon oil in a large skillet over medium heat. Spoon ¼ cup batter per fritter into the skillet to make 4 fritters. Cook until golden, about 2 minutes on each side. Repeat with the remaining batter. Serve immediately with salsa.

TIPS FROM OUR TEST KITCHEN

This makes a nice meatless entrée.

Tomato Casserole

Mrs. Ivor Stephenson, Winnsboro, South Carolina

½ cup (1 stick) butter
1 medium onion, chopped
½ green bell pepper, chopped
2½ cups drained stewed tomatoes
¼ cup all-purpose flour
1 cup milk
½ teaspoon salt
¼ teaspoon black pepper
6 hard-cooked eggs, sliced
1 cup shredded sharp Cheddar
1 sleeve butter cracker crumbs

"This is an old recipe of my mother's that I serve on special occasions such as Thanksgiving."

1. Preheat the oven to 400°F.

2. Melt 1 tablespoon butter in a skillet. Add the onion and bell pepper and sauté until soft. Remove from the heat and add the tomatoes.

3. Make a white sauce by melting 4 tablespoons of the butter in a small saucepan. Stir in the flour and cook for 1 minute. Add the milk gradually, whisking until smooth. Stir in the salt and black pepper and remove from the heat.

4. Arrange half of the sliced eggs in the bottom of a 13 × 9-inch baking dish. Spoon half of the tomato mixture over the eggs. Cover with half of the white sauce. Repeat the layers. Sprinkle with the Cheddar and cracker crumbs. Dot with the remaining butter.

5. Bake for 30 minutes, or until well browned.

Tomatoes Florentine

Martha Wolf, Brighton, Michigan

SERVES 8

One 10-ounce package frozen chopped
spinach

2 large tomatoes, cut into ¾-inch-thick
slices

½ cup dried Italian seasoned bread
crumbs

½ cup chopped green onions (white and
green parts)

3 eggs, beaten

½ cup (1 stick) butter, melted

¼ cup grated Parmesan

¼ teaspoon garlic powder

¼ teaspoon salt, or to taste

¼ teaspoon dried thyme

2 to 3 dashes hot pepper sauce

TIPS FROM OUR TEST KITCHEN

You may use smaller tomatoes, if
desired. Cut into ¾-inch-thick slices
and cover the bottom of the baking
pan. Top with the spinach mixture
and use the back of a spoon to
spread evenly over all. Bake as
directed.

"My family insists that I serve this at our Christmas dinner, along with a standing rib roast. One of our sons doesn't like tomatoes, so I make a tiny casserole for him using all of the other ingredients—except the tomatoes—and sprinkle grated cheese on top."

1. Preheat the oven to 350°F. Grease a 13 × 9-inch glass baking dish.

2. Cook the spinach according to the package directions. Drain well in a colander.

3. Arrange the tomato slices in a single layer on the bottom of the prepared pan. Combine the bread crumbs, green onions, eggs, butter, Parmesan, garlic powder, salt, thyme, and hot sauce in a medium bowl. Add the spinach; mix well.

4. Spoon equal amounts of the spinach mixture on top of each tomato slice. Bake, uncovered, for 15 minutes.

Southern Pecan Praline Yams

Jennifer Pybus, Lockhart, Alabama

One 40-ounce can yams, drained
½ cup orange juice
½ cup chopped pecans
½ cup packed dark brown sugar
¼ cup self-rising flour
¼ teaspoon ground cinnamon
¼ cup (½ stick) butter or margarine,
    melted

"We usually don't need a reason to get together for a fabulous meal, but our family enjoys this sweet side dish, especially when we celebrate Thanksgiving. For that special down-home flavor, I use pecans gathered from my grandmother's backyard pecan orchard. This dish is also great served for dessert with vanilla ice cream."

1. Preheat the oven to 350°F. Grease a 2-quart baking dish.

2. Arrange the yams in the prepared dish. Pour the juice evenly over the yams.

3. Combine the pecans, brown sugar, flour, cinnamon, and butter in a bowl; mix well.

4. Spread the pecan mixture evenly over the yams in a thin layer.

5. Bake, uncovered, for 45 minutes, or until bubbly. Let stand for 15 to 20 minutes before serving.

Fourth of July Zucchini Bake

Carolyn Ruff, Shelbyville, Illinois

SERVES 6 TO 8

4 small zucchini, diced (about 3 cups total)

2 cups club cracker crumbs, about 50 crackers

¼ cup (½ stick) butter

3 eggs

1 small onion, grated

½ cup milk

1½ cups shredded Cheddar

1 teaspoon salt

½ teaspoon pepper

¼ cup grated Parmesan

TIPS FROM OUR TEST KITCHEN

For variety, use yellow crookneck squash instead of the zucchini.

"Our neighbors gave us some zucchini, and I decided instead of frying it I would try some other ideas of my own. This dish is fitting for Independence Day."

1. Preheat the oven to 350°F. Grease a 9-inch deep-dish pie pan or a 9-inch square baking dish.

2. Bring 4 cups water to a boil in a large saucepan. Add the zucchini; reduce the heat and simmer, covered, until tender, about 3 minutes. Drain well in a colander.

3. Press the cracker crumbs on the bottom of the prepared pan to form a crust. Dot with the butter. Spoon the zucchini on top.

4. Whisk the eggs in a medium bowl until fluffy. Stir in the onion, milk, 1 cup of the Cheddar, the salt, and pepper. Pour over the zucchini and sprinkle with the remaining ½ cup Cheddar and the Parmesan.

5. Bake, uncovered, for 35 minutes, or until golden on the edges.

Entrées

Whether it's a traditional baked ham for Easter or Christmas, turkey and dressing for Thanksgiving, or corned beef and cabbage for St. Patrick's Day, a family recipe, handed down through the years, is the centerpiece of the holiday meal.

Michaela Rosenthal of Woodland Hills, California, created the perfect seasonal blend of flavors for fall celebrations in her Pan-Seared Pork Loin with Apples and Onions. Her recipe was the entrée category winner in the *American Profile* Holiday Recipe Contest.

Juanita Barnhart of Greenfield, Indiana, wanted to find a different entrée to serve her family for Christmas dinner after they tired of ham and turkey. Her Creamy Beef Burgundy was a winner—and fills her home with delicious aromas while it cooks.

American Profile readers kicked up the flavors of several of the recipes with spices reminiscent of the season. In Sedalia, Missouri, Wanda White uses cinnamon sticks, whole cloves, and a red wine mari-nade to give her Easter Ham in Burgundy and Sweet Spiced Marinade a rich, distinctive taste, while Leah Kline of Sunset, South Carolina, uses allspice, bay leaves, curry powder, and garlic to season her Deviled Turkey each November. She says it "wouldn't seem right to have Thanksgiving without it."

Those who don't want to spend a lot of time in the kitchen on a holiday might learn from the example of Helgard Suhr-Hollis of New Braunfels, Texas. Suhr-Hollis has time to visit with her guests when Triple Onion Chicken is on her menu. It's assembled the day before and baked the day she serves it.

And Dana Turberville of Uriah, Alabama, found herself on a mission to improve on her grandmother's signature eggplant casserole. Grandma's version was not a family favorite, but Turberville came up with Eggplant Mushroom Casserole, Evolved, which honors her grandmother's memory but yields a tastier result.

Texas-Style Beef Brisket with Panhandle Sauce

Gail Van Osdell, St. Charles, Illinois **SERVES 12 TO 16**

2¼ cups ketchup

1½ cups beer

½ cup packed brown sugar

½ cup white wine vinegar

2 tablespoons Worcestershire sauce

2 tablespoons chili powder

3 garlic cloves, minced

1 cup chopped onions

¼ teaspoon cayenne pepper

One 5- to 7-pound beef brisket

2 tablespoons liquid smoke

TIPS FROM OUR TEST KITCHEN

The brisket may be prepared in advance and refrigerated whole. Next day, slice and pour the reserved sauce over it. Cover the pan lightly with foil. Heat in a 300°F oven for 30 minutes, or until hot.

"Over the years, I've tried quite a few brisket recipes, and this one is by far the best! When fixing it for the family, I'll make the brisket and serve it the same day. But when we're having friends over for dinner, it's a great time saver to fix the beef the day before."

1. Combine the ketchup, beer, brown sugar, vinegar, Worcestershire sauce, chili powder, garlic, onions, and cayenne in a large saucepan. Bring to a boil; reduce the heat and simmer, stirring occasionally, until the sauce thickens, about 30 minutes. Remove from the heat. Pour 2 cups sauce into a bowl, cover, and refrigerate.

2. Preheat the oven to 250°F. Trim excess fat from the brisket. Brush both sides with the liquid smoke and place in a roasting pan. Pour the remaining sauce over the brisket, turning to coat evenly. Bake, covered, for 4 hours, or until tender.

3. To serve, remove the brisket from the pan juices; slice thinly across the grain. Heat the reserved sauce and serve over the sliced brisket.

Creamy Beef Burgundy

Juanita Barnhart, Greenfield, Indiana

SERVES 8 TO 10

4 pounds boneless chuck roast or round
  steak, cut into 1-inch cubes
One 10-ounce can cream of celery soup
Three 10-ounce cans cream of
  mushroom soup
1 cup burgundy or other dry red wine
One 13-ounce can mushroom slices or
  pieces, drained
One 1-ounce envelope dried onion-
  mushroom soup mix
Cooked rice, egg noodles, or mashed
  potatoes

TIPS FROM OUR TEST KITCHEN

This may be assembled a day in
advance and stored in the
refrigerator until baking time.

"My family was tired of the traditional ham or turkey for Christmas dinner, so I decided to fix this recipe for our celebration. It was a big hit, and I have been preparing it each year by request. The house smells delicious when it's in the oven."

1. Preheat the oven to 250°F. Grease a roasting pan.

2. Combine the roast, soups, wine, mushrooms, and soup mix in the prepared pan. Cook, covered, for 4 hours, or until the beef is very tender.

3. Serve over cooked rice, egg noodles, or mashed potatoes. May be served over thick slices of bread as well.

Ben's Swiss Steak

Bernadette Swancer, Medina, Ohio

SERVES 8

2 cups all-purpose flour

4 pounds cube steak, cut into 8 pieces

Salt and black pepper

1/3 cup vegetable oil

2 large green bell peppers, chopped

One 8-ounce package sliced mushrooms

1 large onion, chopped

2 jalapeño chiles, finely chopped

2 large tomatoes, chopped

TIPS FROM OUR TEST KITCHEN

The cube steaks will break down and become smaller, but will create a thick, rich gravy. Remove the seeds from the jalapeño chiles for a very mild dish.

"My son Ben loves Swiss Steak. He's always asking for it and enjoys it with a big helping of mashed potatoes. The jalapeño chiles add a little spice and heat."

1. Place the flour in a 13 × 9-inch baking dish. Add some of the steak pieces and coat evenly with the flour; shake off the excess. Season lightly with salt and black pepper. Remove to a platter. Repeat with the remaining steak.

2. Heat the oil in a large skillet over medium-high heat. Working in four batches, add 2 pieces of beef and brown for 3 minutes on each side. When browned, transfer to a Dutch oven. Repeat with the remaining pieces of beef. Add additional oil if needed.

3. Add 1 cup water to the pan drippings. Bring to a boil, scraping the bottom and sides of the skillet to loosen browned bits. Pour over the beef. Top with the bell peppers, mushrooms, onion, jalapeños, and tomatoes.

4. Bring to a boil, reduce the heat, cover tightly, and simmer for 1 hour and 45 minutes until very tender when pierced with a fork. Rearrange the cube steak pieces occasionally to keep them from sticking to the bottom of the pan.

Slow Cooker Beer Stew

Mary J. Lewis, Eatonton, Georgia

SERVES 12

1 pound bacon slices

2 large onions, chopped

2 large green bell peppers, chopped

2 jalapeño chiles, chopped

2 medium garlic cloves, minced

½ teaspoon black pepper

One 12-ounce can or bottle dark beer

10 medium tomatoes, diced, or four
    14-ounce cans diced tomatoes

One 6-ounce can tomato paste

One 1-ounce package chili mix

One 1-ounce package taco mix

4 pounds ground sirloin

Salt and black pepper

3 cups shredded mozzarella or Mexican-
    style cheese

Sour cream

TIPS FROM OUR TEST KITCHEN

This stew freezes well. Remove the seeds from the jalapeño chiles for a very mild dish. Add canned dark kidney beans for a heartier stew.

"Like most good recipes, this one developed over time. It is tried and true and always makes a hit. This stew is all meat and taste."

1. Place a large skillet over medium-high heat. Add the bacon and cook until browned, stirring frequently. Remove the bacon with a slotted spoon and drain on paper towels. Crumble.

2. Add the onions, bell peppers, and jalapeño chiles to the bacon drippings. Cook, stirring frequently, until the onions are translucent, about 6 minutes. Add the garlic and black pepper; cook for 15 seconds. Add the beer and bring to a boil.

3. Remove the skillet from the heat and transfer the mixture to a greased 6-quart slow cooker. Add the tomatoes, tomato paste, and chili and taco mixes.

4. Add one-third of the ground sirloin to the skillet and cook over high heat until browned, stirring frequently. Add the browned sirloin to the slow cooker and repeat with the remaining beef. Cover and cook on high for 4 to 5 hours. Season with salt and black pepper.

5. At serving time, spoon the stew into soup bowls. Top each portion with 2 tablespoons mozzarella, sour cream, and bacon.

FEBRUARY
[2]

Camp House Stew

James Harvey, Dayton, Texas

SERVES 10 TO 12

1 tablespoon olive oil

¼ cup chopped bacon or washed salt pork

2 to 3 pounds stew meat, such as beef, venison, or any wild game

3 large sweet onions, sliced

1½ beef bouillon cubes

2 tablespoons paprika

1 teaspoon salt

1 teaspoon dried marjoram

1 teaspoon black pepper

One 12-ounce beer, optional

One 6-ounce can tomato paste

1 tablespoon Worcestershire sauce

4 large white or red potatoes, cubed

6 carrots, thickly sliced

3 garlic cloves, crushed

2 small turnips, diced

1 tablespoon Tabasco sauce, optional

"I love to deer-hunt, and my wife loves to camp, but there are times she is unable to go with me to our deer camp, so I had to learn to feed myself. My wife has found out I really can cook, so guess who does the cooking at camp now? I should have stuck to sandwiches!"

1. Heat the olive oil in a large stewpot. Add the bacon and cook. Add the meat; cook and stir over medium-high heat until lightly browned on all sides. Remove the meat.

2. Reduce the heat to medium and add the onions, ½ cup water, and the bouillon cubes. Cook, stirring, until the onions are tender. Add the paprika, salt, marjoram, pepper, beer, if using, tomato paste, Worcestershire, and ½ cup water; mix well. If not using beer, add 1 cup water. Return the meat to the pot, cover, and simmer, stirring often, until tender, about 1 hour. Add the potatoes, carrots, garlic, turnips, Tabasco, if using, and 1 cup water. Cover and simmer, stirring often, for 45 minutes, or until the vegetables are cooked.

Grandpa K's Chile Rolls

John Konitzer Jr., Albuquerque, New Mexico

SERVES 8

3 tablespoons vegetable oil

1 cup chopped onions

4 to 6 poblano chiles, seeded and
    chopped

1 tablespoon minced garlic
    (about 6 garlic cloves)

1 teaspoon salt

1 teaspoon black pepper

1 pound lean ground beef

¼ cup chopped cilantro

Two 8-ounce cans refrigerated crescent
    dinner rolls

Two 8-ounce packages cream cheese,
    softened

4 cups shredded Cheddar

Sour cream, optional

Additional cilantro, optional

TIPS FROM OUR TEST KITCHEN

For a milder dish, use two 4-ounce
cans chopped mild green chiles
instead of the poblanos and add
them after the beef is browned.

"On special occasions, I make my famous green chile stew for my family and close friends. On many festive occasions, I make fruit pies using crescent roll dough. I thought I would combine some of those ideas and see if I could make something new and different. These Chile Rolls were a big surprise and successful with my family."

1. Preheat the oven to 350°F. Grease a baking sheet.

2. Heat 1 tablespoon of the oil in a large skillet over medium heat. Add the onions, poblanos, garlic, salt, and black pepper. Cook for about 4 minutes, stirring frequently. Add the beef and cook until browned, stirring frequently. Remove the skillet from the heat. Stir in the cilantro.

3. Unroll the crescent rolls on the baking sheet; press the 2 pieces of dough together. Do not separate the rolls. Spread the cream cheese evenly over the dough and spread the meat mixture down the center lengthwise. Sprinkle with 2 cups of the Cheddar. Fold the sides of the rolls in toward the center, overlapping slightly. Pinch the seam to seal. Brush the top of the dough with the remaining 2 tablespoons oil and sprinkle with the remaining 2 cups Cheddar.

4. Bake for 30 minutes, or until the crust is golden. Let stand for 10 minutes to absorb the flavors. Cut into 2–inch slices and serve topped with sour cream and additional cilantro, if desired.

Irish Beef Potpies

Mary J. Lewis, Eatonton, Georgia

SERVES 8 TO 12

6 tablespoons butter or margarine

2 pounds top sirloin, cut into ½-inch cubes

¾ cup Irish whiskey

2 medium onions, chopped

3 medium carrots, chopped

4 medium garlic cloves, minced

10 dried bay leaves

1 teaspoon pepper

1 teaspoon garlic powder

One 10-ounce can beef consommé

One 10-ounce can cream of mushroom soup

One 13-ounce can whole mushrooms, drained

One 15-ounce can green peas, drained

4 frozen pie shells (not deep-dish), thawed

Butter-flavored nonstick cooking spray

TIPS FROM OUR TEST KITCHEN

The potpies may be served in shallow bowls, if desired.

"My father's side of the family is Irish. This recipe has been developed from the basic meat pie to a rich, delicious delicacy. The vegetables, spices, and Irish whiskey give it a distinctive flavor that fits in perfectly with a St. Patrick's Day menu."

1. Preheat the oven to 350°F.

2. Melt the butter in a large skillet over medium-high heat. Add half of the beef and cook until browned, stirring frequently. Remove with a slotted spoon to a large bowl. Repeat with the remaining beef. Pour the whiskey over the beef, cover with plastic wrap, and set aside.

3. Add the onions, carrots, garlic, bay leaves, pepper, and garlic powder to the pan drippings. Reduce the heat to medium and cook, stirring frequently, until the onions are translucent, about 4 minutes. Add the consommé and cook over medium heat until reduced slightly, about 10 minutes. Remove and discard the bay leaves.

4. Add the consommé mixture to the beef. Stir in the mushroom soup; mix well. Add the mushrooms and peas and stir.

5. Spoon the beef mixture into 2 pie shells, place a pie shell on top of each, and pinch the edges. Make several ½-inch slits in each top crust. Spray with butter-flavored nonstick cooking spray.

6. Line the oven rack with foil. Bake for 1 hour and 20 minutes, or until the crusts are golden.

World's Easiest Pot Roast

Sandra H. Bennett, Washington, Missouri

SERVES 6

One 3- to 4-pound boneless chuck roast
   or arm roast

5 large russet potatoes, quartered

4 celery stalks, cut into 2-inch pieces

1 pound baby carrots

One 1-ounce package dried onion
   soup mix

One 14-ounce can whole peeled
   tomatoes, sliced in thirds and liquid
   reserved

TIPS FROM OUR TEST KITCHEN

To decrease the cooking time,
preheat the oven to 325°F and roast
for 3 hours.

"This method of cooking an inexpensive cut of meat makes it so tender that this recipe quickly became one of our favorite meals. It is assembled very quickly, in 15 minutes or less, and then requires no more attention until it is done."

1. Preheat the oven to 275°F.

2. Arrange two 24-inch-long pieces of heavy-duty foil crosswise in a 15 × 10-inch baking dish. Place the roast in the center of the foil and arrange the potatoes, celery, and carrots around it.

3. Sprinkle the onion soup mix over the roast. Place the tomatoes on top. Add water to the reserved tomato liquid to fill the can and pour over the vegetables surrounding the roast.

4. Bring the ends of the foil together all around, creating a seal so that juices do not escape.

5. Place the dish in the oven and roast for 8 hours. Transfer the roast to a serving platter, surround it with the vegetables, and spoon pan juices over all.

1930's Meat Loaf

Juanita Jones, Kingsville, Texas

SERVES 4 TO 6

1 pound regular or lean ground beef

½ pound mild Italian sausage, casings removed

1 medium onion, chopped

1 cup cracker crumbs or cracker meal

One 6-ounce can tomato paste

3 eggs, beaten

3 tablespoons chili powder

1 teaspoon salt

½ teaspoon pepper

2 bacon slices, halved

TIPS FROM OUR TEST KITCHEN

You may chop the bacon before placing it in the bottom of the pan for more even distribution of flavor, if desired.

"This is the oldest recipe I have. It was given to me by my aunt in Vivian, Louisiana, in 1931. This makes the most delicious cold sandwiches."

1. Preheat the oven to 350°F.

2. Combine the ground beef, sausage, onion, cracker crumbs, tomato paste, eggs, chili powder, salt, and pepper in a large bowl; mix well.

3. Place the bacon strips on the bottom of an 8 × 4-inch loaf pan. Place the ground beef mixture on top of the bacon. Pat down with fingertips to spread evenly.

4. Bake for 1 hour and 5 minutes, or until a meat thermometer reaches 175°F. Remove from the oven and let stand for 10 minutes. Invert on a cutting board and slice.

FEBRUARY

[2]

Mexican Casserole with Corn Bread Topping

Matilda McLane, Cave City, Arkansas

SERVES 8

1 pound ground beef

1 pound mild Italian sausage, casings removed

1 cup frozen corn or Mexican corn, thawed

1 medium green bell pepper, finely chopped

1 medium onion, finely chopped

1 medium garlic clove, minced

1 teaspoon paprika

¼ teaspoon cayenne pepper, optional

One 1-ounce package taco seasoning mix

One 8-ounce can tomato sauce

One 10-ounce can diced tomatoes with green chiles

2 to 3 cups shredded Cheddar or Monterey Jack

One 6-ounce package corn bread mix

⅔ cup milk

1 egg

TIPS FROM OUR TEST KITCHEN

You may substitute any vegetable for the corn.

"For an extra kick, serve the casserole with salsa."

1. Preheat the oven to 350°F. Grease a 13 × 9-inch glass baking pan.

2. Place a large skillet over medium-high heat. Add the ground beef and cook until browned, stirring frequently. Drain on paper towels.

3. Add the sausage to the skillet; cook until browned. Return the beef to the skillet. Add the corn, bell pepper, onion, garlic, paprika, cayenne, if using, taco seasoning mix, tomato sauce, tomatoes with green chiles, and ¾ cup water. Bring to a boil, reduce the heat, and simmer, uncovered, stirring frequently, until slightly thickened, 10 to 15 minutes.

4. Spoon the beef mixture into the prepared pan. Sprinkle evenly with the Cheddar. Combine the corn bread mix, milk, and egg in a bowl; mix well. Pour evenly over the beef mixture. Bake, uncovered, for 30 minutes, or until golden.

Beer Can Grilled Chicken

Marcia Trescott, Council Bluffs, Iowa

SERVES 4

2 tablespoons brown sugar

2 tablespoons paprika

2 teaspoons black pepper

2 teaspoons salt

1 teaspoon garlic powder

1 teaspoon onion powder

1 teaspoon celery seeds

¼ teaspoon cayenne pepper, optional

1 whole chicken

One 12-ounce can beer

TIPS FROM OUR TEST KITCHEN

Use a can of beer only, not a bottle.

"We love to cook and experiment, and we especially love to cook outdoors, where food tastes best. I love to share with others and watch their eyes light up and their appetites get conquered. My job is done."

1. Preheat the grill to medium-high.

2. Combine the brown sugar, paprika, black pepper, salt, garlic powder, onion powder, celery seeds, and cayenne in a bowl; mix well.

3. Rinse the chicken and pat dry. Apply the rub to the chicken, pressing down heavily to allow the seasonings to adhere. Sprinkle any remaining rub in the cavity of the chicken.

4. Remove the tab on the beer can and make additional holes or slits in the top with a can opener. Place the full beer can into the cavity of the chicken. Arrange the chicken on the grill rack in an upright position, pulling the legs apart to form a tripod. Cover the grill and cook until done, 1 to 1¼ hours.

Sausage-Stuffed Chicken Breasts

Ken Kercher, Hillsboro, Illinois

4 boneless, skinless chicken breast halves

¼ pound Italian sausage, casings removed

1 teaspoon Italian seasoning

1 teaspoon garlic powder

½ teaspoon chili powder

1 tablespoon horseradish mustard

1 egg, well beaten

¾ cup all-purpose flour

1½ cups Italian seasoned bread crumbs

"This recipe is derived from an old family recipe for Pheasant Kiev, adjusted for my wife and children, who will not eat wild game. Placing the chicken rolls on a broiling pan allows the juices to drain off and keeps the breasts from getting soggy."

1. Pound the chicken breasts to ¼-inch thickness. Wrap tightly in plastic wrap and refrigerate for at least 2 hours.

2. Break up the sausage and place in a bowl. Add the Italian seasoning, garlic powder, chili powder, and horseradish mustard; mix well. Shape the sausage mixture into 4 links. Wrap tightly in plastic wrap and refrigerate for at least 2 hours.

3. Preheat the oven to 375°F. Brush one side of each chicken breast with the beaten egg. Place 1 sausage link on that side. Roll up and secure with a wooden pick.

4. Roll each breast in flour; dip in the remaining beaten egg; roll in bread crumbs.

5. Place the chicken on a broiler pan. Bake for 45 to 50 minutes until a meat thermometer inserted into the center reads 160°F.

Curry-Flavored Chicken

Michelle Smith, New Castle, Kentucky

SERVES 4 TO 6

6 tablespoons butter or margarine

6 tablespoons all-purpose flour

3 teaspoons curry powder, or to taste

1½ teaspoons salt

¼ teaspoon ground ginger

1½ teaspoons sugar

½ cup chopped onions

2 cups chicken broth

2 cups milk

4 cups shredded or cubed cooked
chicken

1 teaspoon lemon juice

6 to 8 cups cooked white rice

TIPS FROM OUR TEST KITCHEN

Fresh chicken broth is best, but canned or broth made from bouillon is good, too. This dish is also great served over mashed potatoes or egg noodles instead of rice. You may add sautéed vegetables, such as broccoli and red peppers, to this dish.

"I am certain this recipe came from my grandparents, but it may go even further back. I liked this dish so much that I requested it to be made for my birthday each year."

1. Melt the butter over low heat in a heavy saucepan. Blend in the flour, curry powder, salt, ginger, and sugar. Add the onions; cook until translucent.

2. Gradually stir in the chicken broth and milk. Bring to a boil and cook for 1 minute, stirring constantly. Reduce the heat to a simmer; add the cooked chicken and lemon juice. Heat thoroughly, about 3 minutes. Serve over cooked rice.

Chicken Supreme

Barbara Schindler, Napoleon, Ohio

3 tablespoons butter

Six 4-ounce boneless, skinless chicken
  breast halves

1 pound sliced mushrooms

One 2-ounce can sliced black olives

6 green onions, chopped

Salt, pepper, and garlic salt

12 ounces mozzarella, sliced

"This is my own special recipe and is requested often by my family. It keeps the chicken very moist."

1. Preheat the oven to 300°F. Butter a 13 × 9-inch baking dish.

2. Melt the butter in a skillet. Add the chicken and sauté until slightly browned. Remove from the skillet. Sauté the mushrooms, olives, and green onions in the same skillet.

3. Place the chicken in the prepared dish. Season with salt, pepper, and garlic salt. Pour the vegetable mixture over the chicken. Place a cheese slice on top of each chicken breast. Cover with foil. Bake for 45 minutes.

Chili Cheese Chicken

Mary L. Daring, Carey, Ohio

SERVES 4

2 tablespoons extra virgin olive oil

½ teaspoon chili powder

½ teaspoon ground cumin

¼ teaspoon cayenne pepper

½ teaspoon garlic powder

½ teaspoon chopped cilantro, or to taste

¼ teaspoon salt

¼ teaspoon black pepper

4 boneless, skinless chicken breast halves, rinsed and patted dry

2 tablespoons finely chopped red onion

1 medium tomato, seeded and diced

½ medium green bell pepper, cut into thin strips

1 cup shredded Cheddar

TIPS FROM OUR TEST KITCHEN

This dish has great flavors and is low in carbohydrates, too.

"With everyone being more health conscious, this is my family's favorite. I serve it with a large salad and fresh fruit. It is a good dish for the end of summer when vegetables are garden fresh."

1. Combine the olive oil, spices, salt, and black pepper in a jar. Secure with a lid and shake vigorously until well blended.

2. Arrange the chicken in a shallow pan, such as a pie pan, and pour the marinade over the top. Turn the chicken a few times to coat evenly. Let stand for 15 minutes.

3. Preheat the oven to 400°F. Line a baking sheet with foil and arrange the chicken on the sheet. Top with the onion, tomato, and bell pepper.

4. Bake, uncovered, for 20 minutes until the chicken is no longer pink in the center. Remove from the oven, sprinkle evenly with the Cheddar, and bake for 3 minutes, or until the cheese has melted.

5. Remove the chicken to a serving platter. Drizzle any remaining pan drippings over all.

Cornflake Chicken Strips

Deborah Carson, Fort Morgan, Colorado

4 cups crushed plain cornflakes

½ cup all-purpose flour

1 teaspoon Lawry's seasoned salt

½ teaspoon pepper

1 teaspoon poultry seasoning

2 eggs

4 boneless, skinless chicken breast halves, cut into thin strips

Vegetable oil

"In 1983, my children were begging for KFC extra-crispy chicken. Unfortunately, it didn't fit into my budget. I came up with a way to make extra-crispy chicken. It worked, they loved it, and now they all make chicken this way."

1. Combine the cornflakes, flour, seasoned salt, pepper, and poultry seasoning.

2. Beat the eggs with 1 tablespoon water. Dip the chicken strips in the egg mixture and then roll in the cornflake mixture, pressing firmly to coat well.

3. Pour the oil into a large skillet to a depth of about 2 inches. Heat the oil to 250°F. Fry the chicken strips for 6 to 8 minutes, or until done. Serve warm with your favorite dipping sauce.

Never-Fail Slow Cooker Stuffing

Wanda White, Sedalia, Missouri

SERVES 6 TO 12

1 whole chicken, cooked, boned, and
    chopped
One 6-ounce package corn bread
    stuffing mix
1 large onion, chopped
1 cup chopped celery
3 eggs, beaten
One 10-ounce can cream of mushroom
    soup
2 cups chicken broth, or to taste
1 to 1½ teaspoons poultry seasoning
1 teaspoon salt
¼ teaspoon pepper
2 tablespoons butter, cut into small pieces
Chicken gravy, optional

1. Grease a 3½- to 4-quart slow cooker.

2. Combine the chicken, stuffing mix, onion, celery, eggs, soup, broth, and seasonings in a bowl; mix gently. Transfer to the slow cooker. Top with the butter.

3. Cook, covered, on high for 3 hours. Do not remove the lid during cooking time. Serve with chicken gravy, if desired.

TIPS FROM OUR TEST KITCHEN

You may substitute a rotisserie chicken or a 20-ounce bag of frozen, precooked, diced chicken for the whole chicken. Reduce the salt to ½ teaspoon if using an alternative. You may also use herb stuffing rather than the corn bread stuffing, but reduce the poultry seasoning to ¾ teaspoon.

Sour Cream Chicken Enchiladas

Karen E. Nelson, Brookings, Oregon

SERVES 6 TO 8

2 boneless chicken breast halves (about 14 ounces)

2 tablespoons olive oil

1 tablespoon butter

1 medium white onion, finely chopped

2 to 3 medium jalapeño chiles, seeded and finely chopped

3 medium garlic cloves, minced

One 4-ounce can chopped mild green chiles

1 bunch cilantro leaves, chopped

Three 10-ounce cans cream of chicken soup

One 16-ounce container sour cream

Salt and black pepper

Ten 7-inch flour tortillas

2 cups shredded Cheddar

Green or red bell pepper strips, optional

Additional cilantro or sliced olives, optional

Chopped tomatoes or pimientos, optional

TIPS FROM OUR TEST KITCHEN

Substitute 3 cups frozen, precooked chicken strips in place of the chicken breasts for an even quicker dish. Thaw before using.

"Sour Cream Chicken Enchiladas is my signature dish. It is comfort food, and can be both elegant or Tuesday night supper. I have gotten calls from friends across the country who want me to mail them a pan of my enchiladas."

1. Preheat the oven to 350°F. Grease a 13 × 9-inch glass baking pan.

2. Bring 4 cups water to a boil in a deep skillet. Add the chicken, return to a boil, reduce the heat, and simmer, covered, until no longer pink in the center, 10 to 15 minutes. Remove the chicken to a cutting board; cool slightly. Shred using two forks.

3. Return the skillet to medium heat. Add the olive oil, butter, onion, jalapeños, garlic, mild green chiles, cilantro, soup, and sour cream. Cook for 10 minutes, or until thoroughly heated. Remove from the heat and season with salt and pepper.

4. Arrange the tortillas on a work surface. Spoon about ¼ cup of the sauce onto each tortilla, roll up, and place, seam side down, crosswise in the prepared pan. Pour the remaining sauce evenly over the top and sprinkle evenly with the Cheddar.

5. Bake for 30 to 35 minutes until the cheese has melted and the sauce is bubbly around the outer edges. Let stand for 10 minutes. Garnish with green or red pepper strips, cilantro, olives, tomatoes, and pimientos, if desired.

Spicy Chicken Over Angel Hair Pasta

Cheryl Ludemann, Boonville, New York   SERVES 6

3 to 4 tablespoons olive oil

4 cherry peppers, seeded and chopped

1 onion, chopped

1 red bell pepper, chopped

1½ pounds boneless, skinless chicken
   breast halves, cut into bite-sized
   pieces

2 garlic cloves, chopped

One 14-ounce can chopped tomatoes

1 pound angel hair pasta

Parmesan

TIPS FROM OUR TEST KITCHEN

Cherry peppers are round, bright red peppers with a sweet and mildly hot flavor.

"Watch out—the cherry peppers make this a spicy dish! They will also cause you to cough when they are cooked in the hot oil."

1. Heat the olive oil in a large skillet over medium-high heat. Add the cherry peppers, onion, and bell pepper. Sauté for 2 minutes. Add the chicken; sauté for 3 to 4 minutes. Add the garlic and sauté for 1 minute longer. Add the tomatoes, reduce the heat to medium, and simmer.

2. Cook the pasta according to the package directions; drain.

3. Divide the pasta among 6 serving plates. Spoon the chicken mixture on top. Sprinkle with Parmesan.

Triple Onion Chicken

Helgard Suhr-Hollis, New Braunfels, Texas

SERVES 4

2 bacon slices, chopped

2 cups sliced mushrooms

3 leeks, well rinsed, trimmed, and cut into julienne strips

1 medium onion, chopped

½ cup sour cream

½ cup heavy cream

½ cup shredded Cheddar

One 1-ounce envelope dried onion–mushroom soup mix

½ teaspoon paprika

¼ teaspoon salt, or to taste

¼ teaspoon pepper, or to taste

4 boneless, skinless chicken breast halves (1 to 1½ pounds)

"I like to fix this dish when we have company because you prepare it the day before and have time to visit the day you serve it. Also, tastes delicious!"

1. Heat a Dutch oven over medium heat. Add the bacon, mushrooms, leeks, and onion. Cook, stirring frequently, until the onion is translucent, about 8 minutes. Add the sour cream, heavy cream, Cheddar, and soup mix; mix well. Cook for 10 minutes, then stir in the paprika, salt, and pepper. Remove from the heat.

2. Grease a 13 × 9-inch glass baking dish. Arrange the chicken in the pan. Pour the mushroom mixture evenly over the chicken. Cool for 30 minutes, cover with plastic wrap, and refrigerate overnight.

3. Preheat the oven to 350°F. Remove the plastic wrap and bake, uncovered, for 1 hour.

FEBRUARY
[2]

Comfort Turkey Casserole

Jo Ann Reid, Salisbury, North Carolina

SERVES 6

One 16-ounce package frozen broccoli
 florets

3 cups cooked rice, preferably long grain

4 cups cubed cooked turkey or chicken

One 7-ounce jar sliced mushrooms,
 drained

One 6-ounce package or 8 slices
 American cheese

½ cup chicken broth

One 10-ounce can cream of mushroom
 soup

½ cup mayonnaise (not light or fat free)

One 2-ounce can French-fried onions

TIPS FROM OUR TEST KITCHEN

This is a great way to use up leftover
turkey and rice. No leftovers? You
may use a 20-ounce package frozen,
precooked, diced chicken breasts, if
desired.

"I like to make this recipe after Thanksgiving or Christmas because it's a good way to use up leftover turkey. If I don't have turkey, chicken is just as good. My family enjoys this dish very much."

1. Preheat the oven to 350°F. Grease a 13 × 9-inch glass baking dish.

2. Cook the broccoli according to the package directions; drain well. Layer the rice, broccoli, turkey, mushrooms, and cheese in the prepared pan. Pour the broth evenly over the top.

3. Combine the soup and mayonnaise in a small bowl; mix well. Spoon over the top of the casserole, using the back of a spoon to spread evenly. Sprinkle the onions over the soup mixture. Bake, uncovered, for 35 to 40 minutes until golden.

Deviled Turkey

Leah Kline, Sunset, South Carolina

One 12-pound whole turkey, thawed,
   if frozen
2 tablespoons chopped sage
2 teaspoons curry powder
2 teaspoons garlic powder
2 teaspoons dried parsley
2 teaspoons celery seeds
1 teaspoon paprika
½ teaspoon dry mustard
¼ teaspoon ground allspice
4 dried bay leaves
1 to 2 tablespoons salt
1 to 2 tablespoons pepper
⅓ cup vegetable oil

"With all the seasonings, this turkey recipe has the best taste. It wouldn't seem right to have Thanksgiving without it. I love to make gravy from the pan drippings and serve it with mashed potatoes."

1. Rinse the turkey and pat dry with paper towels.

2. Combine the sage, curry powder, garlic powder, parsley, celery seeds, paprika, mustard, allspice, bay leaves, salt, and pepper in a bowl; mix well.

3. Using a paring knife, make ½-inch slits in the turkey breast, twisting the knife to make a slight gap. Rub the entire surface of the turkey evenly with the oil. Put the sage mixture inside the slits and then rub on the outside. Place any remaining sage mixture inside the cavity. Cover with plastic wrap and refrigerate overnight.

4. Preheat the oven to 325°F. Place 2 inches of water in a large roasting pan that is at least 6 inches deep. Place a rack in the pan. Remove the plastic wrap from the turkey and place on the rack, breast side down.

5. Cook, covered, for 3 hours, or until the internal temperature reaches 180°F. Remove from the oven, place on a cutting board, and let stand for 15 minutes before slicing. Remove and discard the bay leaves before serving.

Cabbage and Corned Beef with Sweet Tangy Glaze

Barbara Coffelt, Estill Springs, Tennessee　　　SERVES 8

One 4-pound corned beef brisket

2/3 cup packed dark brown sugar

2 tablespoons prepared mustard

2 tablespoons ketchup

1/4 cup vegetable oil

2 heads green cabbage (about 3 pounds), cored and coarsely sliced

3/4 teaspoon sugar

1 1/2 teaspoons salt

"My family loves this recipe anytime, but it's a requirement for St. Patrick's Day."

1. Bring 12 cups water to a boil in an 8-quart stockpot. Add the corned beef, return to a boil, and cook according to package directions.

2. Remove the corned beef to a cutting board and cool for about 10 minutes. Slice thinly against the grain and arrange in an open roasting pan or broiler pan, overlapping the slices slightly.

3. Preheat the oven to 350°F. Combine the brown sugar, mustard, and ketchup in a small bowl; mix well. Spread evenly on top and between the corned beef slices. Bake, uncovered, for 20 minutes, or until the glaze is browned.

4. Heat the oil in the stockpot over medium-high heat. Add the cabbage, sugar, and salt. Cook, stirring frequently with a long-handled spoon, until crisp-tender, 10 to 12 minutes. Arrange the cabbage on a serving platter. Top with the corned beef.

Ham in Burgundy and Sweet Spiced Marinade

Wanda J. White, Sedalia, Missouri

SERVES 20

One 10-pound bone-in ham, shank
    portion
10 to 12 cinnamon sticks, broken in half
24 whole cloves
Two 750ml bottles burgundy wine

TIPS FROM OUR TEST KITCHEN

An alternate way to marinate the ham is to place it in a large turkey bag, add the wine, seal the bag with a twist tie, and turn several times to coat. Place in a 13 × 9-inch glass baking dish and refrigerate for 48 hours, turning occasionally.

"The first time I baked this ham, my eight-year-old daughter was really fascinated with the procedure. The ham has a slightly pink color and smells wonderful."

1. Trim off the rind and make 20 to 24 holes in the ham with a paring knife, twisting the knife to form a ½-inch gap. Insert the halved cinnamon sticks in each of the slits, with the jagged side in the ham, leaving ¼ inch showing. Insert the cloves over the entire ham surface, particularly near the cinnamon sticks.

2. Place the ham in a nonreactive stockpot. Cover the ham with several layers of cheesecloth and pour the wine through the cheesecloth, soaking the ham thoroughly. Refrigerate for 48 hours, turning and basting the ham occasionally.

3. Preheat the oven to 325°F.

4. Remove the ham from the stockpot; discard the cheesecloth. Place the ham in a 13 × 9-inch glass baking dish and bake for 18 to 20 minutes per pound until the internal temperature reaches 160°F. Remove the ham from the oven and let stand for 15 minutes before slicing.

Dotty's Ham Loaf

Dorothy Williams, Greencastle, Indiana

LOAF

2 pounds smoked ham, coarsely chopped

8 ounces bulk pork sausage

1 cup cracker crumbs or cracker meal

2 tablespoons minced onion

2 eggs, beaten

1 teaspoon salt, or to taste

1¼ cups milk

1 tablespoon finely chopped parsley

GLAZE

¾ cup packed brown sugar

¼ cup cider vinegar

¾ teaspoon dry mustard

SAUCE

¾ cup mayonnaise

¾ cup sour cream

¼ cup prepared mustard

1 to 2 tablespoons prepared horseradish

1 teaspoon lemon juice

⅛ teaspoon salt

TIPS FROM OUR TEST KITCHEN

If desired, heat the sauce over medium heat until thoroughly heated. Do not boil or it will separate.

"This is my special Ham Loaf. It is wonderful, especially around Christmas. We look forward to it. It is so good and is different from any I have ever tasted anywhere else."

1. Preheat the oven to 350°F. Grease an 8 × 4-inch loaf pan.

2. To prepare the loaf, place the ham in a food processor and process until it is the texture of ground beef. Combine the ground ham with the sausage, cracker crumbs, onion, eggs, salt, milk, and parsley in a large bowl; mix well.

3. Place the ham mixture in the prepared pan and flatten slightly.

4. To prepare the glaze, combine the brown sugar, vinegar, and dry mustard in a small bowl; whisk to blend and set aside.

5. To prepare the sauce, combine the mayonnaise, sour cream, prepared mustard, horseradish, lemon juice, and salt in another bowl. Refrigerate until serving time.

6. Bake the ham loaf for 40 minutes. Remove from the oven and spoon the glaze over the loaf; bake for 1 hour longer. Remove from the oven, pour off any grease, and let stand for 10 minutes before slicing. Serve with the sauce.

Grilled Kielbasa Kabobs with Pineapple

Gloria Smith, Nixa, Missouri

1 pound kielbasa sausage, cut into 22 pieces

18 whole mushrooms

1 large green bell pepper, cut into 18 cubes

2 medium zucchini, halved lengthwise and cut into 1-inch pieces (18 total)

One 20-ounce can pineapple chunks, drained, 18 pieces, reserve remaining chunks for later use

1/3 cup olive or canola oil

1 1/2 tablespoons Dijon mustard

1 teaspoon lemon juice

1 teaspoon soy sauce

Salt and black pepper

Brown rice or couscous

"I came up with this easy recipe when I was thinking of dishes for my son to make to earn a cooking badge for his Ranger troop. Since he was the first one to make this recipe, he *really* loves it."

1. Preheat a grill or the broiler to high.

2. Thread six 12-inch skewers, alternating the sausage, vegetables, and pineapple. Combine the olive oil, mustard, lemon juice, and soy sauce in a jar. Season with salt and pepper. Secure the lid and shake to blend thoroughly.

3. Place the skewers on the grill rack and brush with half of the sauce. Cook for 6 minutes, turn, and brush with the remaining sauce. Cook until browned, about 4 minutes.

Pan-Seared Pork Loin with Apples and Onions

Michaela Rosenthal, Woodland Hills, California.

¼ cup all-purpose flour

Two 2-pound whole pork tenderloins

1 tablespoon seasoned salt

¼ cup peanut oil

2 tablespoons unsalted butter

1 teaspoon extra virgin olive oil

1 teaspoon dark brown sugar

1 teaspoon grated lemon zest

1 teaspoon lemon juice

¼ cup apple juice or apple cider

2 teaspoons orange marmalade or 1½ teaspoons sugar plus ¼ teaspoon grated orange zest

¼ teaspoon ground nutmeg

2 large tart apples, such as Granny Smith, peeled and chopped (about 1 pound total)

2 large red onions, peeled and chopped (about 3 cups)

"Pan-Seared Pork Loin is perfect for a special fall dinner for the family or guests."

1. Preheat the oven to 425°F.

2. Place the flour in a shallow pan and coat the pork evenly with the flour. Shake off excess flour and sprinkle the seasoned salt evenly over all.

3. Heat the oil in a large skillet over high heat. Add the pork and cook until richly browned. Place in a 13 × 9-inch baking pan and bake for 15 minutes. Reduce the heat to 325°F and cook for 22 to 25 minutes until the internal temperature reaches 165°F on a meat thermometer.

4. Combine the butter and olive oil in a large skillet over medium-high heat. When the butter is melted, add the brown sugar, lemon zest, lemon juice, apple juice, marmalade, and nutmeg; mix well. Add the apples and onions, reduce the heat to medium, and cook, stirring frequently, until the apples are tender and the onions begin to turn brown, 20 to 25 minutes.

5. Remove the cooked tenderloins to a cutting board and let stand for 10 minutes before slicing into ½-inch slices. Tent with a sheet of foil to keep warm, if desired.

Bourbon Pork Tenderloin

Louise Vilsack, Glenshaw, Pennsylvania

SERVES 8

MARINADE AND MEAT

¼ cup soy sauce

2 tablespoons brown sugar

¼ cup bourbon

One 2½-pound pork tenderloin

SAUCE

⅓ cup sour cream

½ cup mayonnaise

1 tablespoon chopped onion

1 tablespoon dry mustard

1½ teaspoons red wine vinegar

¼ teaspoon salt

"I am a senior citizen who still likes to cook and entertain. This recipe has become a favorite of many of my friends and family."

1. To prepare the marinade, combine the soy sauce, brown sugar, and bourbon. Stir well to dissolve the sugar. Place the tenderloin in a zip-top plastic bag. Pour in the marinade. Refrigerate for 3 hours.

2. Preheat the oven to 325°F. Place the pork in a baking dish. Bake for 2 hours, basting frequently with the marinade. Cool the roast and slice for serving.

3. To prepare the sauce, combine the sour cream, mayonnaise, chopped onion, dry mustard, vinegar, and salt in a saucepan. Bring to a boil. Remove from the heat, cool slightly, and place in a dish to serve with the pork.

Roast Pork with Cherry Sauce

Bobbie E. Bankston, Midland, Texas

SERVES 8 TO 10

1 teaspoon salt

1 teaspoon pepper

1 teaspoon dried rubbed sage

One 3- to 4-pound boneless pork loin roast

One 14-ounce can red, tart, pitted cherries in water

1½ cups sugar

¼ cup cider vinegar

12 whole cloves

1 cinnamon stick

⅓ cup cornstarch

1 tablespoon lemon juice

1 tablespoon butter

3 to 4 drops red food coloring, optional

TIPS FROM OUR TEST KITCHEN

For a sweet/tart sauce, use less sugar.

"My teenager would make a sandwich from the leftovers and a hamburger bun. Christmas Eve was a time to have fruit salad on the table, too."

1. Preheat the oven to 325°F.

2. Combine the salt, pepper, and sage in a small bowl; mix well. Rub the pork roast with the mixture and place in an 11 × 7-inch baking dish, fat side up. Bake, uncovered, for 1 hour and 15 minutes until the internal temperature reaches 160°F on a meat thermometer.

3. Drain the cherries, reserving the liquid. Add enough water to the cherry liquid to measure ¾ cup. Pour ½ cup of the liquid into a medium saucepan. Add the sugar, vinegar, cloves, and cinnamon stick. Bring to a boil, reduce the heat, and simmer, uncovered, for 10 minutes. Remove the cloves and cinnamon and discard.

4. Combine the cornstarch with the reserved ¼ cup liquid and stir until the cornstarch has dissolved completely. Using a whisk, stir the cornstarch mixture into the hot cherry liquid. Bring to a boil and cook for 2 minutes, stirring constantly. Stir in the lemon juice, butter, cherries, and food coloring, if desired. Cook for 1 minute longer to heat thoroughly. Place the pork on a cutting board and let stand for 15 minutes before slicing. Serve with the cherry sauce.

Lamb with Curry Sauce

Helen F. Hough, Rockport, Texas

SERVES 6 TO 8

½ cup dry sherry

½ cup chopped pitted dates or seedless
   raisins

1 tablespoon chopped crystallized ginger

1 tablespoon chicken bouillon granules
   (or 3 bouillon cubes)

2 tablespoons soy sauce

½ teaspoon curry powder, or to taste

¼ teaspoon garlic salt, or to taste

1 tablespoon olive oil

3 to 3½ pounds whole lamb leg roast

Parsley, optional

"My husband's parents did not like turkey, so we had lamb for Thanksgiving. The recipe works well with lamb chops or shanks, too."

1. Preheat the oven to 350°F.

2. Combine the sherry, dates, ginger, bouillon, soy sauce, curry powder, garlic salt, and 3 tablespoons water in a small bowl; mix well.

3. Heat the olive oil in a large skillet over medium heat. Add the lamb and brown on all sides. Place the lamb in a Dutch oven on a wire rack. Pour the sherry mixture over the lamb, cover tightly, and bake, basting frequently with the sherry mixture, for 1 hour and 15 minutes, or until the internal temperature reaches 165°F.

4. Remove the lamb from the oven. Place on a cutting board and let stand for 10 minutes before slicing. Slice the lamb and arrange on a serving platter.

5. Skim the fat from the pan liquids and pour the sauce evenly over all. Garnish with parsley, if desired.

Aunt Peggy's Salmon Pasta Salad

Peggy Galletley, Porterville, California

SERVES 4 TO 6

8 ounces dried angel hair or vermicelli
    pasta, broken into thirds

1 small zucchini or yellow squash,
    chopped

½ cup chopped celery

⅓ cup finely chopped red onion

One 2-ounce can sliced ripe olives,
    drained

One 7-ounce jar marinated artichoke
    hearts, drained and coarsely chopped

3 tablespoons chopped basil or cilantro,
    or to taste

2 tablespoons chopped parsley, or to taste

½ teaspoon garlic salt, or to taste

¼ teaspoon celery seeds, or to taste

¼ teaspoon pepper, or to taste

½ cup mayonnaise, or to taste

1 pound salmon fillets, cooked, flaked,
    and chilled

Spring greens, optional

TIPS FROM OUR TEST KITCHEN

For variety, add water chestnuts, raw chopped cauliflower or broccoli, and jalapeño chiles. You may use rotini instead of angel hair pasta.

"My husband is a truck driver with a gourmet palate. He gets frustrated at the food available on the road and has a large plug-in refrigerator in his truck now. I make cold pasta dishes that are flavorful and have fresh vegetables and protein for his dinners while he's away."

1. Cook the pasta according to the package directions. Drain well and run under cold water to cool quickly. Shake off the excess liquid and place in a large bowl.

2. Add the zucchini, celery, onion, olives, artichoke hearts, basil, parsley, garlic salt, celery seeds, pepper, and mayonnaise. Toss gently, but thoroughly, to coat completely. Fold in the salmon. Serve on a bed of spring greens, if desired.

Salmon with Savory Seafood Rub

Laura Frerich, Napoleon, Ohio

SERVES 4

Four 6-ounce salmon fillets, rinsed and
    patted dry
2 tablespoons olive oil
1 tablespoon dark brown sugar
1 teaspoon dry mustard
1 teaspoon chili powder
1 teaspoon ground cumin

TIPS FROM OUR TEST KITCHEN

It's important to pat the fillets dry.
Otherwise the oil and seasonings
will not adhere properly.

"My husband is a seafood lover. He discovered this
quick, easy meal one night when he was in charge of
our July 4 entrée."

1. Place the fillets on a foil-lined baking sheet. Spoon the olive oil evenly over all. Combine the brown sugar, dry mustard, chili powder, and cumin in a small bowl; mix well. Sprinkle the rub over the salmon; press down to allow the spices to adhere. Refrigerate for at least 30 minutes to overnight.

2. Preheat the oven to 400°F. If refrigerated for 30 minutes, bake the salmon for 8 to 10 minutes until opaque in the center. If refrigerated overnight, bake for 10 to 12 minutes until opaque in the center. Do not overcook.

Payette's Seafood Gumbo

Carol Payette, Friendswood, Texas

SERVES 18

1 small bunch green onions, chopped

1½ cups chopped onions

1 medium green or red bell pepper, chopped

1 medium celery stalk, chopped

4 medium garlic cloves, minced

1 cup vegetable oil

1 cup all-purpose flour

2 dried bay leaves

1 tablespoon salt

1 teaspoon black pepper

½ teaspoon cayenne pepper

½ teaspoon dried oregano

½ teaspoon dried thyme

3 pounds uncooked shrimp, peeled and deveined

1 pound crabmeat, picked clean

½ cup chopped parsley

Gumbo filé, optional

TIPS FROM OUR TEST KITCHEN

To cool the mixture quickly, place the gumbo in a large roasting pan or two large pans on wire racks. When cooled, place in gallon-sized plastic storage bags and refrigerate overnight.

"We had a place on the bay in San Leon, Texas, and during holidays and vacations it was always party time with our family, friends, and neighbors. And this gumbo was always a hit."

1. Combine the onions, bell pepper, celery, and garlic in a medium bowl; mix well.

2. Heat the oil in a Dutch oven over medium heat. Gradually add the flour, stirring constantly. Cook for 15 to 17 minutes until the flour mixture is a rich dark brown color, stirring constantly. Be careful not to burn. Add half of the onion mixture and cook for 1 minute, stirring constantly. Add the remaining onion mixture and cook for 2 minutes.

3. Remove from the heat; gradually add 4 cups water, 1 cup at a time, stirring constantly until the flour dissolves. Add another 4 cups water. Increase the heat to high and bring the mixture to a boil, stirring occasionally.

4. Reduce the heat and add the bay leaves, salt, black pepper, cayenne, oregano, and thyme. Simmer, covered, for 1 hour. Add the shrimp and crab and cook until the shrimp is opaque in the center, about 10 minutes. Remove from the heat, discard the bay leaves, and add the parsley and gumbo filé, if using. Flavors improve greatly if the gumbo is refrigerated overnight.

Shrimp with Arugula and Penne Pasta

Jo Ann Geary, Whispering Pines, North Carolina

SERVES 6

¼ cup plus 2 tablespoons olive oil

2 pounds medium shrimp, peeled and deveined

¼ teaspoon dried red pepper flakes

1 teaspoon dried oregano

½ cup sliced dry or jarred sun-dried tomatoes

2 tablespoons chopped shallots

2 bunches arugula

1½ tablespoons freshly squeezed lemon juice

1 pound penne pasta, cooked

TIPS FROM OUR TEST KITCHEN

Serve this dish with grated Parmesan.

"As a registered nurse living in Manhattan with a miniature galley kitchen, I lived on one- or two-pot dishes, simple and healthy. This delicious combination was one of my favorites."

1. Heat 2 tablespoons of the olive oil in a skillet. Add the shrimp, red pepper flakes, and oregano. Sauté for 2 minutes. Add the sun-dried tomatoes and shallots. Sauté until the shrimp is pink, 2 to 3 minutes longer. Transfer to a large bowl.

2. Add the arugula, the remaining ¼ cup olive oil, and the lemon juice to the shrimp mixture. Fold in the cooked pasta.

Grilled Shrimp on a Stick

Shelia Hake, Bossier City, Louisiana

SERVES 4

One 20-ounce can pineapple chunks in
  syrup
1 cup soy sauce
1 cup sugar
1/2 cup vegetable oil
6 medium garlic cloves, minced
2 teaspoons grated fresh ginger, or to
  taste
2 teaspoons pepper
1/4 cup sesame seeds, toasted
1 bunch green onions, chopped
  (green part only)
1 pound jumbo shrimp, peeled and
  deveined, leave tails on

TIPS FROM OUR TEST KITCHEN

The shrimp may also be cooked in a
preheated broiler, if desired.

"I have a passion for cooking and enjoy making this
awesome crowd-pleaser, which is great for a party—
like on July 4.

1. Drain the pineapple chunks, reserving the syrup. Combine the soy sauce, sugar, oil, garlic, ginger, pepper, sesame
seeds, green onions, and reserved pineapple syrup in a
gallon-sized resealable plastic freezer bag. Seal the bag
tightly and shake to blend thoroughly. Transfer 1 cup of the
marinade to a bowl.

2. Add the shrimp to the bag. Seal tightly and shake to coat
the shrimp thoroughly. Refrigerate the shrimp mixture for
2 to 3 hours, but no longer than 4 hours.

3. Preheat the grill to high. Thread wooden skewers, alternating shrimp and pineapple. Place on the grill rack 4 to 5
inches from the heat source. Grill until the shrimp is opaque
in the center, about 3 minutes on each side, basting with the
reserved marinade.

Best Lasagna

Michelle Kellogg, Heber City, Utah

NOODLES AND CHEESE

1 pound lasagna noodles

16 ounces grated Parmesan

16 ounces shredded mozzarella

16 ounces cottage cheese

MEAT SAUCE

1 pound ground beef

1 onion, chopped

1 garlic clove, crushed

½ pound mild sausage

One 28-ounce can crushed tomatoes

One 12-ounce can tomato paste

1 teaspoon dried oregano

1 teaspoon dried basil

2 teaspoons salt

Pepper

½ teaspoon fennel seeds

¼ cup chopped parsley

CREAM SAUCE

¼ cup butter or margarine

¼ cup all-purpose flour

2 cups milk

"When I married fourteen years ago, my husband would always compare my lasagna recipe to his mother's. My recipe was found lacking. I said I would never make lasagna again until I got his mother's recipe. It took about a year, but I have to admit that this recipe is the best I've tasted."

1. Cook the lasagna noodles according to the package directions. Drain, rinse with hot water, and drain again.

2. To prepare the meat sauce, brown the ground beef in a skillet. Add the onion and garlic. Drain and add the sausage, tomatoes, and tomato paste. Stir in the oregano, basil, salt, pepper to taste, fennel seeds, and parsley. Simmer, covered, for 30 minutes. Uncover and simmer for 30 minutes longer, stirring occasionally.

3. To prepare the cream sauce, melt the butter in a saucepan over medium heat. Stir in the flour. Cook for 1 minute. Add the milk and cook, stirring constantly, until smooth and thick.

4. Preheat the oven to 375°F.

5. To assemble the lasagna, pour one-third of the meat sauce in the bottom of a 15 × 12-inch pan. Arrange 6 or 7 cooked noodles over the sauce. Pour half of the remaining meat sauce over the noodles. Sprinkle with half of the Parmesan. Add another layer of noodles and sprinkle with the mozzarella. Pour the hot cream sauce on top. Layer with the remaining noodles, cottage cheese, remaining meat sauce, and remaining Parmesan. Bake for 30 minutes, or until the cheese melts.

Braciole-Crowned Pasta

Tony T. Greco, Saylorsburg, Pennsylvania

SERVES 4

BRACIOLE

1 pound round steak, flattened to a
   ¼-inch thickness

2 tablespoons Italian bread crumbs

1 tablespoon grated Romano or Parmesan

1 teaspoon finely chopped parsley

1 medium garlic clove, minced

1 tablespoon minced onion

½ teaspoon salt

¼ teaspoon pepper

2 hard-cooked eggs, sliced

2 tablespoons olive oil

TOMATO SAUCE

2 tablespoons olive oil

2 tablespoons finely chopped onion

2 medium garlic cloves, minced

One 28-ounce can crushed tomatoes

½ teaspoon sugar

6 basil leaves

1 teaspoon dried oregano

¼ teaspoon salt, or to taste

⅛ teaspoon pepper, or to taste

12 ounces uncooked penne pasta

¼ cup grated Romano, or to taste

"Braciole is a traditional dish. Though it is a little extra work, Italians serve it on a regular basis. This stuffed steak would be a real taste treat to help celebrate any holiday or dinner."

1. To prepare the braciole, sprinkle the beef evenly with the bread crumbs, cheese, parsley, garlic, onion, salt, and pepper. Arrange the eggs evenly over the top. Roll tightly, starting at one of the short ends. Secure with kitchen string at the ends and in the center.

2. Heat the olive oil in a large skillet over medium-high heat. Add the beef roll and cook on all sides until browned. Remove the beef roll.

3. To prepare the sauce, add the olive oil to the pan and place over medium heat. Add the onion and cook, stirring frequently, until translucent, 2 to 3 minutes. Add the garlic and cook for 15 seconds, stirring constantly. Add the remaining ingredients. Return the beef roll to the pan and spoon some of the sauce over the beef.

4. Bring the mixture to a boil, reduce the heat, and simmer, covered, for 1½ hours, or until very tender. Turn the beef occasionally and spoon the sauce over the roll.

5. During the last 15 minutes of cooking, prepare the pasta according to the package directions; drain.

To flatten the beef, place it on a sheet of plastic wrap, place another sheet of plastic wrap on top of the beef. Using a meat mallet, pound the beef to a ¼-inch thickness.

6. Transfer the beef to a cutting board; let stand for 10 minutes before carefully slicing. Place the pasta in a shallow bowl or platter. Spoon the sauce on top of the pasta. Arrange the beef slices on top and sprinkle with Romano.

Mexican Lasagna

Gwen Swanson, Pukwana, South Dakota

1½ pounds ground beef, browned

One 16-ounce can refried beans

½ teaspoon dried oregano

2 teaspoons ground cumin

¾ teaspoon garlic powder

12 uncooked lasagna noodles

2½ cups salsa

2 cups sour cream

¾ cup sliced green onions

One 2-ounce can sliced black olives

½ cup shredded Mexican-style cheese

"I created this recipe to save time by not having to precook, cool, and drain the lasagna noodles. We think it tastes just as good without all the steps of noodle preparation."

1. Preheat the oven to 350°F. Lightly spray a 13 × 9-inch baking dish with nonstick cooking spray.

2. Combine the browned beef, beans, oregano, cumin, and garlic powder in a bowl; mix well.

3. Place 4 lasagna noodles in the bottom of the baking dish. Spread half of the beef mixture over the noodles. Top with 4 more noodles and the remaining beef mixture. Cover with the remaining noodles.

4. Combine 2½ cups water and the salsa in a bowl. Pour over the noodles. Cover with foil and bake for 1½ hours, or until the noodles are tender.

5. Combine the sour cream, green onions, and olives. Spoon over the casserole and top with the cheese. Return to the oven and bake, uncovered, until the cheese melts. Let stand to set before serving.

Almost Lasagna Zucchini Casserole

Marcella Stewart, Madison, Indiana

SERVES 4

2 to 3 small zucchini, peeled and sliced

1 pound lean ground beef

1 cup chopped onions

One 8-ounce can tomato sauce

One 14-ounce can petite diced tomatoes, drained

One 8-ounce package shredded mozzarella

6 butter-flavored crackers, crushed

Salt and pepper

¼ cup grated Parmesan, or to taste

TIPS FROM OUR TEST KITCHEN

If petite cut tomatoes are not available, chop the plain diced variety into smaller pieces, and drain for a thicker consistency.

"Growing up in the country, we always had a big garden. Zucchini grows so quickly and is so plentiful, we were always looking for new recipes. This one is our favorite."

1. Grease an 8-inch square baking pan. Arrange the zucchini in the bottom of the pan.

2. Heat a large skillet over medium-high heat. Add the beef and onions and cook until browned, stirring frequently. Remove from the heat. Add the tomato sauce and tomatoes to the beef mixture; toss gently, yet thoroughly, to blend. Add the mozzarella; toss gently.

3. Spoon the mixture on top of the zucchini and sprinkle evenly with the cracker crumbs, salt, pepper, and Parmesan. Bake, uncovered, for 45 minutes, or until the top is golden and the zucchini is tender. Remove from the oven and let stand for 20 minutes before serving.

Sausage Penne Family Supper

Trisha Kruse, Eagle, Idaho

SERVES 6

1 pound mild Italian sausage, casings removed

1 cup thinly sliced red onion

1 cup thinly sliced red bell pepper

1 cup thinly sliced mushrooms

8 ounces uncooked penne pasta

2 cups beef broth

1 cup evaporated milk

1 teaspoon minced garlic

2 teaspoons Italian seasoning

¾ cup shredded Cheddar

¼ cup grated Parmesan

"This hearty, family-style meal is quick and tasty. I get a lot of requests for it, and I love it too, so I'm glad to oblige. The mix of veggies gives it nice contrasting colors and flavors. Even kids eat vegetables when they have cheese and pasta along for the ride!"

1. Crumble the sausage into a large skillet. Add the onion, bell pepper, and mushrooms. Sauté until the sausage is cooked through and the vegetables are wilted.

2. Stir in the pasta and broth, bring to a boil, and stir. Reduce the heat and simmer until the pasta is tender, about 15 minutes. Stir in the milk, garlic, and Italian seasoning and heat thoroughly; do not boil. Remove from the heat and add the Cheddar; stir until the cheese is melted. Sprinkle with Parmesan and serve.

Tortellini in Sun-Dried Tomato Sauce

Kathleen Peterson, West End, North Carolina

SERVES 6 TO 8

1 pound cheese or mushroom tortellini

One 8-ounce jar sun-dried tomatoes in oil, undrained

4 ounces pepperoni, sliced

3 tablespoons Dijon mustard

4 medium garlic cloves

1 tablespoon fennel seeds

½ cup olive oil

2 tablespoons lemon juice

One 11-ounce can pitted ripe or Kalamata olives, halved (1½ cups), drained

One 14-ounce can artichoke heart quarters, drained

½ cup finely chopped parsley

3 tablespoons chopped basil

"The sauce part of this recipe was given to me by a friend who is a wonderful Italian cook."

1. Cook the pasta according to the package directions. Drain, but do not rinse, and place in a large bowl. Combine the tomatoes, pepperoni, mustard, garlic, fennel seeds, oil, and lemon juice in a blender or food processor; process until smooth.

2. Add the tomato mixture to the pasta; toss gently to coat. Add the remaining ingredients; mix well. Serve at room temperature or chilled.

Parsley Tortellini Toss

Bobbie E. Bankston, Midland, Texas

SERVES 5 TO 6

One 16-ounce package frozen cheese
    tortellini
1½ cups cubed provolone
1½ cups cubed mozzarella
1 cup cubed cooked ham
1 cup cubed cooked turkey
1 cup frozen green peas, thawed
2 medium carrots, shredded
½ medium green or red bell pepper,
    chopped
½ cup olive oil
3 tablespoons cider vinegar
2 tablespoons grated Parmesan
2 medium garlic cloves, minced
¼ cup chopped parsley
Salt and black pepper

TIPS FROM OUR TEST KITCHEN

You may use 2 cups ham or 2 cups
turkey instead of 1 cup of each, if
desired.

"Everything in this recipe is good for your body. I like to cook good things—for our health."

1. Cook the tortellini according to the package directions. Drain the cooked pasta in a colander and run under cold water to cool quickly. Shake off excess water.

2. Combine the provolone, mozzarella, ham, turkey, peas, carrots, and bell pepper in a large bowl; mix well. Add the tortellini to the cheese mixture.

3. Mix the oil, vinegar, Parmesan, garlic, and parsley in a jar. Secure the lid and shake to blend. Pour over the pasta. Toss gently to coat completely. Cover with plastic wrap and refrigerate for 2 hours to allow the flavors to blend. Season with salt and black pepper.

Mary's 5-a-Day Vegetable Parmesan

Mary H. Hammann, Waggoner, Illinois

SERVES 8 TO 10

4 cups thinly sliced zucchini

1 small onion, sliced

1 green bell pepper, cut into strips

1 medium carrot, grated

2 tablespoons butter or margarine

1 teaspoon salt

Black pepper, optional

1 cup diced tomatoes, seeds removed

3 tablespoons grated Parmesan

Chopped green onions (white and green
    parts)

TIPS FROM OUR TEST KITCHEN

Serve over cooked pasta for a fresh
vegetarian meal.

"In the summer, I like to use all the vegetables from
our garden, especially fresh green onions. I dice
them and use the tops to make this dish colorful."

1. Combine the zucchini, onion, bell pepper, carrot, 1 tablespoon water, butter, salt, and black pepper, if using, in a
large skillet. Cover and cook 1 minute. Uncover and cook,
turning with a wide spatula, until the vegetables are barely
tender, 5 to 10 minutes.

2. Add the tomatoes and Parmesan. Toss and cook for 1 minute longer. Sprinkle chopped green onions on top.

Eggplant Mushroom Casserole, Evolved

Dana Turberville, Uriah, Alabama

7 tablespoons extra virgin olive oil

3 to 4 medium eggplants, sliced about ½ inch thick (about 3 pounds total)

½ teaspoon garlic powder

Salt and black pepper

2 cups shredded Italian Four-Cheese Blend

1½ cups grated Parmesan

1 egg white, beaten

2 cups sliced mushrooms

Two 16-ounce jars spaghetti sauce

"When I was growing up, my grandmother had a summer garden full of every vegetable that could be grown in our southern Alabama climate. One of her personal favorites was eggplant, and she always prepared her Eggplant Mushroom Casserole for our July 4 cookout. It always came out a gray mass of mush, and she was the only one who would eat it. I decided to evolve her eggplant effort, and my family loved it."

1. Preheat the oven to 450°F. Grease a 13 × 9-inch glass baking dish.

2. Line two large cookie sheets with foil. Brush the foil with 3 tablespoons of the olive oil. Arrange the eggplant slices in a single layer on the cookie sheets and brush with the remaining ¼ cup olive oil. Sprinkle the slices with the garlic powder, salt, and black pepper.

3. Place pans on top and bottom racks of the oven. Bake for 7 minutes. Switch the pans from top to bottom racks and bake for 8 minutes, or until the eggplant is lightly browned. Remove from the oven and let stand for 5 minutes. The eggplant may stick to the foil if removed immediately. Reduce the heat to 350°F.

4. Combine the Italian cheese with 1 cup of the Parmesan in a bowl; toss until well blended. Add the egg white and stir until blended.

204   **Hometown Recipes for the Holidays**

The casserole will retain its heat even after standing for 30 minutes at room temperature.

5. Place one-third of the eggplant in the bottom of the prepared pan. Top with half of the mushrooms, one-third of the spaghetti sauce, and half of the cheese mixture. Repeat the layers once and then top with the remaining eggplant and spaghetti sauce.

6. Cover with foil and bake for 45 minutes. Remove the foil, sprinkle with the remaining ½ cup Parmesan, and bake, uncovered, for 15 minutes. Let stand for 30 minutes before serving.

Desserts

"Life's short—eat dessert first" is the mantra of many, and it's certainly justified with holiday desserts such as these.

Barbara Peters of Salem, Illinois, begins her holiday baking in October, making forty varieties of cookies, cakes, and candy to give to lucky family members and friends. Her Luscious Apricot Bars are always included.

Cherry Coconut Bars have been Patty Strickland's favorite ever since a neighbor brought them over when her daughter was born at Christmastime in 1959.

Two Pennsylvania bakers, Heather Stine of Catawissa and Martha Zeleniak of Taylor, have successfully developed variations on a theme. Stine came up with Raspberry Cheesecake Bars to incorporate the taste of her beloved cheesecake into a simpler-to-make bar. And Zeleniak's Pumpkin Pie Squares satisfy pumpkin pie lovers and make life easier on the cook.

For Laura Frerich of Napoleon, Ohio, a quiet Valentine's Day at home with her husband and their new son was the perfect way to celebrate. Her Ooey-Gooey Caramel Turtle Cake was a hit and came in first in the dessert category of the *American Profile*'s Holiday Recipe Contest.

And for Phyllis Willink of Baldwin, Wisconsin, Cranberry Cake with Hot Butter Sauce is an important part of the holidays. She says it's "our Christmas cake," much looked forward to by her three daughters and their families. And we liked it so much that we named it the grand prize winner in our Holiday Recipe Contest.

Luscious Apricot Bars

Barbara J. Peters, Salem, Illinois

One 7-ounce package dried apricots

½ cup (1 stick) butter, softened

¼ cup granulated sugar

1⅓ cups sifted all-purpose flour

½ teaspoon baking powder

¼ teaspoon salt

1 cup packed light brown sugar

2 eggs, beaten

½ teaspoon vanilla extract

½ cup chopped walnuts or pecans

Confectioners' sugar

TIPS FROM OUR TEST KITCHEN

The apricot bars freeze well.

"I bake about forty different kinds of cookies, cakes, and candy for the holidays. I start baking in October and freeze and give everyone plates of baked goods at Christmas. Luscious Apricot Bars is one recipe I always include."

1. Preheat the oven to 350°F. Grease an 8-inch square baking pan.

2. Combine the apricots and 1½ cups water in a medium saucepan. Cook for 10 minutes over medium heat; drain well. Set aside.

3. Combine the butter, granulated sugar, and 1 cup of the flour in a small bowl. Using a fork, mix until crumbly and press into the prepared pan. Bake for 25 minutes, or until the crust is lightly golden.

4. Chop the apricots. Sift together the remaining ⅓ cup flour, the baking powder, and salt in a small bowl. Combine the brown sugar and eggs in a medium bowl, stirring with a fork until well blended. Add the flour mixture; blend well. Stir in the vanilla, walnuts, and chopped apricots. Spread evenly over the crust and bake for 30 minutes, or until lightly browned.

5. Set the pan on a wire rack to cool completely. Cut into bars and roll in confectioners' sugar.

Corn Scallop (page 134)   *Eggplant Casserole (page 136)*

Gramma Tillie's Cheese Potatoes (page 143)

Butternut Squash Bake (page 152)

Autumn Rum-Glazed Carrots (page 131)   *Red, White, and Blue Potatoes (page 142)*

Texas-Style Beef Brisket with Panhandle Sauce (page 160)

Camp House Stew (page 164)   *Spicy Chicken Over Angel Hair (page 178)*

Pan-Seared Pork Loin with Apples and Onions (page 186)

Shrimp with Arugula and Penne Pasta (page 193)

Sausage Penne Family Supper (page 200)

Butterfingers Dessert (page 270)

*Banana Nut Cake with
Banana Nut Frosting (page 221)*

Strawberry Torte (page 273)

Blueberry Bread Pudding with Blueberry Ginger Sauce (page 269)

Banana Oatmeal Cookies (page 264)   *Peppermint Stick Cookies (page 265)*

Georgia Corn Bread Cake (page 231)

Ooey-Gooey Caramel Turtle Cake (page 22

C ranberry Cake with Hot Butter Sauce (page 223)

Cream Cheese Cupcakes (page 271)

Cherry Coconut Bars

Patty Strickland, Waverly, Ohio

CRUST

1 cup all-purpose flour
3 tablespoons confectioners' sugar
½ cup (1 stick) butter, softened

FILLING

2 eggs, beaten
1 cup granulated sugar
¼ cup all-purpose flour
½ teaspoon baking powder
¾ cup chopped walnuts
½ cup sweetened shredded coconut
½ cup maraschino cherries, drained
    and quartered
1 teaspoon vanilla extract
¼ teaspoon salt

"These Cherry Coconut Bars have been a family favorite for forty-eight years. I was a new mother in December 1959 when a neighbor brought over a plate of these bars along with a baby gift. That baby, my daughter Stephanie, passed away in 2005, but I continue to bake these to carry on the Christmas tradition for her husband and three boys."

1. Preheat the oven to 350°F.

2. To prepare the crust, combine the flour, confectioners' sugar, and butter in a medium bowl; mix well. Press the mixture into an 8-inch square baking dish. Bake for 22 minutes, or until lightly golden.

3. To prepare the filling, combine the eggs, granulated sugar, flour, baking powder, walnuts, coconut, cherries, vanilla, and salt in the bowl; mix well. Spoon on top of the crust and spread evenly. Bake for 22 minutes, or until golden brown. Remove from the oven to a wire rack. Cool completely before cutting.

Lemon Bars

Tillie B. Vaughan, Victorville, California

MAKES 24 BARS

2 cups plus 4 tablespoons all-purpose
  flour
1 cup (2 sticks) butter or margarine,
  softened
½ cup confectioners' sugar
4 eggs
2 cups granulated sugar
6 tablespoons freshly squeezed lemon
  juice
1 tablespoon grated lemon zest
1 teaspoon baking powder

"I tried to teach my ten-year-old granddaughter how to make this recipe while we were camping and waiting for her mom and dad to arrive at the campground. Thank goodness they were late, as we made it three times before we got it right. For some reason, I gave her baking soda instead of baking powder, and the batter fizzed all over. After the third try, it came out great, and we have enjoyed it on many campouts since then."

1. Preheat the oven to 350°F.

2. Combine 2 cups of the flour with the butter and confectioners' sugar in a 13 × 9-inch baking pan. Mix together with a fork and press firmly into the bottom of the pan.

3. Bake for 20 to 25 minutes until lightly done but not browned.

4. Beat the eggs in a large bowl using a mixer. Add the granulated sugar; blend well. Add the lemon juice and zest; beat well. Add the baking powder and remaining 4 tablespoons flour; beat well. Pour the mixture over the hot crust; do not let it cool. Bake for 20 to 25 minutes. Sprinkle the top with additional confectioners' sugar.

Holiday Mincemeat Bars

Marjorie Reif, Spearfish, South Dakota

MAKES 16 BARS

¾ cup shortening or margarine

¾ cup sugar

⅓ cup molasses

1½ cups all-purpose flour

2 cups old-fashioned oats

¾ teaspoon salt, optional

One 27-ounce jar mincemeat

"A favorite of our family all these years, this recipe was from my mother. It always brings back happy memories of Christmas and our family of three children. We lived through the Depression, but never felt depressed with goodies like this. Mom could always make do, and I can, too."

1. Preheat the oven to 350°F. Grease a 9-inch square baking pan.

2. Combine the shortening, sugar, molasses, flour, oats, and salt, if desired, in a large bowl. Using two knives or a pastry blender, mix to a coarse crumble.

3. Press half of the oat mixture into the prepared pan. Spoon the mincemeat over the top. Crumble the remaining oat mixture evenly over the mincemeat. Bake for 25 minutes, or until lightly browned. Cool completely on a wire rack before cutting.

Pumpkin Pecan Butterflies

Connie Lindsey, Sauk City, Wisconsin

MAKES 30 COOKIES

2 cups whole wheat pastry flour

1 cup quick oats

1 teaspoon baking powder

1½ tablespoons pumpkin pie spice or cinnamon

½ teaspoon salt

1 cup (2 sticks) butter, cut into small pieces

1½ cups packed brown sugar

1 egg, slightly beaten

1½ teaspoons vanilla extract

1 cup canned pumpkin

½ cup chopped pecans

30 almonds

½ cup chocolate chips

60 (1-inch) pieces pull-and-peel licorice, optional

"Our children have enjoyed this tasty treat for years. There's so much nutrition packed into these little cookies, including loads of vitamin A and fiber, that we eat them for breakfast sometimes."

1. Preheat the oven to 375°F.

2. Combine the flour, oats, baking powder, pumpkin pie spice, and salt in a large bowl.

3. In a separate bowl, blend the butter and brown sugar. Add the egg and vanilla; mix well. Add the butter mixture to the flour mixture. Stir in the pumpkin. Add the pecans. Mix well by hand.

4. Roll the dough into sixty 1-inch balls. Press 2 balls together, pressing the top center of the wings out a bit. Press an almond in the center where the 2 balls come together. Decorate the wings with chocolate chips. Repeat with the remaining dough balls.

5. Bake for about 15 minutes. While still hot, quickly push in the licorice pieces for antennas, if using.

Pumpkin Pie Squares

Martha Zeleniak, Taylor, Pennsylvania

CRUST

1 cup all-purpose flour

½ cup old-fashioned oats

½ cup packed dark brown sugar

½ cup (1 stick) butter or margarine,
  softened

FILLING

One 15-ounce can pumpkin

One 12-ounce can evaporated milk

2 eggs

¾ cup granulated sugar

½ teaspoon salt

1 teaspoon ground cinnamon

½ teaspoon ground ginger, optional

¼ teaspoon ground cloves

TOPPING

½ cup chopped pecans

½ cup packed dark brown sugar

2 tablespoons butter or margarine

Whipped cream, optional

"Pumpkin Pie Squares are so much easier to serve than a pie. They are delicious and everyone loves them. Simple to make, hard to refuse, and excellent to the taste!"

1. Preheat the oven 350°F. Grease a 13 × 9-inch glass baking dish.

2. To prepare the crust, combine the flour, oats, brown sugar, and butter in a medium bowl: Using a pastry blender or a fork, stir until crumbly. Press the mixture into the prepared pan and bake for 15 minutes, or until partially set.

3. To prepare the filling, combine the pumpkin, evaporated milk, eggs, granulated sugar, salt, and spices in the bowl; mix well. Pour over the crust and bake for 20 minutes.

4. To prepare the topping, combine the pecans, brown sugar, and butter in a small bowl. Sprinkle evenly over the filling. Bake for 15 to 20 minutes until the filling is set. Cool completely on a wire rack before cutting into squares. Serve with whipped cream, if desired.

Sour Cream Raisin Bars

Elsie Probasco, Bartley, Nebraska

MAKES 36 BARS

2 cups raisins

1 cup packed dark brown sugar

1 cup (2 sticks) butter or margarine, softened

1¾ cups old-fashioned oats

1¾ cups all-purpose flour

1 teaspoon baking soda

3 egg yolks

1 cup granulated sugar

1½ cups sour cream

2½ tablespoons cornstarch

½ teaspoon ground cinnamon, optional

1 teaspoon vanilla extract

"When I serve cookies at church, everyone asks for Sour Cream Raisin Bars. And a friend asks me to make a pan of these bars for her for Christmas. So I've made a lot of them!"

1. Preheat the oven to 350°F. Grease a 13 × 9-inch glass baking dish.

2. Combine the raisins and 1½ cups water in a medium saucepan. Cook over medium heat for 10 minutes; drain well and set aside to cool.

3. Combine the brown sugar, butter, oats, flour, and baking soda in a medium bowl; mix well using a spoon. Press half of the oat mixture (about 2 cups) into the bottom of the prepared pan to form a crust. Bake for 7 minutes until partially cooked and slightly set.

4. Combine the egg yolks, granulated sugar, sour cream, cornstarch, and cinnamon, if desired, in a medium saucepan and stir until the cornstarch is dissolved. Cook over medium heat until the mixture thickens and resembles pudding, about 8 minutes. Remove from the heat; stir in the cooked raisins and vanilla.

5. Pour into the crust and crumble the remaining oat mixture evenly over the top. Bake for 25 minutes, or until set. Cool completely on a wire rack before cutting.

Raspberry Cheesecake Bars

Heather Stine, Catawissa, Pennsylvania

MAKES 25 BARS

1 cup sugar

½ cup (1 stick) butter, softened

1¼ cups all-purpose flour

One 8-ounce package cream cheese, softened

½ teaspoon almond extract

1 egg

¼ cup seedless red raspberry jam

"I love cheesecake and wanted to take a recipe, simplify it, and make it my own. Whoever gives these bars a chance will really enjoy how easy they are and how delicious."

1. Preheat the oven to 350°F. Grease a 9-inch square baking pan.

2. Combine ½ cup of the sugar and the butter in a large bowl; mix well. Stir in the flour until the mixture is crumbly. Press into the prepared pan. Bake for 15 to 18 minutes until the edges are lightly golden. The mixture will not be fully cooked.

3. Combine the remaining ½ cup sugar, the cream cheese, almond extract, and egg in the large bowl. Beat using a mixer at high speed until well blended.

4. Pour the cream cheese mixture over the crust. Place 2 tablespoons of the jam in a small bowl and microwave on high for 15 seconds until slightly melted. Stir to blend and spoon over the cream cheese mixture. Using the tip of a spoon, carefully swirl the jam into the cream cheese layer, being careful not to disturb the crust.

5. Bake for 18 to 20 minutes until set. Place the pan on a wire rack and let stand for 30 minutes. Using the back of a spoon, stir the remaining jam and spread evenly over the bars in a thin layer. Refrigerate for 30 minutes before cutting into bars. Store leftovers in the refrigerator.

Salted Nut Rollers

Addibeth Beeler, Miles City, Montana

¼ cup evaporated milk

30 caramels

¼ cup (½ stick) butter

1½ to 2 cups sifted confectioners' sugar

One 16-ounce jar salted peanuts

One 16-ounce jar unsalted peanuts

TIPS FROM OUR TEST KITCHEN

This is a very fast-moving recipe that is quick to prepare.

"I make this candy for Christmas and Easter."

1. Combine the evaporated milk, caramels, and butter in a medium saucepan over medium-low heat. Cook until the caramels and butter are melted, stirring frequently. Blend in the confectioners' sugar. Remove from the heat.

2. Spread the salted and unsalted peanuts on a large sheet of wax paper. Using a tablespoon and working quickly, drop caramel mixture over the peanuts. Cover the mixture with the peanuts and shape into rolls, about 3 inches by 1 inch. The rolls will be sticky.

3. Let stand for 30 minutes before wrapping the rollers individually with wax paper or colorful plastic wrap.

Heavenly Holiday Brownies

Marie Brown, Wilson, North Carolina

MAKES 24 BROWNIES

1 cup self-rising flour

¾ cup sugar

One 3-ounce box chocolate instant
 pudding mix

½ cup vegetable oil

2 eggs

2 cups semisweet chocolate chips

1 cup chopped macadamia nuts

1 tablespoon milk

TIPS FROM OUR TEST KITCHEN

Use a flat spatula to carefully remove soft brownies from the baking dish. Firmer brownies are easier to cut into squares.

"I developed this quick, easy dessert to satisfy my family's sweet tooth. I make the brownies as special gifts on Valentine's Day, but they are great all year round. This is a much tastier brownie than conventional recipes."

1. Preheat the oven to 350°F. Grease an 11 × 7-inch glass baking dish with nonstick cooking spray.

2. Combine the flour, sugar, pudding mix, oil, eggs, chocolate chips, macadamia nuts, and milk in a large bowl; stir until just blended. The mixture will be thick. Spoon the batter into the prepared pan. Using the back of a spoon, spread the mixture evenly. Bake for 30 minutes until a wooden pick inserted 2 inches from the edge comes out clean.

3. Cool in the pan on a wire rack for 1 minute before serving for a very soft brownie or cool for 40 minutes for a firmer brownie.

German Apple Cake

Deborah Johnston, Catonsville, Maryland

SERVES 16

3 tablespoons ground cinnamon

3½ cups sugar

4 cups all-purpose flour

4 teaspoons baking powder

1 teaspoon salt

1 cup orange juice

1 cup vegetable oil

4 eggs

7 apples, peeled, cored, and sliced

"This cake recipe was given to me by my great-aunt during a visit to her home in Germany. She doesn't know who originally developed it, as it has been passed down in our family for many generations."

1. Preheat the oven to 350°F. Grease a tube pan.

2. Combine the cinnamon and 1½ cups of the sugar in a bowl; mix well.

3. Sift together the flour, the remaining 2 cups sugar, the baking powder, and salt. Make a well in the center and add the orange juice, oil, and eggs. Beat well with a wooden spoon.

4. Pour half of the batter into the prepared pan. Top with half of the apples and sprinkle with one-third of the sugar-cinnamon mixture. Pour the remaining batter on top and sprinkle with half of the remaining sugar-cinnamon mixture. Top with the remaining apples and the remaining sugar-cinnamon mixture.

5. Bake for 1 to 1½ hours. Cover loosely with foil if the top is becoming too brown during the last 30 minutes. Cool for about 1 hour before slicing.

Good Apple Cake

Agnes Regnaud, Spring Hill, Florida

CAKE

4 medium McIntosh apples, peeled and
    finely chopped (about 4 cups)
2 medium Rome or Granny Smith
    apples, peeled and finely chopped
    (about 2 cups)
1 tablespoon lemon juice
3 eggs
1 cup vegetable oil
2 cups all-purpose flour
1¼ cups granulated sugar
1 teaspoon baking soda
1 to 2 teaspoons ground cinnamon
½ teaspoon salt
1 teaspoon vanilla extract
½ cup chopped walnuts or pecans

FROSTING

3 tablespoons butter, softened
One 3-ounce package cream cheese,
    softened
1½ cups sifted confectioners' sugar
1 teaspoon vanilla extract

TIPS FROM OUR TEST KITCHEN

You may omit the frosting and
sprinkle with confectioners' sugar.
The flavor improves if the cake is
refrigerated for 24 hours.

"I found this recipe while going through my husband's grandmother's old cookbooks. It was in Gram's original handwriting, didn't specify the pan size, and just said 'Bake 'til done.' I had to do some experimenting, but nonetheless this has become a family favorite."

1. Preheat the oven to 350°F.

2. To prepare the cake, combine the apples and lemon juice in a medium bowl. Using a mixer at medium speed, beat the eggs until light. Add the oil and beat until well blended. Add the flour, sugar, baking soda, cinnamon, and salt; beat until smooth. Stir in the vanilla, apples, and nuts.

3. Spread the mixture in an ungreased 13 × 9-inch glass baking dish. Bake for 40 minutes, or until a wooden pick inserted in the center comes out clean. Cool completely in the pan on a wire rack.

4. To prepare the frosting, combine the butter, cream cheese, confectioners' sugar, and vanilla in a medium bowl; beat with a mixer at medium speed until well blended and fluffy. This will be a very thin layer.

Best Applesauce Cake

Janet Connolly, Orange City, Florida

SERVES 16

3 cups applesauce

2 cups sugar

1 cup vegetable oil

4 cups all-purpose flour

4 teaspoons baking soda

1 teaspoon ground cloves

1 teaspoon ground nutmeg

2 teaspoons ground cinnamon

1 cup nuts, optional

1 cup raisins, optional

1 cup dried cherries, optional

"This recipe has been a well-kept secret."

1. Preheat the oven to 325°F. Spray a tube pan with nonstick cooking spray and flour lightly.

2. Combine the applesauce, sugar, and oil in a bowl; mix well.

3. Mix the flour, baking soda, cloves, nutmeg, and cinnamon in a separate bowl. Add to the applesauce mixture; blend well. Add the nuts, raisins, and dried cherries, if using.

4. Pour the batter into the prepared pan. Bake for 1 hour, or until a wooden pick inserted in the center comes out clean.

Banana Nut Cake with Banana Nut Frosting

Nina Grizzard, Las Cruces, New Mexico SERVES 16

CAKE

2¼ cups granulated sugar

¾ cup vegetable shortening

1½ cups mashed bananas

3 eggs

1½ teaspoons vanilla extract

3 cups all-purpose flour

1 teaspoon salt

1½ teaspoons baking powder

1¼ teaspoons baking soda

1 cup buttermilk

1½ cups chopped pecans

FROSTING

2 mashed bananas

3 tablespoons butter, softened

2 cups confectioners' sugar

1½ cups chopped pecans

"This recipe was handed down through my family from my great-grandmother. I am the only one left who makes it for birthdays, so all the family members fight over it."

1. Preheat the oven to 350°F. Spray three 9-inch cake pans with nonstick cooking spray.

2. To prepare the cake, cream the granulated sugar and shortening in a bowl using a mixer. Add the mashed bananas, eggs, and vanilla; mix well.

3. Combine the flour, salt, baking powder, and baking soda in a separate bowl; mix well. Add to the banana mixture alternately with the buttermilk. Beat for 3 minutes with a mixer at medium speed. Stir in the pecans. Pour into the prepared pans. Bake for 30 minutes.

4. To prepare the frosting, beat the mashed bananas, butter, and confectioners' sugar in a bowl. Add additional confectioners' sugar as needed to achieve a spreading consistency. Stir in the pecans.

5. Spread the frosting on top of one layer, top with another layer, frost the top of that layer, then top with the final layer. Frost the top and sides of the cake.

Butter Rum Cake

Judy Prine and Eloise Dance, Hattiesburg, Mississippi

CAKE

1 cup (2 sticks) butter

1 cup vegetable oil

5 eggs

3 cups sugar

3 cups cake flour

1 cup milk

½ teaspoon baking powder

1 teaspooon rum flavoring

1 teaspoooon butter flavoring

1 teaspoooon almond extract

GLAZE

1 cup sugar

1 teaspoon rum flavoring

1 teaspoon butter flavoring

1 teaspoon almond extract

1 teaspoon coconut flavoring

"As a mother, I understand the love my mother mixed into each Butter Rum Cake she prepared the night before gift exchange at school. Now my son, daughter, and I mix cake after cake for each of their teachers. My wish is that my children will make Butter Rum Cake for their children's teachers."

1. Preheat the oven to 350°F. Grease a Bundt pan.

2. To prepare the cake, combine the butter and oil in a saucepan. Heat until the butter melts. Pour into a mixing bowl. With a mixer, beat in the eggs, 1 at a time. Add the sugar, cake flour, milk, baking powder, and flavorings; blend well. Pour the mixture into the prepared pan.

3. Bake for 1½ hours, or until the cake pulls away from the sides of the pan.

4. To prepare the glaze, combine ½ cup water with the sugar and the flavorings in a saucepan. Heat until the sugar melts; do not boil. Pour over the cake while it is still hot.

Cranberry Cake with Hot Butter Sauce

Phyllis Willink, Baldwin, Wisconsin

SERVES 6 TO 8

CAKE

2 cups all-purpose flour

3 teaspoons baking powder

1 teaspoon salt

3 tablespoons butter, melted

1 cup sugar

2 eggs, beaten

1 cup milk

2 cups fresh cranberries

SAUCE

1 cup (2 sticks) butter

2 cups sugar

1 cup cream or half-and-half

2 teaspoon vanilla extract

TIPS FROM OUR TEST KITCHEN

The cake may be served at room temperature with the hot sauce, if desired. Substitute blueberries, blackberries, or raspberries for the cranberries, if desired.

"This recipe is our Christmas cake—our three daughters, their husbands, and their children say the holiday wouldn't be the same without it."

1. Preheat the oven to 350°F. Grease a 13 × 9-inch glass baking pan.

2. To prepare the cake, sift together the flour, baking powder, and salt in a small bowl. Combine the butter and sugar and beat with a mixer at medium speed until well blended. Add the beaten eggs. Add the milk alternately with the sifted dry ingredients, starting and ending with the dry ingredients; mix well. Stir in the cranberries. Pour into the prepared pan. Bake for 30 minutes until a wooden pick inserted in the center comes out clean.

3. To prepare the sauce, combine the butter, sugar, cream, and vanilla in a medium saucepan. Cook over medium-low heat, stirring frequently, until the sugar melts, about 10 minutes. Serve hot over the cake.

Ooey-Gooey Caramel Turtle Cake

Laura Frerich, Napoleon, Ohio

CAKE

¾ cup unsweetened cocoa powder

1½ cups granulated sugar

6 tablespoons butter, softened

1 teaspoon vanilla extract

2 eggs

1⅔ cups all-purpose flour

1 teaspoon baking soda

¾ teaspoon baking powder

¼ teaspoon salt

FROSTING

2 tablespoons butter, softened

¼ cup packed dark brown sugar

3 tablespoons milk

2 teaspoons vanilla extract

2 cups confectioners' sugar

TOPPING

1 cup caramel apple dip

¼ cup finely chopped pecans, toasted

"My husband is a sucker for anything gooey and delicious. The year our son was born, he was only a few weeks old on Valentine's Day. We decided to stay home and celebrate that year. We had a great evening enjoying our new son, our friends, and this cake."

1. Preheat the oven to 350°F. Coat the bottoms of two 8-inch round cake pans with nonstick cooking spray and line with wax paper. Coat the wax paper with nonstick cooking spray and dust with 1 tablespoon flour.

2. To prepare the cake, combine 1½ cups boiling water and the cocoa in a small bowl; whisk until well blended. Set aside to cool completely.

3. Combine the sugar, butter, and vanilla in a large bowl. Beat with a mixer at medium speed until well blended. Add the eggs, 1 at a time, beating well after each addition.

4. Combine the flour, baking soda, baking powder, and salt in a small bowl; mix well. Add the flour mixture and cocoa mixture alternately to the sugar mixture, beginning and ending with the flour mixture. Pour the batter into the prepared pans; sharply tap the pans once on the counter to remove any air bubbles. Bake for 25 minutes, or until a wooden pick inserted in the center comes out clean. Cool in the pans on a wire rack for 10 minutes. Remove from the pans and cool completely on wire racks.

224   Hometown Recipes for the Holidays

5. To prepare the frosting, melt the butter in a small saucepan over medium heat; add the brown sugar and 2 tablespoons of the milk. Cook for 1 minute until the sugar melts. Remove from the heat; cool slightly.

6. Combine the butter mixture and vanilla in a large bowl. Gradually add the confectioners' sugar. Beat with a mixer at medium speed until smooth. Add the remaining milk, 1 teaspoon at a time, beating until the frosting is of spreading consistency. Place 1 cake layer on a serving plate and spread the top with half of the frosting.

7. To prepare the topping, spoon the caramel dip into a small plastic bag. Snip a small piece off one corner and drizzle half of the caramel dip over the frosting. Top with the second cake layer, spread the remaining frosting over the top of the cake, and drizzle with the remaining caramel dip. Sprinkle with the pecans.

Christmas Carrot Pineapple Cake

Jane Williamson, Hot Springs Village, Arkansas

1 cup raisins

5 tablespoons unsweetened apple juice

4 eggs

½ cup canola oil

¾ cup plain yogurt

½ cup unsweetened applesauce or one
4-ounce jar baby-food applesauce

1 cup packed light brown sugar

1 teaspoon Stevia

1 tablespoon vanilla extract

2 cups all-purpose flour

2 teaspoons baking soda

2 teaspoons baking powder

¼ teaspoon salt

4 teaspoons ground cinnamon

1 cup unsweetened, shredded coconut

3¼ cups grated carrots (about 2 pounds)

2 tablespoons honey

One 15-ounce can unsweetened, crushed
pineapple, drained

1 cup chopped walnuts

"Christmas Carrot Pineapple Cake not only tastes heavenly, but it's truly baked with love. For medical reasons, I can't eat any refined sugar. Last Christmas, my husband, Milt, surprised me with this cake recipe. He has always enjoyed cooking, but this time he has outdone himself by combining his ingenuity with my medical requirements."

1. Preheat the oven to 350°F. Grease and flour a 15 × 10-inch cake pan.

2. Combine the raisins and apple juice in a microwave-safe bowl and cover with wax paper. Cook on high for 30 to 40 seconds until the raisins are plump and soft; set aside.

3. Combine the eggs, oil, yogurt, applesauce, brown sugar, Stevia, and vanilla in a large bowl. Using a mixer at medium speed, beat until well blended.

4. In a separate bowl, sift together the flour, baking soda, baking powder, salt, and cinnamon. Stir in the coconut. Gradually add the coconut mixture to the egg mixture. Stir in the carrots, honey, raisins and juice, and the pineapple. Fold in the walnuts.

5. Pour the batter into the prepared pan, smoothing to make the top level. Bake for 40 to 50 minutes until a wooden pick inserted near the center comes out clean. Cool in the pan for 10 to 15 minutes, then turn onto a wire rack to cool completely.

TIPS FROM OUR TEST KITCHEN

Stevia is a natural, very powerful sweetener available at most natural food centers.

6. Serve plain or with a topping of whipped cream and vanilla sweetened to taste with Stevia, if desired.

Italian Cream Cake

Azalea Stephens, Dayton, Texas

SERVES 12 TO 16

CAKE

1 cup whole buttermilk

1 teaspoon baking soda

5 eggs, separated

2 cups granulated sugar

½ cup (1 stick) butter or margarine, softened

½ cup shortening

2 cups all-purpose flour

1 teaspoon vanilla extract

One 3-ounce can sweetened coconut

FROSTING

One 8-ounce package cream cheese, softened

¼ cup (½ stick) butter or margarine, softened

One 16-ounce box confectioners' sugar

1 teaspoon vanilla extract

1 cup chopped pecans

TIPS FROM OUR TEST KITCHEN

Flavors improve if the cake is refrigerated for 24 hours. It keeps well for one week in the refrigerator and can be frozen for one month.

"This cake recipe was given to me thirty years ago, and I bake it for Christmas and birthdays. I am eighty-nine years old and have to use a walker now, but I can still cook."

1. Preheat the oven to 350°F. Grease three 9-inch cake pans and line with wax paper.

2. To prepare the cake, combine the buttermilk and baking soda in a small bowl; mix well. Place the egg whites in a small mixing bowl and, using a mixer at high speed, beat until stiff.

3. Combine the granulated sugar, butter, and shortening in a large mixing bowl and beat with a mixer at medium speed until light. Add the egg yolks, 1 at a time, beating well. Add the buttermilk mixture to the butter mixture alternately with the flour. Stir in the vanilla, fold in the beaten egg whites, and gently stir in the coconut.

4. Pour about 2 cups of the batter into each prepared pan. Bake for 18 to 20 minutes until a wooden pick inserted in the center comes out clean. Cool in the pans on a wire rack for 10 minutes. Remove from the pans to cool completely.

5. To prepare the frosting, combine the cream cheese and butter in a large bowl. Beat with a mixer at medium speed until smooth. Reduce the speed to low and slowly add the confectioners' sugar and vanilla; mix well. Stir in the pecans and spread the frosting between the layers and over the sides and top of the cake. Store in the refrigerator.

Peanut Buttery Chocolate Cake

Kimberly J. Keller, Richlands, Virginia

SERVES 16

CAKE

2 cups all-purpose flour

2 teaspoons baking soda

1 teaspoon baking powder

1/2 teaspoon salt

2 cups granulated sugar

2/3 cup unsweetened cocoa powder

2 eggs

1 cup milk

2/3 cup vegetable oil

1 teaspoon vanilla extract

1 cup brewed coffee, cooled to room
   temperature, or 1 cup water plus
   1 teaspoon instant coffee granules

FROSTING

One 3-ounce package cream cheese,
   softened

1/4 cup creamy peanut butter

2 cups confectioners' sugar

2 tablespoons milk

1/2 teaspoon vanilla extract

Miniature chocolate chips, optional

TIPS FROM OUR TEST KITCHEN

The addition of cream cheese to the
frosting makes it light and creamy.

"In our house, this cake disappears very quickly. It's one cake we all love—including my ten-year-old daughter. I always make it on the Fourth of July."

1. Preheat the oven to 350°F. Grease a 13 × 9-inch glass baking pan.

2. To prepare the cake, sift the flour, baking soda, baking powder, and salt into a large mixing bowl. Add the granulated sugar and cocoa and mix well. Add the eggs, milk, oil, and vanilla. Using a mixer at medium speed, beat for 2 minutes, scraping down the sides of the bowl. Stir in the coffee; the batter will be thin.

3. Pour the batter into the prepared pan. Bake for 35 to 40 minutes until a wooden pick inserted near the center comes out clean. Cool completely on a wire rack.

4. To prepare the frosting, combine the cream cheese and peanut butter in a large mixing bowl. Using a mixer, beat at medium speed until smooth. Beat in the confectioners' sugar, milk, and vanilla. Beat until smooth. Spread the frosting over the top of the cake and sprinkle with chocolate chips, if desired. Store in the refrigerator.

22-Minute Chocolate Cake

Reginia Napier, Clarksville, Texas

CAKE

2 cups granulated sugar

2 cups all-purpose flour

1/2 cup (1 stick) butter or margarine

1/2 cup vegetable oil

3 1/2 tablespoons unsweetened cocoa powder

1/2 cup buttermilk

2 eggs

1 teaspoon baking soda

1 teaspoon vanilla extract

ICING

1/2 cup (1 stick) butter or margarine

3 1/2 tablespoons unsweetened cocoa powder

1/3 cup milk

1 teaspoon vanilla extract

One 16-ounce box confectioners' sugar

1 cup toasted pecans, optional

1 cup flaked coconut, optional

TIPS FROM OUR TEST KITCHEN

Oven temperatures vary, so be sure to test this cake after baking for 15 minutes.

"I began making this cake in 1967 when I was first married. I make it for every holiday and every family gathering. It is the only dessert that every one of us likes."

1. Preheat the oven to 400°F. Grease and flour a 17 × 12-inch jelly-roll pan.

2. To prepare the cake, combine the granulated sugar and flour in a large bowl. Combine 1 cup water with the butter, oil, and cocoa in a saucepan; bring to a boil. Pour over the flour mixture.

3. Combine the buttermilk, eggs, baking soda, and vanilla in a bowl; mix well. Stir into the batter. Pour into the prepared pan. Bake for 15 to 22 minutes.

4. To prepare the icing, combine the butter, cocoa, and milk in a saucepan; bring to a boil. Stir in the vanilla, confectioners' sugar, pecans, and coconut, if using. Pour over the cake as soon as it is removed from the oven.

Georgia Corn Bread Cake

Stella T. Thompson, Fort Payne, Alabama

SERVES 12 TO 14

1 cup granulated sugar

1 cup packed brown sugar

4 eggs, beaten

1 cup vegetable oil

1½ cups self-rising flour

1 teaspoon vanilla extract

2 cups pecans, finely chopped

Whipped cream, optional

TIPS FROM OUR TEST KITCHEN

Although there's no cornmeal in this cake, the pecans give it the texture of corn bread.

"This cake is perfect for potluck suppers or to pack in lunch boxes."

1. Preheat the oven to 350°F. Lightly grease and flour a 13 × 9-inch baking dish.

2. Combine the granulated sugar, brown sugar, eggs, and oil in a medium bowl; mix well. Stir in the flour and vanilla. Add the pecans and stir until evenly mixed. Spoon into the prepared pan. Bake for 30 to 35 minutes. Serve with whipped cream, if desired.

Black Devil's Food Cake with Egyptian Frosting

Diane Mauch, Hankinson, North Dakota

SERVES 16

CAKE

2 cups all-purpose flour

½ teaspoon salt

3 teaspoons baking soda

1¾ cups sugar

½ cup unsweetened cocoa powder

1 egg

⅔ cup vegetable oil

1 cup buttermilk

1 cup strong coffee or 1 cup water plus
    1½ teaspoons instant coffee granules

FROSTING

2 eggs, beaten

1½ cups sugar

1 rounded tablespoon all-purpose flour

1 cup heavy or whipping cream

1 cup raisins

1 cup chopped nuts

TOPPING

2 teaspoons butter

One 1-ounce square chocolate

TIPS FROM OUR TEST KITCHEN

This cake has a rich, deep chocolate, old-fashioned flavor.

"My mother baked this cake for many birthdays in our family—it is also a special treat at Christmas. It's very rich and melts in your mouth. It will stay moist for several days."

1. Preheat the oven to 350°F. Grease and flour a 13 × 9-inch glass baking dish.

2. To prepare the cake, sift the flour, salt, and baking soda into a large mixing bowl. Add the sugar, cocoa, egg, oil, buttermilk, and coffee. Beat with a mixer at medium speed until smooth, about 2 minutes. Bake for 25 to 30 minutes until a wooden pick inserted near the center comes out clean. Cool in the pan on a wire rack.

3. To prepare the frosting, combine the eggs, sugar, flour, cream, and raisins in a large saucepan. Cook over medium heat until thick, about 15 minutes, stirring constantly. Cool for 20 to 30 minutes. Stir in the nuts. Spread the frosting over the cake.

4. To prepare the topping, combine the butter and chocolate square in a small bowl and heat in the microwave on Low, stirring every 15 seconds until melted. Drizzle over the frosting.

Fudge Upside-Down Cake

Kay Carman, Philpot, Kentucky

CAKE

2 tablespoons butter or margarine

¾ cup granulated sugar

4 tablespoons unsweetened cocoa
  powder

1 cup all-purpose flour

2 teaspoons baking powder

¼ teaspoon salt

1 cup milk

½ cup walnuts

1 teaspoon vanilla extract

SAUCE

½ cup granulated sugar

½ cup packed brown sugar

3 tablespoons unsweetened cocoa
  powder

1 tablespoon butter or margarine

1 cup milk

One 1-ounce square unsweetened
  chocolate

½ teaspoon almond extract

½ cup chopped walnuts

Ice cream or whipped cream

TIPS FROM OUR TEST KITCHEN

While the cake bakes, the sauce goes
to the bottom and makes a creamy
topping.

"This recipe came from my mother back when I was a young cook. She made it many times when I was growing up."

1. Preheat the oven to 350°F. Grease a 13 × 9-inch pan or a large cast-iron skillet.

2. To prepare the cake, melt the butter and pour into a large bowl. Add the granulated sugar and cocoa; mix well. Combine the flour, baking powder, and salt in a medium bowl. Add to the butter mixture alternately with the milk. Add the walnuts and vanilla and pour into the prepared pan.

3. To prepare the sauce, heat the granulated sugar, brown sugar, cocoa, butter, and milk in a saucepan. Add the chocolate and stir until it melts and the sauce is smooth. Stir in the almond extract and walnuts. Pour over the top of the cake batter.

4. Bake for 25 to 30 minutes. Cool slightly. Invert the cake onto a serving platter. Serve with ice cream or whipped cream.

Old-Fashioned Devil's Food Cake

Heidi and Faithe Copp, Rochester, New Hampshire

CAKE

¾ cup milk

2 teaspoons instant coffee granules

¾ cup unsweetened cocoa powder

½ cup sour cream

1¼ cups all-purpose flour

1½ teaspoons baking soda

½ teaspoon baking powder

1 cup (2 sticks) butter, softened

1½ cups granulated sugar

3 eggs

2 teaspoons vanilla extract

FROSTING

Four 1-ounce squares baking chocolate

1⅔ cups confectioners' sugar

¾ cup heavy cream

2 teaspoons vanilla extract

6 tablespoons butter, cut into small cubes

"We made this rich and indulgent cake for July 4 originally, but it has been a favorite for Christmas especially."

1. Preheat the oven to 350°F. Grease three 8-inch cake pans and line the bottoms with wax paper. Grease and flour the wax paper.

2. To prepare the cake, combine the milk and coffee granules in a small saucepan. Cook over medium heat until bubbles form around the outer edges to 180°F. Add the cocoa powder and whisk until well blended. Add the sour cream and whisk until smooth. Remove from the heat; cool.

3. Combine the flour, baking soda, and baking powder in a small bowl.

4. Beat the butter with a mixer at medium speed until light. Add the granulated sugar gradually and beat until light and fluffy. Add the eggs, 1 at a time, and beat until well blended. Beat in the vanilla. Reduce the mixer speed to low and gradually beat in the flour mixture, alternating with the chocolate mixture and beginning and ending with the flour mixture. Beat for 2 minutes at medium speed.

5. Divide the batter among the three pans, about 2 cups per pan. Bake for 20 to 25 minutes, or until the top springs back when touched. Cool in the pans on wire racks for 15 minutes. Gently remove the cakes from the pans, place on wire racks, and peel off the wax paper. Cool completely.

234   **Hometown Recipes for the Holidays**

6. To prepare the frosting, combine the chocolate, confectioners' sugar, and cream in a medium saucepan. Cook over medium heat until smooth, stirring constantly. Remove from the heat and stir in the vanilla.

7. Pour the chocolate mixture into a large bowl. Place the bowl in another bowl filled with ice water. Stir the frosting occasionally and let stand until cold and thick, about 15 minutes. Remove the bowl from the ice water bowl. Gradually add the butter to the frosting while beating with a mixer at high speed until it is stiff enough to hold its shape.

8. To assemble, place one layer on a serving plate and spread the top evenly with 3/4 cup frosting. Repeat with the remaining two layers and frosting.

Holiday Cake

Billie J. Rogers, Durant, Oklahoma

SERVES 12 TO 16

CAKE

2 cups chopped prunes (12 ounces)

2½ cups all-purpose flour

2 teaspoons baking soda

1 teaspoon ground cinnamon

1 teaspoon ground nutmeg

1 teaspoon ground allspice

4 eggs

1 cup prune juice

6 tablespoons butter, softened

2 cups granulated sugar

ICING

½ cup (1 stick) butter or margarine,
softened

One 8-ounce package cream cheese,
softened

One 16-ounce package confectioners'
sugar

1 teaspoon vanilla extract

¾ cup chopped pecans

"My mother gave me this recipe when I first married back in 1958. I still have the copy in her handwriting, although it is now in four pieces. When I get the recipe out, it brings back wonderful memories of my mother. I call it Holiday Cake because when my children were younger, they would not eat Prune Cake!"

1. Preheat the oven to 325°F. Grease and flour three 9-inch round cake pans.

2. To prepare the cake, combine the prunes and hot water to cover. Let stand for 5 to 10 minutes to soften.

3. Sift together the flour, baking soda, and spices. Place the eggs in a large mixing bowl and beat with a mixer at medium-high speed. Add the prune juice and butter; beat well. Add the flour mixture; beat until smooth, about 2 minutes. Drain the prunes; stir into the batter.

4. Divide the batter evenly among the pans (about 1 cup each). Bake for 16 to 20 minutes until a wooden pick inserted near the center comes out clean. Cool in the pans on a wire rack for 10 minutes. Remove the layers from the pans and cool completely on wire racks.

5. To prepare the icing, combine the butter and cream cheese in a medium mixing bowl. Using a mixer at medium-high speed, beat until smooth. Add the confectioners' sugar and vanilla; beat until smooth. Stir in the pecans.

6. Spread the icing over the top of one cake layer. Add the second layer; ice the top. Top with the third layer; ice the top and sides. Store in the refrigerator. Refrigerate for 24 hours before serving for better flavor.

Old-Fashioned Jam Cake

Bernice Stahl, Auburn, Kentucky

SERVES 12 TO 16

CAKE

3 cups self-rising flour

1 teaspoon ground cinnamon

1 teaspoon ground nutmeg

1 teaspoon ground cloves

1 teaspoon ground allspice

2 cups granulated sugar

1 cup (2 sticks) butter, softened

1 cup blackberry jam

1 cup raspberry jam

4 eggs

1 cup milk

1 teaspoon vanilla extract

1 cup chopped nuts, optional

CARAMEL ICING

2 cups packed light brown sugar

½ cup milk

8 teaspoons butter

⅛ teaspoon salt

4 cups confectioners' sugar

1 cup chopped nuts, optional

TIPS FROM OUR TEST KITCHEN

The flavors improve if the cake is refrigerated for 24 hours.

"We gather at my granddaughter's house each Thanksgiving and Christmas to keep our family traditions going strong. One of my family's favorites is this Jam Cake."

1. Preheat the oven to 350°F. Grease and flour three 9-inch round cake pans.

2. To prepare the cake, sift the flour and spices into a large mixing bowl. Stir in the granulated sugar. Using a mixer at medium speed, beat the butter, jams, eggs, milk, and vanilla until smooth, 2 minutes. Stir in the nuts, if desired.

3. Divide the batter evenly among the prepared pans. Bake for 18 to 23 minutes until a wooden pick inserted near the center comes out clean. Cool in the pans on a wire rack for 10 minutes. Remove the layers from the pans to cool completely on a wire rack.

4. To prepare the icing, combine the brown sugar, milk, butter, and salt in a large saucepan. Bring to a boil over medium heat, stirring constantly. Remove from the heat and add the confectioners' sugar. If the icing is too thick, add a little milk. Stir in nuts, if desired. Spread over one cake layer. Top with the second layer; ice the top. Top with the third layer; ice the top.

Mom's Oatmeal Cake

Rhonda Stella, Bonner's Ferry, Idaho

CAKE

1 cup old-fashioned oats

½ cup (1 stick) butter, softened

1 cup packed brown sugar

1 cup granulated sugar

2 eggs

1½ cups all-purpose flour

1 teaspoon baking soda

1 teaspoon salt

1 teaspoon ground cinnamon

FROSTING

½ cup (1 stick) butter

¼ cup milk

½ cup packed brown sugar

1 teaspoon vanilla extract

½ cup chopped pecans, lightly toasted

½ cup flaked coconut

"My mom's moist, delicious oatmeal cake has always been a family favorite. Everyone who tastes it requests a copy of the recipe. This scrumptious dessert remains to this day my mom's 'signature cake.'"

1. Preheat the oven to 350°F. Grease a 13 × 9-inch baking pan.

2. To prepare the cake, pour 1½ cups boiling water over the oats in a small bowl.

3. Cream the butter, brown sugar, granulated sugar, and eggs with a mixer. Add the flour, baking soda, salt, and cinnamon to the creamed mixture alternately with the oat mixture.

4. Pour into the prepared pan. Bake for 25 to 30 minutes.

5. To prepare the frosting, combine the butter, milk, brown sugar, and vanilla in a saucepan. Bring to a boil and boil for 3 to 4 minutes, stirring constantly. Add the pecans and coconut. Spread over the cake.

Oatmeal Cake with Broiled Coconut Icing

Barbara J. Peters, Salem, Illinois

CAKE

1 cup old-fashioned oats

1/2 cup (1 stick) butter or margarine, softened

1 cup packed light brown sugar

1 cup granulated sugar

2 eggs

1 teaspoon vanilla extract

1 1/2 cups all-purpose flour

1/2 to 1 teaspoon ground nutmeg

1 teaspoon ground cinnamon

1 teaspoon baking soda

1/2 teaspoon salt

ICING

3 tablespoons butter or margarine, softened

2/3 cup packed brown sugar

3 tablespoons milk

1 egg, beaten

1 cup sweetened flaked coconut

1/2 cup pecans

"I make about forty different cookies and cakes for the holidays—Oatmeal Cake is one of them. It freezes well. I received this recipe in the 1960s."

1. Preheat the oven to 350°F. Grease a 13 × 9-inch glass baking dish.

2. To prepare the cake, combine 1 1/2 cups hot water and the oats in a small bowl; set aside to cool. Combine the butter, sugars, eggs, and vanilla; beat with a mixer at medium speed.

3. Sift the flour, spices, baking soda, and salt over the sugar mixture. Add the cooled oat mixture; beat well.

4. Pour the batter into the prepared pan and bake for 35 minutes, or until a wooden pick inserted in the center comes out clean.

5. Preheat the broiler.

6. To prepare the icing, combine all of the ingredients in a medium bowl; stir until well blended. Spread on the hot cake and broil until golden brown. Cool completely on a wire rack.

Peach Upside-Down Cake

Ruth R. Fegley, Barnesville, Pennsylvania

CAKE

3 tablespoons butter, softened

⅔ cup granulated sugar

1 egg

1½ cups all-purpose flour

2 teaspoons baking powder

⅛ teaspoon salt

⅔ cup milk

1 teaspoon vanilla extract

TOPPING

5 tablespoons butter

1 cup packed light brown sugar

2 cups sliced peaches

TIPS FROM OUR TEST KITCHEN

The recipe may be doubled. Use a 12-inch cast-iron skillet for the larger recipe.

"Peach Upside-Down Cake is one of my family's favorites. I make it in the summer with fresh peaches, and in the winter I drain my canned peaches and it is just as delicious."

1. Preheat the oven to 350°F.

2. To prepare the cake, combine the butter, granulated sugar, and egg; beat with a mixer at medium speed until creamy and smooth.

3. Combine the flour, baking powder, and salt in a small bowl; mix well. Gradually add the flour mixture alternately with the milk to the butter mixture, beating at low speed and beginning and ending with the flour mixture. Increase the speed to medium and beat until smooth, about 2 minutes. Add the vanilla; beat well.

4. To prepare the topping, heat the butter in a 10-inch cast-iron skillet over medium heat. Add the brown sugar and stir until well blended. Remove from the heat.

5. Arrange the peaches in the skillet. Pour the batter over the peaches.

6. Bake for 28 to 30 minutes until a wooden pick inserted in the center comes out clean. Invert the cake onto a large plate.

Hall Family Pineapple Cake

Kate L. Settles, Point Clear, Alabama

SERVES 12 TO 16

CAKE

1 cup (2 sticks) butter, softened

2 cups granulated sugar

5 extra-large eggs

2 cups sifted, self-rising cake flour

½ cup pineapple juice or water

½ teaspoon lemon extract

FILLING

One 20-ounce can crushed pineapple

½ cup granulated sugar

⅓ cup light corn syrup

GLAZE

½ teaspoon grated lemon zest

1 tablespoon fresh lemon juice

½ cup confectioners' sugar

"This cake was passed down to me by my aunt, and the filling came from my mother. I added the lemon glaze and pineapple juice."

1. Preheat the oven to 325°F. Grease and flour three 9-inch round cake pans.

2. To prepare the cake, combine the butter and granulated sugar in a large bowl. Using a mixer, beat at medium-high speed until light and fluffy. Add the eggs, 1 at a time; beat well. Add the flour and juice alternately, starting and ending with the flour. Add the lemon extract; beat until light and fluffy. Divide the batter evenly among the pans.

3. Bake for 20 to 25 minutes until a wooden pick inserted near the center comes out clean. Cool in the pans on a wire rack for 5 minutes. Remove from the pans and cool completely on the wire rack.

4. To prepare the filling, combine the pineapple, sugar, and corn syrup in a heavy saucepan. Bring to a boil over medium heat, stirring constantly. Reduce the heat and simmer, uncovered, until thickened, about 40 minutes; stir frequently. Remove from the heat.

5. To assemble, place one cake layer on a cake plate and spoon half of the pineapple mixture (about 1 cup) over the cake, letting the cake absorb the juices. Place the second layer on top and spoon the remaining pineapple mixture over this layer. Top with the third layer and cool for 1 hour.

TIPS FROM OUR TEST KITCHEN

Store this fruity, refreshing cake in the refrigerator. The flavor improves if the cake is refrigerated for 24 hours before serving.

6. To prepare the glaze, combine the lemon zest, lemon juice, and confectioners' sugar in a small bowl; stir until well blended. When the cake is cool, spread the glaze over the top layer.

Spiced Pumpkin Roll with Cream Cheese

Kenny Hoefle Jr., McAdenville, North Carolina

SERVES 12 TO 16

CAKE

3 eggs

1 cup granulated sugar

¾ cup canned pumpkin

1 teaspoon lemon juice

¾ cup self-rising flour

1 teaspoon baking powder

½ teaspoon salt

1 teaspoon ground ginger

2 teaspoons ground cinnamon

½ teaspoon ground nutmeg

FILLING

8 ounces cream cheese, softened

1 cup confectioners' sugar

¼ cup (½ stick) butter, softened

1¼ teaspoons vanilla extract

"I've been making pumpkin rolls for about ten years—I started with one for Christmas Eve dinner. Now I make three for dinners, one for a birthday gift, and three for gifts. I wouldn't be surprised if that number changes again this year!"

1. Preheat the oven to 375°F. Grease a 15 × 10-inch jelly-roll pan and line the bottom with wax paper.

2. To prepare the cake, place the eggs in large mixing bowl. Beat the eggs for 5 minutes with a mixer at medium speed. Add the granulated sugar, pumpkin, and lemon juice; beat until smooth. Sift together the flour, baking powder, salt, and spices; add to the egg mixture; mix well. Pour the batter into the prepared pan.

3. Bake for 12 to 15 minutes until the cake springs back when touched and a wooden pick inserted near the center comes out clean.

4. Unroll a clean dish towel on the counter and put a piece of wax paper on top. Sprinkle with confectioners' sugar. Immediately loosen the edges of the cake from the pan and turn it out onto the wax paper–lined towel. Starting at the long edge, roll up into a small roll. Place in the refrigerator until cool.

5. To prepare the filling, combine the cream cheese, confectioners' sugar, butter, and vanilla in a small mixing bowl; beat until smooth.

This cake has a nice springy texture and the filling is light and creamy.

6. To assemble, gently unroll the cake and spread the filling on the cake. Roll again, wrap in plastic wrap, and refrigerate until serving time.

Holiday Cranberry-Raisin Spice Cake

Mary Helen Jeffrey, Robertsdale, Alabama

SERVES 12 TO 16

CAKE

2 cups all-purpose flour

1 teaspoon baking soda

1 teaspoon ground nutmeg

1 teaspoon ground cinnamon

1 teaspoon salt

½ cup shortening

1 cup packed dark brown sugar

2 eggs

1 cup cranberry sauce

¾ cup sour milk

1 cup raisins

1 cup chopped nuts

ICING

One 3-ounce package cream cheese, softened

½ teaspoon vanilla extract

2 cups confectioners' sugar

2 tablespoons milk

Maraschino cherries, optional

TIPS FROM OUR TEST KITCHEN

To make sour milk, combine ¾ cup milk with 2 teaspoons cider vinegar in a small bowl. Let stand for 10 minutes.

"My mother always made this spice cake for the Christmas holiday. She made it a couple of days ahead of time, because it got moister the longer it sat. Just like Mother, I bake it every year."

1. Preheat the oven to 350°F. Grease a 10-inch tube pan.

2. To prepare the cake, sift together the flour, baking soda, spices, and salt. Combine the shortening and brown sugar in a large mixing bowl. Using a mixer at high speed, beat until fluffy. Add the eggs, 1 at a time. Blend in the cranberry sauce. Add the sour milk alternately with the flour mixture, starting and ending with the flour mixture. Stir in the raisins and nuts.

3. Pour the batter into the prepared pan. Bake for 55 to 60 minutes until a wooden pick inserted near the center comes out clean. Cool in the pan on a wire rack. Invert onto a serving plate.

4. To prepare the icing, combine the cream cheese and vanilla in a bowl; mix well. Add the confectioners' sugar and milk, stirring until smooth. Pour over the top of the cake, allowing it to run down the sides. Decorate with cherries or other holiday fruits, if desired. Store the cake in the refrigerator.

Walnut Cake

Mary Murry, Gatesville, Texas

CAKE

3 cups all-purpose flour

½ teaspoon baking soda

½ teaspoon salt

1 cup (2 sticks) butter or margarine, softened

2 cups granulated sugar

2 eggs, separated

1 cup milk

1 teaspoon vanilla extract

1 teaspoon almond extract

1 pound walnuts, finely chopped

1 teaspoon cream of tartar

GLAZE

¼ cup confectioners' sugar

1 tablespoon milk

Whole walnuts, optional

"This recipe has been in our family as long as I can remember. My mother made this cake each Christmas. As she got into her later years, she was on a fixed income and would bake one cake and split it between my family and my brother's. This was a great gift made with lots of love."

1. Preheat the oven to 350°F. Grease a 9-inch tube pan.

2. Sift the flour, baking soda, and salt into a medium bowl. Combine the butter, granulated sugar, and egg yolks in a large mixing bowl. Using a mixer, beat at medium speed until creamy and smooth. Reduce the speed to low and gradually beat in the flour mixture alternately with the milk, beginning and ending with the flour mixture and beating after each addition. Add the extracts; beat well. Stir in the walnuts.

3. Using clean beaters, place the egg whites in a small mixing bowl. Beat at high speed until foamy. Add the cream of tartar and beat until stiff. Fold the egg white mixture into the batter mixture.

4. Pour the batter into the prepared pan. Bake for 1 hour and 5 minutes, or until a wooden pick inserted in the center comes out clean. Cool in the pan on a wire rack for 10 minutes. Invert onto a plate.

5. For the glaze, combine the confectioners' sugar with the milk in a small bowl and stir until the sugar is dissolved. Drizzle evenly over the warm cake. Garnish with whole walnuts, if desired. The flavors improve overnight.

Fresh Strawberry Amaretto Shortcake

Terry Ramirez-McCarty, Helendale, California

SERVES 16

FILLING

¼ cup plus 3 tablespoons granulated
    sugar
2 pounds fresh strawberries
¼ cup amaretto liqueur

CAKE

4 eggs
⅓ cup vegetable oil
One 18-ounce box white cake mix
    (supermoist variety)
1 teaspoon orange extract

FROSTING

Two 8-ounce packages cream cheese,
    softened
¼ cup (½ stick) butter, softened
1 cup confectioners' sugar
1¾ cups heavy cream
1 tablespoon orange extract
2 cups toasted sliced almonds

"My family and I look forward to Easter every year. We just love fresh strawberries and try to eat them as often as possible during the season. I started making this cake many years ago. It was very complicated and time consuming. Being a working mom, I needed to simplify the recipe. I have made changes so it's quick and easy to make."

1. Preheat the oven to 350°F. Spray three 8-inch round cake pans with nonstick cooking spray and dust with 3 tablespoons granulated sugar.

2. To prepare the filling, reserve 6 whole strawberries with stems on. Slice the remaining strawberries and combine them with the liqueur and ¼ cup sugar in a medium bowl; toss to coat. Cover with plastic wrap and refrigerate until needed.

3. To prepare the cake, combine the eggs and oil in a large bowl and beat with a mixer at high speed for 30 seconds. Add the cake mix and 1 cup water; beat at medium speed for 3 minutes. The batter may be slightly lumpy. Add the orange extract and beat for 30 seconds.

4. Divide the batter evenly among the prepared pans (about 1½ cups each). Bake for 20 to 25 minutes until just golden and the layers spring back when touched. Cool in the pans on a wire rack.

If a pastry bag is not available, use a quart-sized plastic bag and snip a piece off of one corner, about ½ inch wide. Fill with the cream cheese mixture and squeeze through the hole in the plastic bag.

5. To prepare the frosting, combine the cream cheese and butter in a medium bowl. Using a mixer at medium speed, beat until smooth. Reduce the speed to medium-low. Add the confectioners' sugar and about half of the cream; beat until just combined. Add the remaining cream and orange extract. Increase the speed to medium-high and beat until stiff peaks form, 2 to 3 minutes. Be careful not to overmix. Refrigerate until needed.

6. When the layers are cool, lightly trim the tops of the cakes if not level. Fill a pastry bag without a tip with 1 cup of the cream cheese mixture and pipe an even circle of frosting around the edge of one of the layers, creating a dam effect. Spoon half of the sliced strawberries and liquid in the center of the first layer. Top with the second layer and repeat with the remaining cream cheese mixture in the pastry bag and sliced strawberries and liquid. Place the final layer on top. Frost the cake with the remaining frosting, top with the whole strawberries, and press almonds on the sides. Refrigerate until serving time. The flavors improve overnight.

Light and Lemony Tiramisù Cake

Mary Ann Lee, Clifton Park, New York

SERVES 8 TO 12

CAKE

6 eggs, separated

1/8 teaspoon salt

1/2 teaspoon cream of tartar

1 1/4 cups granulated sugar

1 teaspoon lemon extract

1 teaspoon vanilla extract

1 1/2 cups sifted cake flour

FILLING

1/2 cup whipping cream

1 teaspoon granulated sugar

8 ounces mascarpone

1/2 cup confectioners' sugar

1 cup ricotta

1 teaspoon vanilla extract

2 tablespoons grated lemon zest

One 10-ounce jar lemon curd

GLAZE

1/4 cup lemon liqueur

1/2 cup prepared lemonade

Confectioners' sugar

Lemon slices, optional

"This cake is extremely good after a heavy meal. It is also refreshing in the warm summer weather."

1. Preheat the oven to 350°F. Grease the bottom of a 9-inch springform pan. Line with wax paper. Grease the wax paper.

2. To prepare the cake, place the egg whites in a large bowl. Add the salt and cream of tartar. Using a mixer at high speed, beat until frothy. Add the granulated sugar gradually. Beat until the egg whites form peaks, 3 to 5 minutes.

3. Place the egg yolks in a small bowl and stir with a fork. Add the lemon and vanilla extracts. Fold the yolk mixture into the beaten egg whites. Gradually fold in the flour by hand. Spread the batter evenly in the prepared pan.

4. Bake for 35 to 40 minutes until a wooden pick inserted in the center comes out clean. Cool in the pan on a wire rack for 5 minutes. Remove the cake from the pan and cool completely on the wire rack.

5. To prepare the filling, beat the whipping cream and granulated sugar with a mixer at high speed until stiff peaks form. Refrigerate.

6. Combine the mascarpone and confectioners' sugar; beat well with a mixer at medium speed. Blend in the ricotta. Add the vanilla, lemon zest, and 1/3 cup lemon curd; mix well. Fold in the whipped cream. Spoon 2 to 3 tablespoons of the mascarpone mixture into the remaining lemon curd. Set aside.

This cake is very flavorful without being too sweet. It is a good dessert for a summer party.

7. To prepare the glaze, combine the lemon liqueur and lemonade.

8. To assemble, remove the wax paper from the cake. Using a serrated knife, carefully slice the cake into three layers. Place one layer on a serving plate. Brush with about ¼ cup of the glaze and spread with about 1½ cups of the mascarpone filling mixture. Repeat with the second layer. Top with the third layer and brush with the remaining glaze. Spread with the remaining lemon curd. Frost the sides of the cake with the remaining mascarpone filling. Refrigerate for several hours to overnight.

9. Just before serving, dust the cake with confectioners' sugar and garnish with lemon slices, if desired.

Darla's Blueberry Cheesecake

Darla Gregory, Port Henry, New York

CRUST

20 honey-flavored graham crackers,
  crushed
½ cup (1 stick) butter, softened
1½ teaspoons sugar

FILLING

Three 8-ounce packages cream cheese,
  softened
1 cup sugar
2 tablespoons all-purpose flour
¼ teaspoon salt
1 teaspoon vanilla extract
4 eggs, separated
1 cup sour cream

TOPPING

½ cup sugar
1 tablespoon cornstarch
⅛ teaspoon salt
1 cup fresh or frozen and thawed
  blueberries

"The family gets together for Easter, Thanksgiving, and Christmas; everyone looks for Darla's cheesecake."

1. Preheat the oven to 300°F.

2. To prepare the crust, combine the crackers, butter, and sugar in a bowl; mix well. Press in the bottom of a 9-inch springform pan. Bake for 10 minutes. Cool in the pan on a wire rack.

3. To prepare the filling, increase the oven temperature to 350°F. Place the cream cheese in a large bowl and beat with a mixer at high speed until smooth. Add the sugar, flour, salt, and vanilla. Beat until well blended. Add the egg yolks, 1 at a time, mixing after each addition. Add the sour cream and beat until well blended.

4. Place the egg whites in a medium bowl. Using clean beaters, beat at high speed until stiff. Fold into the cream cheese mixture and pour the batter into the cooled crust.

5. Bake for 40 minutes or until set. Leave in the oven. Turn off the heat and open the oven door for 10 minutes. Remove from the oven and cool on a wire rack until room temperature. Cover with plastic wrap and refrigerate overnight.

6. To prepare the topping, combine the sugar, cornstarch, and salt with ½ cup water in a medium saucepan. Stir until the cornstarch is dissolved. Add the berries and bring to a boil. Boil for 1 full minute, stirring occasionally. Cool, cover with plastic wrap, and refrigerate overnight. At serving time, top the cheesecake with the blueberry mixture.

Chocolate Cheesecake

Bonnie Rickenbaugh, Sturtevant, Wisconsin

SERVES 12

CRUST

1½ cups chocolate graham cracker
   crumbs

¼ cup sugar

⅓ cup butter, melted

FILLING

Three 8-ounce packages reduced-fat or
   regular cream cheese, softened

One 14-ounce can sweetened condensed
   milk

One 12-ounce package semisweet
   chocolate chips, melted

4 eggs

2 teaspoons vanilla extract

"This cheesecake is very rich and creamy, and I have been asked to make it for many occasions. I like to make it because I usually have all the ingredients on hand. I especially like to serve it to guests because this is a dessert that is meant to be shared."

1. Preheat the oven to 300°F.

2. To prepare the crust, combine the chocolate crumbs, sugar, and butter in a small bowl; mix well. Press in the bottom of a 9-inch springform pan.

3. To prepare the filling, place the cream cheese in a large bowl and beat with a mixer at high speed until smooth. Add the condensed milk; beat well. Add the remaining ingredients and beat until smooth.

4. Pour the batter into the prepared crust and bake for 1 hour and 5 minutes, or until a knife inserted in the center comes out clean. Cool in the pan on a wire rack to room temperature. Cover with plastic wrap and refrigerate overnight.

De Lime in De Coconut Cheesecake

Sheila Suhan, Scottdale, Pennsylvania   SERVES 12

CRUST

1 cup graham cracker crumbs

½ cup sweetened shredded coconut

3 tablespoons sugar

1 teaspoon grated lime zest

3 tablespoons butter or margarine, melted

FILLING

Four 8-ounce packages cream cheese, softened

4 eggs

One 15-ounce can sweetened cream of coconut milk

½ cup sour cream

2 teaspoons grated lime zest

Juice of 2 medium limes

1 teaspoon vanilla extract

Whipped cream, optional

Lime wedges, optional

TIPS FROM OUR TEST KITCHEN

To soften cream cheese quickly, unwrap and place on a microwave-safe plate. Microwave on high for 30 seconds.

"This light, creamy cheesecake has a wonderful combination of lime and coconut without the coarse texture. I first served it as an Easter dessert. It was such a hit that the meal wouldn't have been complete without it. I named it after a popular song of my generation."

1. Preheat the oven to 325°F.

2. To prepare the crust, combine the graham cracker crumbs, coconut, sugar, zest, and butter in a food processor. Process until just blended. Press in the bottom and about ½ inch up the sides of a 10-inch springform pan.

3. To prepare the filling, place the cream cheese in a large bowl and beat with a mixer at high speed until smooth. Reduce the speed to low and add the eggs, 1 at a time; beat well.

4. Add the remaining filling ingredients and beat well. Scrape the bottom and sides of the bowl and pour the filling over the crust. Bake for 1 hour and 15 minutes, or until a knife inserted in the center comes out clean. Cool to room temperature on a wire rack. Cover with plastic wrap and refrigerate overnight. Garnish with whipped cream and lime wedges, if desired.

Blueberry Cream Cheese Pound Cake

Dee Williams, Kingsland, Georgia

One 8-ounce package cream cheese, softened

½ cup vegetable oil

One 18-ounce package yellow butter cake mix

One 3-ounce package instant vanilla pudding mix

4 eggs, beaten

2 teaspoons vanilla extract

2¼ cups fresh or frozen, thawed blueberries

Confectioners' sugar

"This is a combination of recipes from my grandmother and aunt and my husband's aunt. We would have this cake at July 4 parties when we were kids, or on Labor Day weekend for the last party of the summer. It doesn't stay around very long!"

1. Preheat the oven to 325°F. Lightly spray a 9-inch Bundt pan with nonstick cooking spray and dust with flour.

2. Combine the cream cheese and oil in a medium bowl; beat with a mixer at high speed until smooth and creamy. Add the cake mix, pudding mix, eggs, and vanilla. Beat at medium speed until blended. Fold in the berries. Pour the batter into the prepared pan.

3. Bake for 60 to 65 minutes until a wooden pick inserted in the center comes out clean. Cool the cake in the pan on a wire rack for 20 minutes. Remove from the pan and cool completely on the wire rack. Sprinkle with confectioners' sugar before serving.

Retro Cherry Pound Cake

Janet Redding, Stanley, North Carolina

SERVES 12 TO 16

CAKE

1½ cups shortening or 1 cup shortening
    plus ½ cup (1 stick) margarine,
    softened

3 cups granulated sugar

6 eggs

½ teaspoon almond extract

½ teaspoon vanilla extract

3¾ cups sifted all-purpose flour

¾ cup milk

One 10-ounce jar maraschino cherries,
    drained and chopped

ICING

One 3-ounce package cream cheese,
    softened

¼ cup (½ stick) margarine or butter,
    softened

2 cups confectioners' sugar

1 teaspoon vanilla or almond extract

½ cup sweetened flaked coconut,
    optional

½ cup chopped nuts

"Easy to make and so elegant, this is our favorite cake. I like to surprise my husband and bake it on Valentine's Day."

1. Grease and flour a 9-inch tube pan. Do not preheat the oven.

2. To prepare the cake, combine the shortening and sugar in a large bowl; beat with a mixer at medium speed until well blended. Add the eggs, 1 at a time, and beat until well blended. Add the extracts and beat well. Add the flour alternately with the milk, starting and ending with the flour. Beat well after each addition. Fold in half of the cherries.

3. Pour the batter into the prepared pan. Bake at 300°F for 1½ hours, or until a wooden pick inserted in the center comes out almost clean. Cool the cake in the pan on a wire rack for 10 minutes and then invert onto a plate.

4. To prepare the icing, combine the cream cheese, margarine, sugar, and vanilla in a medium bowl; beat with a mixer at low speed until smooth. Spread the icing on the top and the sides of the cake. Sprinkle the remaining maraschino cherries, the coconut if using, and the nuts on top.

Overseas Chocolate

Kathy Greer, Spokane, Washington

MAKES 96 SQUARES

4½ cups sugar

¾ cup (1½ sticks) butter or margarine

One 12-ounce can evaporated milk

Three 5-ounce chocolate bars with almonds, broken into small pieces

One 12-ounce package semisweet chocolate chips

One 7-ounce jar marshmallow cream

"Overseas Chocolate has been in the family for years. We love the fudge during the holidays."

1. Grease a 13 × 9-inch glass baking dish. Combine the sugar, butter, and evaporated milk in a large saucepan. Place over medium heat. Bring to a rolling boil, stirring frequently. Boil for 5 minutes, stirring constantly.

2. Remove from the heat, add the remaining ingredients, and stir until melted. Pour the mixture into the prepared pan and let stand overnight. Cut into squares. Store in an airtight container with sheets of wax paper between the layers.

Quick-and-Easy Family Peanut Brittle

Mildred S. Fettig, Petoskey, Michigan

½ cup light corn syrup

½ cup sugar

1 cup raw peanuts

1 teaspoon baking soda

"My brother handed this recipe down to the rest of the family. It's great—everyone I give it to loves it."

1. Lightly butter a foil-lined baking sheet.

2. Combine the corn syrup and sugar in a 1½-quart saucepan. Cook over high heat until bubbly. Add the peanuts. Cook for 6 minutes exactly, stirring constantly with a wooden spoon and taking care not to burn the mixture.

3. Remove from the heat and add the baking soda. Be careful; the mixture bubbles up when the soda is added. Stir quickly for 5 seconds.

4. Pour the mixture onto the prepared baking sheet into a very thin layer. Cool completely before breaking into pieces. Store in an airtight container.

Homemade Peanut Butter Cups

Shirley Glaser, Ridgeland, Wisconsin

MAKES 72 PIECES

1½ cups graham cracker crumbs or
    21 graham cracker halves, crushed
1 cup (2 sticks) butter, softened
1 cup peanut butter
One 16-ounce package confectioners'
    sugar
One 12-ounce package milk chocolate
    chips
2 teaspoons shortening

TIPS FROM OUR TEST KITCHEN

To help measure out 72 balls evenly, divide the cracker crumb mixture into eighths and make 9 balls out of each section.

"Always a special treat at Christmas, weddings, and special parties, the peanut butter cups look pretty in printed paper liners."

1. Combine the graham cracker crumbs, butter, peanut butter, and confectioners' sugar in a large bowl; mix well.

2. Using a teaspoon as a scoop, roll the mixture into 72 small balls and press into petite paper liners, such as paper or foil mini-muffin liners or candy liners.

3. Combine the chocolate chips and the shortening in a microwave-safe bowl. Microwave on Medium for 1 minute. Watch closely so the mixture does not burn. Stir until the chips are melted.

4. Using a teaspoon, spoon the melted chocolate mixture over each peanut butter ball. Refrigerate for at least 2 hours to set. For peak flavor and texture, prepare 2 days in advance.

Cornflake Cookies

Norma Jo Drewette, Jackson, North Carolina

MAKES ABOUT 2 DOZEN COOKIES

1 cup (2 sticks) butter or margarine,
    softened
1 cup sugar
1 teaspoon vanilla extract
1½ cups self-rising flour
½ cup pecans
2 cups cornflakes

"My father's aunt gave this recipe to my mom many years ago when I was a very young child. Everyone loves these cookies and always wants to know what is in them. They are surprised when I tell them I use cornflakes to make the cookies."

1. Preheat the oven to 350°F. Spray a baking sheet with non-stick cooking spray.

2. Cream the butter, sugar, and vanilla in a large bowl. Gradually add the flour. Stir in the pecans and cornflakes. Drop by tablespoonfuls on the prepared baking sheet.

3. Bake for about 10 minutes until lightly browned around the edges and the middle looks firm. Remove from the pan immediately with a spatula.

Passover Macaroons

Ida Tenor, Pittsburgh, Pennsylvania

MAKES 6 DOZEN COOKIES

6 egg whites

1 cup sugar

2 teaspoons vanilla extract

One 14-ounce package sweetened flaked
coconut

2 cups chopped nuts

"Jewish people are not allowed to use flour or baking powder on Passover, so this is a perfect recipe. I am ninety-six years old and have used this recipe for years."

1. Preheat the oven to 350°F. Line two large baking sheets with parchment or wax paper.

2. Place the egg whites in a large bowl; beat with a mixer at high speed until peaks begin to form. Gradually add the sugar, 1 tablespoon at a time, beating constantly. Beat in the vanilla. Slowly fold the coconut and nuts into the egg mixture.

3. Drop by slightly rounded tablespoons onto the baking sheets. Bake for 18 minutes or until slightly golden. Cool on the baking sheets on a wire rack.

Molasses Cookies

Theresa Slemp, Afton, Tennessee

MAKES 2 DOZEN COOKIES

1½ cups all-purpose flour

1 cup sugar

1 teaspoon baking soda

½ teaspoon ground allspice

½ teaspoon ground nutmeg

½ teaspoon ground cloves

½ teaspoon kosher salt

½ cup shortening, melted and cooled

1 egg

¼ cup unsulfured molasses

¾ cup old-fashioned oats

"I've always been fascinated with my family history and cooking, and combining the two just seemed natural. This is my great-grandmother's recipe. While these cookies are baking, the house is filled with a rich, spicy scent that takes a person back to cold winters and wood stoves."

1. Preheat the oven to 375°F.

2. Sift together the flour, sugar, baking soda, spices, and salt. Add the melted, cooled shortening, egg, and molasses; mix well. Stir in the oats.

3. Drop by tablespoonfuls on an ungreased baking sheet. Flatten with the bottom of a glass that has been dipped in sugar. Bake for 10 to 12 minutes.

Monster Cookies

Becky Jackson, Spring Hill, Florida

3 eggs

1 cup packed dark brown sugar

1 cup granulated sugar

¾ teaspoon vanilla extract

¾ teaspoon light corn syrup

2 teaspoons baking soda

½ cup (1 stick) butter, softened

1¼ cups peanut butter (12 ounces)

4½ cups old-fashioned oats

⅔ cup semisweet chocolate chips

⅔ cup raisins or M&Ms

TIPS FROM OUR TEST KITCHEN

Keeping the cookies on the baking sheet after removing them from the oven allows the cookies to continue to bake without drying out.

"I baked Monster Cookies for a new friend not long after I had moved to town. He wasn't home when I dropped them off, but he told his roommate he would marry the person who had baked the cookies. He married the baker—me—a year later. That was nearly twenty years ago, and I'm still baking them."

1. Preheat the oven to 350°F. Lightly grease two baking sheets.

2. Combine the eggs, sugars, vanilla, corn syrup, baking soda, and butter in a large bowl; beat with a mixer at medium-high speed until smooth. Add the peanut butter and beat until well blended. Stir in the remaining ingredients until well blended.

3. Using a ½-cup measure or an ice cream scoop, place 2 scoops of the dough onto each cookie sheet. Flatten each to a 4-inch-round, ½-inch-thick cookie.

4. Bake for 12 minutes. Remove from the oven and place the baking sheets on a wire rack for 4 minutes. Remove the cookies. Repeat with the remaining dough.

Banana Oatmeal Cookies

Ann Langenfeld, Burns, Oregon

MAKES 4 DOZEN COOKIES

¾ cup shortening

1 cup sugar

1 egg

1 cup mashed bananas

1½ cups all-purpose flour

½ teaspoon baking soda

1 teaspoon salt

1 teaspoon ground cinnamon

½ teaspoon ground nutmeg

2 cups quick-cooking oats

1 cup chocolate chips

"This is a childhood favorite. My grandma would always make these cookies for my sisters and me. She would call the chocolate chips 'chocolate bitties.' When I make these cookies, the way my home smells really brings back the memories of my grandma."

1. Preheat the oven to 400°F. Combine the shortening, sugar, egg, and bananas in a bowl; mix well. Add the flour, baking soda, salt, cinnamon, and nutmeg; mix well. Stir in the oats and chocolate chips.

2. Drop by rounded tablespoons onto a baking sheet. Bake for 8 to 10 minutes. Cool on a wire rack.

Peppermint Stick Cookies

Marva Brubaker, New Carlisle, Ohio

MAKES 5 DOZEN COOKIES

¾ cup (1½ sticks) butter, softened

6 tablespoons sugar, plus additional for dipping

1 egg yolk

1 teaspoon vanilla extract

2 cups sifted all-purpose flour

½ cup crushed peppermint sticks or candies

1 egg white

Chocolate chips

TIPS FROM OUR TEST KITCHEN

These cookies are a great way to use up leftover Christmas peppermints. If you prefer a little more chocolate, use a Hershey's Chocolate Kiss instead of the chocolate chips.

"This recipe came from my grandmother and was one she always baked at Christmas. It is one of my favorites."

1. Preheat the oven to 350°F. Place a sheet of parchment paper on a baking sheet.

2. Cream the butter and 6 tablespoons sugar with a mixer. Mix in the egg yolk and vanilla. Blend in the flour, ¼ cup at a time. Stir in the crushed peppermint sticks.

3. Beat the egg white in a small bowl until frothy.

4. Roll the dough into 1-inch balls. Dip the top of each ball into the egg white and then into extra sugar. Place on the baking sheet, sugared side up. Put a thumbprint in the top of each cookie and top with a chocolate chip. Bake for 10 to 15 minutes.

No-Roll Sugar Cookies

Mary Newton, Winterset, Iowa

MAKES 4 TO 5 DOZEN COOKIES

1½ cups confectioners' sugar

6 tablespoons granulated sugar

1½ cups (3 sticks) butter, softened

2 eggs

3¼ cups all-purpose flour

1½ teaspoons baking soda

1½ teaspoons cream of tartar

1½ teaspoons vanilla extract

"Grandma Abbott always had her wafer-thin sugar cookies waiting for us in the brightly colored old tin sitting in the back pantry on the farm. She raised eight children, babysat nine grandchildren, and fed many a laborer in her big farm kitchen. The tin was never empty."

1. Preheat the oven to 350°F.

2. Cream together the sugars and butter with a mixer at medium speed. Add the eggs and mix well. Add the flour, baking soda, cream of tartar, and vanilla; mix well.

3. Roll the dough into walnut-sized balls. Place on an ungreased baking sheet. Flatten with a glass that has been dipped in sugar. Bake for about 10 minutes until lightly golden.

Bill's Zucchini Cookies

Jean Boutwell, Troy, Alabama

MAKES ABOUT 4 DOZEN COOKIES

½ cup (1 stick) butter, softened

1 cup granulated sugar

1 egg, beaten

2 cups all-purpose flour

1 teaspoon baking soda

1 teaspoon ground cinnamon

½ teaspoon salt

1 cup grated zucchini

1 cup golden raisins

1 cup chopped pecans

1 cup semisweet chocolate chips

"My friend Bill Harden and his wife, Ernestine, developed this cookie recipe to use the abundance of zucchini they grow in their garden. It's mouthwatering and the best cookie I have ever tasted."

1. Preheat the oven to 350°F. Grease two nonstick baking sheets.

2. Combine the butter and sugar in a large bowl; beat with a mixer at medium-high speed until light and fluffy. Gradually add the egg, flour, baking soda, cinnamon, and salt. Beat until smooth. The dough will be stiff at this point. Stir in the remaining ingredients. Drop the batter by teaspoonfuls 2 inches apart onto the baking sheets.

3. Bake for 13 to 15 minutes until light brown. Do not overbake. Place the baking sheets on wire racks to cool for 2 minutes. Remove the cookies and cool completely on wire racks.

Apple Crunch

Pat Gore, Grain Valley, Missouri

SERVES 6 TO 8

6 large apples, peeled, cored, and thinly
    sliced
½ cup granulated sugar
½ teaspoon ground nutmeg or
    cinnamon
1 cup all-purpose flour
1 cup packed brown sugar
½ cup (1 stick) butter
Ice cream or whipped cream

"This recipe was given to me by my mother-in-law in 1949. I have used it so much that the recipe card is soiled, and I have taped it together in several places. I want to keep the original card for my children."

1. Preheat the oven to 325°F. Grease an 8-inch square baking pan.

2. Spread the apples in the pan. Cover with the granulated sugar and sprinkle with nutmeg.

3. Combine the flour and brown sugar in a bowl; mix well. Cut in the butter using a pastry cutter or your fingers until the mixture resembles coarse meal. Spread over the apples.

4. Bake for 1 hour. Serve with ice cream or whipped cream.

Blueberry Bread Pudding with Blueberry Ginger Sauce

Candace McMenamin, Lexington, South Carolina

BLUEBERRY GINGER SAUCE

2 cups fresh or frozen blueberries

½ cup sugar

1 tablespoon chopped crystallized ginger
    or ½ teaspoon ground ginger

PUDDING

1½ cups sugar

4 eggs

1 cup whipping cream

2 cups milk

1 teaspoon vanilla extract

½ teaspoon ground nutmeg

One 16-ounce loaf challah bread, cut into
    2-inch cubes

1 cup fresh or frozen blueberries

Whipped cream, optional

TIPS FROM OUR TEST KITCHEN

If you can't find challah bread, use a
1-pound loaf of French bread or a
baguette.

"I developed this recipe to use my abundance of blueberries. My family and I have a tradition of going to the blueberry patch every July 4. With the sometimes stifling heat here in the South, it is not always easy to get my teenage boys to adhere to this tradition. This recipe helps serve as a reward for their hard efforts, and I get to enjoy some great togetherness with my boys."

1. To prepare the sauce, combine the blueberries, sugar, ginger, and ¼ cup water in a medium saucepan. Bring to a boil, reduce the heat to a simmer, and cook for 3 to 5 minutes until the sauce thickens.

2. To prepare the pudding, preheat the oven to 375°F. Lightly grease a 13 × 9-inch baking pan.

3. Beat the sugar and eggs with a mixer at medium speed until fluffy. Add the whipping cream, milk, vanilla, and nutmeg; beat until blended. Fold in the bread cubes and blueberries. Pour into the baking pan. Let stand for 5 minutes.

4. Bake for 40 to 45 minutes. Cool in the pan for 5 minutes. To serve, top with Blueberry Ginger Sauce and whipped cream, if desired.

Butterfingers Dessert

Joan Reed, Canton, Illinois

SERVES 10 TO 12

2 cups milk

1 quart vanilla ice cream

Two 3-ounce packages instant vanilla
    pudding

½ cup (1 stick) butter

1½ cups crushed graham cracker crumbs

½ cup crushed saltine crackers

One 8-ounce container whipped topping

Four 2-ounce Butterfinger candy bars,
    crushed

Chocolate sauce, optional

1. Combine the milk, ice cream, and pudding mix in a large bowl; beat well. Place in the refrigerator.

2. Melt the butter in a saucepan; pour over the cracker crumbs in a large bowl. Stir well. Pour into a 13 × 9-inch pan, patting into an even layer on the bottom and reserving one-third of the mixture for the topping. Pour the ice cream mixture over the crust. Freeze for 1 hour.

3. Spread the whipped topping over the filling. Mix the crushed Butterfingers with the reserved crumb mixture. Sprinkle over the top and return to the freezer to set. Serve with chocolate sauce, if desired.

Cream Cheese Cupcakes

Wilma Mahon, Honesdale, Pennsylvania

Three 8-ounce packages cream cheese
1¼ cups sugar
5 eggs
1¾ teaspoons vanilla extract
1 cup sour cream
2 tablespoons jam
Fresh berries

"These are great at holiday get-togethers or picnics."

1. Preheat the oven to 325°F. Line 24 muffin tin cups with paper liners.

2. Beat the cream cheese with 1 cup sugar and the eggs in a large bowl. Add 1½ teaspoons vanilla. Pour the batter into the muffin liners, filling two-thirds full. Bake for 40 minutes.

3. Combine the sour cream, the remaining ¼ cup sugar, and the remaining ¼ teaspoon vanilla in a bowl; mix well.

4. Remove the cupcakes from the oven. They will fall in the middle. Fill the center with the sour cream mixture. Spoon ¼ teaspoon jam on top. Return to the oven and bake for 5 minutes. Garnish with fresh berries.

Lovely Lemon Meringues

Karen Van Beek, Pipestone, Minnesota

SERVES 16

MERINGUES

6 egg whites

¼ teaspoon cream of tartar

2 cups sugar

1 teaspoon cider vinegar

FILLING

6 egg yolks

Grated zest and juice of 1 medium lemon

1 cup sugar

2 tablespoons cornstarch

2 cups whipping cream

Fresh berries, optional

TIPS FROM OUR TEST KITCHEN

If the sides of the meringue are too high, press down slightly with the back of a spoon. Store the meringues in the refrigerator for up to four days, if desired.

"When I made these Lovely Lemon Meringues, everybody loved them and wanted the recipe."

1. Grease a 13 × 9-inch glass baking dish.

2. To prepare the meringues, place the egg whites in a medium bowl; beat with a mixer at high speed until stiff peaks form. Add the cream of tartar and gradually add 1 cup of the sugar, beating constantly. Add the vinegar and gradually add the remaining 1 cup sugar.

3. Spoon into the prepared pan. Place in the oven and heat to 300°F. Do not preheat the oven. Bake for 1 hour. Remove from the oven and cool on a wire rack.

4. To prepare the filling, combine the egg yolks, lemon juice, 1 cup sugar, and cornstarch in a medium saucepan. Whisk until well blended and place over medium heat. Cook until thickened, stirring frequently. Remove from the heat, stir in the grated lemon zest, and cool completely.

5. Pour the whipping cream into a medium bowl; beat with a mixer at high speed until stiff peaks form. Fold into the cooled egg yolk mixture.

6. To assemble, spoon the whipped cream mixture on top of the cooled meringue. Spread evenly. Cover with plastic wrap and refrigerate for 24 hours. Cut into squares to serve. Serve with fresh berries, if desired.

Strawberry Torte

Linda Robinson, Jamaica, Vermont

CAKE

½ cup shortening

½ cup sugar

4 egg yolks, beaten

4 tablespoons milk

½ cup plus 2 tablespoons all-purpose
    flour

1 teaspoon baking powder

TOPPING

4 egg whites

1 cup sugar

⅛ teaspoon cream of tartar

⅛ teaspoon salt

2 cups sliced fresh strawberries

2 cups sweetened whipped cream

"This recipe was given to me by a coworker many years ago. It became a family favorite, especially for my son."

1. Preheat the oven to 350°F. Grease two 8-inch round cake pans.

2. To prepare the cake, combine the shortening and sugar in a bowl and beat with a mixer. Blend in the egg yolks, milk, flour, and baking powder. Spread over the bottoms of the pans.

3. To prepare the topping, beat the egg whites until stiff peaks form. Add the sugar, cream of tartar, and salt; beat until thick and glossy. Spread over the cake layers.

4. Bake for 20 to 25 minutes. Cool for 5 minutes and then remove to plates. When completely cool, arrange the strawberries over the egg-white-topping side of one layer. Top with the second layer, with the egg-white-topping side down. Spread whipped cream on top.

Apple Cream Pie

Gina Kendall, Taylorsville, Kentucky

FILLING

One 8-ounce package cream cheese,
    softened
1 egg
½ teaspoon vanilla extract
¾ cup sugar
2 tablespoons all-purpose flour
2 cups finely chopped apples
1 frozen 9-inch deep-dish pie shell,
    thawed

TOPPING

⅓ cup sugar
⅓ cup all-purpose flour
1 teaspoon ground cinnamon
¼ cup (½ stick) butter

"This is my all-time favorite pie to make. It's requested at every family picnic I go to, plus I am asked to make a few extras for others to take home. Try it—it could become your favorite pie."

1. Preheat the oven to 450°F.

2. To prepare the filling, combine the cream cheese, egg, and vanilla in a medium bowl; beat with a mixer at medium speed until smooth. Add the sugar and flour; beat until well blended. Stir in the apples and mix thoroughly. Pour the apple mixture into the pie shell and bake for 15 minutes. Reduce the heat to 325°F and bake for 30 minutes longer.

3. To prepare the topping, combine the sugar, flour, and cinnamon in a medium bowl. Using two knives or a pastry cutter, cut the butter into the flour mixture until it resembles pea-sized crumbs.

4. Remove the pie from the oven and sprinkle evenly with the topping. Bake for 20 to 30 minutes until lightly golden.

Dewberry Pie

Brenda Morgan, Brenham, Texas

CRUST AND FILLING

4 cups fresh or frozen dewberries or
    blackberries

2 unbaked 9-inch pie shells

$1\frac{1}{2}$ cups sugar

2 eggs, beaten

$\frac{1}{2}$ cup all-purpose flour

$\frac{1}{2}$ cup sour cream or $\frac{1}{4}$ cup sweetened
    condensed milk

$\frac{1}{8}$ teaspoon salt

TOPPING

$\frac{1}{2}$ cup all-purpose flour

$\frac{1}{2}$ cup sugar

$\frac{1}{4}$ cup ($\frac{1}{2}$ stick) butter or margarine, cut
    into small cubes

TIPS FROM OUR TEST KITCHEN

Dewberries are any of several
varieties of the trailing form of
blackberries.

"Dewberry Pie is my little granddaughter's favorite
pie—mine, too!"

1. Preheat the oven to 325°F.

2. To prepare the filling, place 2 cups of the berries into each
of the pie shells; set aside. Combine the sugar, eggs, flour,
sour cream, and salt in a bowl; whisk to blend. Pour equal
amounts over each of the two pies. Allow the liquid to settle
to the bottom.

3. To prepare the topping, combine the flour and sugar in a
medium bowl. Using two knives or a pastry blender, cut the
butter into the flour mixture until it resembles small peas.
Sprinkle evenly over both pies. Bake for 1 hour and 15 minutes, or until browned.

Callie's Buttermilk Pie

Kaye Ray, Borger, Texas

SERVES 8

½ cup (1 stick) butter, melted
1¾ cups sugar
3 tablespoons all-purpose flour
3 eggs, beaten
1 cup whole buttermilk
1 teaspoon vanilla extract
¼ to ½ teaspoon ground nutmeg
¼ teaspoon salt
1 unbaked 9-inch deep-dish piecrust

"Growing up on a farm in the Texas Panhandle, I enjoyed country life very much. We had freshly churned butter and buttermilk weekly. My mom would make a buttermilk pie often. We could always look forward to having it for Father's Day because it was my father's favorite."

1. Preheat the oven to 350°F.

2. Combine the butter, sugar, flour, eggs, buttermilk, vanilla, nutmeg, and salt in a large bowl; whisk until smooth.

3. Pour the buttermilk mixture into the piecrust. Bake for 45 to 50 minutes until golden and a wooden pick inserted in the center comes out clean.

4. Cool completely on a wire rack. Cover with plastic wrap and refrigerate until serving time.

Mom's Custard Pie

Mary L. Daring, Carey, Ohio

1 unbaked 9-inch piecrust

4 eggs

½ cup sugar

¼ teaspoon salt

1 teaspoon vanilla extract

2½ cups whole milk

¼ teaspoon ground nutmeg

"I have made this pie many times, and it's my brother's favorite. I highly recommend this recipe. It's good any time of the year."

1. Preheat the oven to 450°F. Line the piecrust with heavy-duty foil. Bake for 8 minutes. Remove the foil and bake for 5 minutes longer.

2. Reduce the oven temperature to 350°F. Separate 1 egg; place the egg white in a small mixing bowl. Combine the egg yolk, the remaining eggs, sugar, salt, vanilla, and milk in a large bowl; whisk until well blended.

3. Beat the egg white with a mixer until stiff peaks form. Fold into the egg mixture. Carefully pour into the crust. Sprinkle ⅛ teaspoon of the nutmeg over the top, cover with foil, and bake for 25 minutes. Remove the foil and bake for 15 to 20 minutes longer until a knife inserted in the center comes out clean.

4. Sprinkle with the remaining nutmeg and place on a wire rack to cool completely. When cool, cover with plastic wrap and refrigerate until serving time.

Sophisticatedly Serious Chocolate Fudge Pie

Perry Schwartz, Athens, Alabama

SERVES 8

CRUST

¼ cup granulated sugar

⅛ teaspoon salt

½ cup shortening

2 tablespoons light corn syrup

½ teaspoon vanilla extract

1 egg

¾ cup cake flour

⅔ cup bread flour

FILLING

1 cup (2 sticks) butter

4 ounces semisweet chocolate

2 cups granulated sugar

4 eggs

2 tablespoons vanilla extract

¾ cup all-purpose flour

⅔ cup cocoa powder

TOPPING

4 ounces cream cheese, softened

2 tablespoons orange liqueur or
  1 tablespoon lemon juice

¾ cup confectioners' sugar

"I used to be an executive chef at a country club in Nashville, Tennessee. The board of directors asked me to come up with some signature desserts, and I created this fudge pie filling recipe myself."

1. Preheat the oven to 375°F. Grease a 9-inch deep-dish pie pan.

2. To prepare the crust, combine the granulated sugar, salt, and shortening in a medium bowl; beat with a mixer at medium-low speed for 10 minutes. Add the corn syrup, vanilla, and egg; beat well. Scrape the sides of the bowl, if necessary. Sift the cake flour and bread flour over the bowl. Fold in until just blended. Do not overmix.

3. Roll out the dough on a lightly floured work surface to ⅛-inch thickness. Arrange in the prepared pan. Prick the bottom and sides with a fork in several places. Bake for 5 minutes. Remove the piecrust from the oven. Reduce the heat to 325°F.

4. To prepare the filling, melt the butter and chocolate in a double boiler over low heat. Mix well and remove from the heat.

5. Combine the granulated sugar and eggs in a medium bowl; beat with a mixer at medium-high speed until ribbons form, about 10 minutes. Add the vanilla.

"Ribbons" means that a continuous string of batter forms, giving a ribbonlike effect when beaters are lifted from the batter.

6. Combine the all-purpose flour and the cocoa in a medium bowl; mix well. Using a firm spatula, fold the melted chocolate into the egg mixture. Add the flour mixture and stir until just blended. Pour into the cooled piecrust and bake for 25 to 30 minutes. The pie is done when it is inflated in appearance and cracks all over the top. Remove from the oven and cool on a wire rack for 30 minutes. Put a 10-inch piece of parchment paper on top and place a large plate on its surface. Refrigerate overnight.

7. To prepare the topping, combine the cream cheese and liqueur in a medium bowl; beat with a mixer at medium-high speed until blended. Reduce the speed to low, gradually add the confectioners' sugar, and beat until smooth. To serve, cut the pie in wedges and top with the cream cheese topping.

End-of-the-Crop Fruit Pie

Kathy Karaba, Ashland, Wisconsin

SERVES 6 TO 8

CRUST

1 cup milk

1 tablespoon cider vinegar

1¾ cups lard or shortening

4 cups all-purpose flour

¼ teaspoon salt

1 egg, lightly beaten

FILLING

¾ cup plus 2 tablespoons sugar

5 tablespoons all-purpose flour

½ to ¾ teaspoon ground cinnamon

1 cup fresh or frozen, thawed blueberries

1½ cups fresh strawberries

1½ cups fresh or frozen, thawed raspberries

1½ tablespoons cold butter or margarine, cut into small pieces

TIPS FROM OUR TEST KITCHEN

Making the crust is usually the time-consuming part of making a pie. Having one in the freezer will save on time, energy, and cleanup.

"When blueberries, raspberries, and strawberries were all available, something needed to be made with them. I put the three varieties together and tried these pies. My family loved the combination."

1. To prepare the crust, combine the milk and vinegar in a small bowl; mix well. Combine the shortening, flour, and salt in a large bowl. Using two knives or a pastry blender, cut the shortening into the flour until it resembles pea-sized crumbs. Stir in the milk mixture and the egg; blend well.

2. Divide the dough in half, wrap one half in plastic wrap, and freeze for later use. Cover the remaining half with plastic wrap and refrigerate for at least 1 hour.

3. Preheat the oven to 425°F.

4. Divide the refrigerated dough in half and place on a lightly floured work surface. Roll out the dough to make two crusts. Arrange one crust in a 9-inch deep-dish pie pan.

5. To prepare the filling, combine the sugar, flour, and cinnamon in a large bowl; mix well. Add the berries; stir gently, yet thoroughly, to coat completely.

6. Pour the berry mixture into the piecrust and top with pieces of butter. Place the remaining piecrust on top and seal the edges tightly. Using a fork, poke holes in several areas on top. Bake for 35 to 45 minutes until the crust is brown and the berries are bubbly.

Cranberry Orange Pecan Pie

Irene Radke, Bayfield, Wisconsin

SERVES 6 TO 8

1 cup chopped fresh cranberries

Grated zest of 1 medium orange

1 unbaked 9-inch piecrust

1 cup pecan halves

3 eggs

1 cup dark corn syrup

⅔ cup sugar

¼ cup (½ stick) butter, melted

"My husband's favorite pie is pecan pie—but it was always a little too rich for me. One day when I was making cranberry relish, I experimented with the cranberry and orange zest, and it came out great."

1. Preheat the oven to 350°F.

2. Combine the cranberries with the orange zest in a small bowl; mix well. Spoon into the bottom of the piecrust. Arrange the pecan halves on top of the cranberry mixture and press down slightly.

3. Combine the eggs, corn syrup, sugar, and butter in a medium bowl; whisk until smooth. Pour evenly over the pecans. Bake for 1 hour, or until set.

Pumpkin Bottom Pecan Pie

Debi Hendrix, Ardmore, Oklahoma

SERVES 6 TO 8

PUMPKIN FILLING

1 egg, slightly beaten

1 cup canned solid pumpkin

1/3 cup sugar

1 tablespoon heavy cream, half-and-half,
   or whole milk

1/2 teaspoon ground cinnamon

1/4 teaspoon ground nutmeg

1/4 teaspoon ground ginger

1 unbaked 9-inch piecrust

PECAN FILLING

2 eggs, slightly beaten

2/3 cup light corn syrup

1/2 cup sugar

3 tablespoons butter, melted

1/2 teaspoon vanilla extract

1 cup chopped pecans

"I received this recipe from my aunt Gwen. She's a fantastic cook. This is an excellent pie to serve at Thanksgiving—the flavors complement each other beautifully."

1. Preheat the oven to 375°F.

2. To prepare the pumpkin filling, combine the egg, pumpkin, sugar, cream, and spices in a medium bowl; mix well. Pour into the bottom of the piecrust.

3. To prepare the pecan filling, combine the eggs, corn syrup, sugar, butter, and vanilla in a bowl; mix well. Stir in the pecans and carefully pour over the pumpkin filling.

4. Bake for 10 minutes; reduce the heat to 350°F. Bake for 50 minutes, or until a knife inserted in the center comes out clean. Cool completely on a wire rack. Cover with plastic wrap and refrigerate until serving time.

Crusty Rhubarb Pie

Barbara Maggs, Cle Elum, Washington

SERVES 8

NO-ROLL PASTRY

1½ cups all-purpose flour

1 teaspoon salt

1 tablespoon sugar

½ cup vegetable oil

2 tablespoons milk

FILLING

4 cups diced, unpeeled rhubarb

1¼ to 2 cups sugar

5 tablespoons all-purpose flour

1 tablespoon butter, cut into small pieces

TOPPING

¼ cup (½ stick) butter

¼ cup sugar

½ cup all-purpose flour

Ice cream or whipped cream

"I grew up in rural Massachusetts, where we had a large rhubarb patch. I remember my mother trying to be creative to get the family to eat it. This pie was our favorite by far."

1. Preheat the oven to 350°F.

2. To prepare the pastry, combine the flour, salt, and sugar in a bowl; mix well. Add the vegetable oil and milk; mix well with a fork. Transfer to a pie pan and press with your fingers to spread over the bottom and up the sides of the pan.

3. To prepare the filling, combine the rhubarb with the sugar and flour; mix well. Pour into the piecrust. Top with butter.

4. To prepare the topping, combine the butter, sugar, and flour in a bowl; mix until crumbly. Sprinkle over the pie filling.

5. Bake for 1 hour. Let cool to set. Serve with ice cream or whipped cream.

List of Contributors

Amunrud, Debra *Glencoe, Arkansas*

Babin, Sheila *Orange, Texas*

Baker, Marsha *Pioneer, Ohio*

Bankston, Bobbie E. *Midland, Texas*

Barlett, Lisa *Sapello, New Mexico*

Barnhart, Juanita *Greenfield, Indiana*

Barnwell, Frances *Marion, North Carolina*

Barron, Sonya *Hamilton, Texas*

Beeler, Addibeth *Miles City, Montana*

Bennett, Sandra H. *Washington, Missouri*

Berry, Margee *Trout Lake, Washington*

Bertsch, Pearl Anna *Ypsilanti, South Dakota*

Boutwell, Jean *Troy, Alabama*

Bradshaw, Lois *Kingsville, Texas*

Brooks, Connie *Hayti, Missouri*

Brown, Marie *Wilson, North Carolina*

Brubaker, Marva *New Carlisle, Ohio*

Burlinson, Nancy *Horseshoe Bend, Arkansas*

Carlucci, Mickey *Peralta, New Mexico*

Carman, Kay *Philpot, Kentucky*

Carson, Deborah *Fort Morgan, Colorado*

Casola, Barb *Venice, Florida*

Cathelyn, Lucille *Geneseo, Illinois*

Cheshire, Mrs. Billy *Luling, Texas*

Coffelt, Barbara *Estill Springs, Tennessee*

Connolly, Janet *Orange City, Florida*

Copp, Heidi and Faithe *Rochester, New Hampshire*

Courson, Rita *Seneca, Pennsylvania*

Curtis, Janet *North Platte, Nebraska*

Dance, Eloise *Hattiesburg, Mississippi*

Daring, Mary L. *Carey, Ohio*

David, Cora and Kandi *Cassville, Pennsylvania*

Decker, Robin *Kalispell, Montana*

Disciascio, Nancy *New Alexandria, Pennsylvania*

Drewette, Norma J. *Jackson, North Carolina*

Eakin, Barbara *Utica, Pennsylvania*

Emig, Marcia *Goodland, Kansas*

Fahrenkamp, Linda *New Prague, Minnesota*

Feazell, Jo K. *Worthham, Texas*

Fegley, Ruth R. *Barnesville, Pennsylvania*

Fettig, Mildred S. *Petoskey, Michigan*

Fortschneider, Betty *Brussels, Illinois*

Frandson, Norma *Grand Forks, North Dakota*

Frerich, Laura *Napoleon, Ohio*

Fulks, Betty   *Onia, Arkansas*

Fyfe, Michelle   *Mesa, Arizona*

Galletley, Peggy   *Porterville, California*

Gates, Joyce   *Clovis, New Mexico*

Geary, Jo Ann   *Whispering Pines, North Carolina*

Glaser, Shirley   *Ridgeland, Wisconsin*

Gore, Pat   *Grain Valley, Missouri*

Greco, Tony T.   *Saylorsburg, Pennsylvania*

Greer, Kathy   *Spokane, Washington*

Gregory, Darla   *Port Henry, New York*

Griffith, Virgie   *Washington, Texas*

Grizzard, Nina   *Las Cruces, New Mexico*

Hake, Shelia   *Bossier City, Louisiana*

Hammann, Mary H.   *Waggoner, Illinois*

Hammond, Kimberly   *Kingwood, Texas*

Hankin, Marion E.   *Boynton Beach, Florida*

Hartman, Dorothea   *Decatur, Indiana*

Harvey, James   *Dayton, Texas*

Heart, Duaine   *Hartselle, Alabama*

Heino, Helen   *Dunlevy, Pennsylvania*

Heitkamp, Rita   *New Bremen, Ohio*

Hendrix, Debi   *Ardmore, Oklahoma*

Hilton, Joni   *Rocklin, California*

Hoefle Jr., Kenny   *McAdenville, North Carolina*

Hoff, Mrs. W.   *Coldwater, Michigan*

Hough, Helen F.   *Rockport, Texas*

Jackson, Becky   *Spring Hill, Florida*

Jackson, Ruth   *Sturgis, Missouri*

James, Barb   *Iola, Wisconsin*

Jeffrey, Mary Helen   *Robertsdale, Alabama*

Jensen, Marlene   *Rochester, Minnesota*

Johnston, Deborah   *Catonsville, Maryland*

Jonas, Mary Louise   *Karnes City, Texas*

Jones, Barb   *Panama, Illinois*

Jones, Juanita   *Kingsville, Texas*

Junker, Kathie   *Lafayette, Tennessee*

Karaba, Kathy   *Ashland, Wisconsin*

Kechnie, Kathleen   *Weatherford, Texas*

Keller, Kimberly J.   *Richlands, Virginia*

Kellogg, Michelle   *Heber City, Utah*

Kendall, Gina   *Taylorsville, Kentucky*

Kercher, Ken   *Hillsboro, Illinois*

Klapal, Bryon   *Castle Rock, Colorado*

Kline, Leah   *Sunset, South Carolina*

Konitzer Jr., John   *Albuquerque, New Mexico*

Kopach, Margaret   *Charleroi, Pennsylvania*

Kruse, Trisha   *Eagle, Idaho*

Lahey, Connie   *Bethalto, Illinois*

Langenfeld, Ann   *Burns, Oregon*

Lature, Ruth Fuller   *Hopkinsville, Kentucky*

Lee, Mary Ann   *Clifton Park, New York*

Lewis, Mary J.   *Eatonton, Georgia*

Lindsey, Connie   *Sauk City, Wisconsin*

Ludemann, Cheryl   *Boonville, New York*

Lynn, Judy   *Huntley, Illinois*

Maggs, Barbara   *Cle Elum, Washington*

Mahon, Wilma   *Honesdale, Pennsylvania*

Makalinao, Chris   *Dallas, Texas*

Martin, Gay *Albertsville, Alabama*

Martin, Terri *Dublin, Virginia*

Mauch, Diane *Hankinson, North Dakota*

McCoy, Sue E. *Lexington, Virginia*

McDaniel, Sam *Cary, North Carolina*

McFarland, Susan *Racine, Wisconsin*

McLane, Matilda *Cave City, Arkansas*

McMenamin, Candace *Lexington, South Carolina*

Miller, Barbara *New Bern, North Carolina*

Montagano, Diane *Plymouth, Michigan*

Morgan, Brenda *Brenham, Texas*

Mulvaney, Barbara *Billings, Montana*

Murry, Mary *Gatesville, Texas*

Napier, Reginia *Clarksville, Texas*

Navarrete, Vicky *Hesperia, California*

Nelson, Karen E. *Brookings, Oregon*

Newton, Mary *Winterset, Iowa*

Onuffer, Dawn *Crestview, Florida*

Pantalone, Marie *Fairfax, Virginia*

Parker, Joy *Covington, Georgia*

Patton, Loyd *Spokane, Washington*

Payette, Carol *Friendswood, Texas*

Payette, Gloria *Friendswood, Texas*

Peters, Barbara J. *Salem, Illinois*

Peterson, Kathleen *West End, North Carolina*

Porter, Carmela *Holland, Michigan*

Prine, Judy *Hattiesburg, Mississippi*

Probasco, Elsie *Bartley, Nebraska*

Pybus, Jennifer *Lockhart, Alabama*

Radke, Irene *Bayfield, Wisconsin*

Ramirez-McCarty, Terry *Helendale, California*

Rau, Elizabeth *Westphalia, Iowa*

Ray, Kaye *Borger, Texas*

Redding, Janet *Stanley, North Carolina*

Reed, Joan *Canton, Illinois*

Regnaud, Agnes *Spring Hill, Florida*

Reich, Anna Victoria *Stafford, Virginia*

Reid, Jo Ann *Salisbury, North Carolina*

Reif, Marjorie *Spearfish, South Dakota*

Rhodes, Mike and Melinda *Capron, Illinois*

Rickenbaugh, Bonnie *Sturtevant, Wisconsin*

Robert, J. B. *Murphy, North Carolina*

Robinson, Linda *Jamaica, Vermont*

Rogers, Billie J. *Durant, Oklahoma*

Rose, Doris Ann *Eddy, Texas*

Rosenthal, Michaela *Woodland Hills, California*

Ruff, Carolyn *Shelbyville, Illinois*

Schindler, Barbara *Napoleon, Ohio*

Schirmer, Ellen *Spokane, Washington*

Schroeder, Grace *Livonia, Michigan*

Schwartz, Perry *Athens, Alabama*

Seibert, Eva *Allentown, Pennsylvania*

Senter, Ann *Graeagle, California*

Settles, Kate L. *Point Clear, Alabama*

Shank, Pamela *Parkersburg, West Virginia*

Shanklin, Dee *New Smyrna Beach, Florida*

Sheriff, Amber *Cumming, Georgia*

Shivers, Mary *Ada, Oklahoma*

Shranko, Robert *Prescott, Arizona*

Sickbert, Cindy *Rushville, Indiana*

Simon, Joann *Wilkes-Barre, Pennsylvania*

Slemp, Theresa *Afton, Tennessee*

Smith, Gloria *Nixa, Missouri*

Smith, Michelle *New Castle, Kentucky*

Spires, Robin *Tampa, Florida*

St. Martin, Oggie *Menominee, Michigan*

Stahl, Bernice *Auburn, Kentucky*

Stella, Rhonda *Bonner's Ferry, Idaho*

Stephens, Azalea *Dayton, Texas*

Stephenson, Mrs. Ivor *Winnsboro, South Carolina*

Stewart, Marcella *Madison, Indiana*

Stine, Heather *Catawissa, Pennsylvania*

Stoos, June *St. Cloud, Florida*

Strickland, Patty *Waverly, Ohio*

Stubblefield, Claudia *Lebanon, Missouri*

Suhan, Shelia *Scottdale, Pennsylvania*

Suhr-Hollis, Helgard *New Braunfels, Texas*

Swancer, Bernadette *Medina, Ohio*

Swanson, Gwen *Pukwana, South Dakota*

Taylor, Judy *Kenna, West Virginia*

Tenor, Ida *Pittsburgh, Pennsylvania*

Thomas, Sue *Canyon, Texas*

Thompson, La Juan *Washington, Arkansas*

Thompson, Stella T. *Fort Payne, Alabama*

Trescott, Marcia *Council Bluffs, Iowa*

Turberville, Dana *Uriah, Alabama*

Van Beek, Karen *Pipestone, Minnesota*

Van Osdell, Gail *St. Charles, Illinois*

Vaughan, Tillie B. *Victorville, California*

Vilsack, Louise *Glenshaw, Pennsylvania*

Wall, Julia M. *Rushville, Illinois*

Warren, Chris *Cedar Rapids, Iowa*

Wesson, Julie *Wilton, Wisconsin*

White, Wanda J. *Sedalia, Missouri*

Williams, Dee *Kingsland, Georgia*

Williams, Dorothy *Greencastle, Indiana*

Williamson, Jane *Hot Springs Village, Arkansas*

Willink, Phyllis *Baldwin, Wisconsin*

Wilson, Donna *Washington, Missouri*

Wolf, Martha *Brighton, Michigan*

Wong, Phyllis *Laughlin, Nevada*

Wood, Christina *Martinsburg, Missouri*

Yantz, DeeDee *Smithfield, Kentucky*

Zeleniak, Martha *Taylor, Pennsylvania*

Recipes Index

Holidays Index

Note: Boldfaced entries are category winners.

American Profile, one of America's most widely circulated magazines, celebrates hometown life, and in *Hometown Recipes for the Holidays* editors Candace Floyd, Anne Gillem, Nancy S. Hughes, and Jill Melton do just that.

Candace Floyd is the food editor of both *Relish* and *American Profile* magazines and coeditor of the best-selling *American Profile Hometown Cookbook*. Anne Gillem is a journalist and has served as editor for independent cookbooks and is a freelance editor. Nancy S. Hughes is a cookbook author and has developed recipes for more than thirty cookbooks. Jill Melton is a registered dietician, chef, author, and editor of *Relish* magazine.

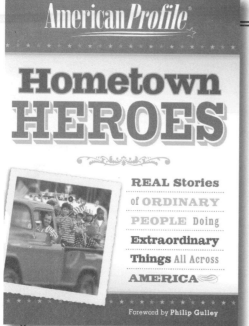

American *Profile*

Hometown HEROES

REAL Stories
of ORDINARY
PEOPLE Doing
Extraordinary
Things All Across
AMERICA

Foreword by **Philip Gulley**

"A wonderful collection of sharing and caring, of passion and purpose. *Hometown Heroes* is a blueprint for building the kind of communities in which we all want to live."

—Jeffrey Marx, Pulitzer Prize–winning author of *Season of Life*

ISBN: 978-0-06-125238-9
$12.95 (paperback)

All across America, ordinary people are going out of their way to help one another and make our country a better place. Unheralded, unrecognized, and often taken for granted, these citizens continue their good deeds, happy just to make a difference. Based on *American Profile*'s most popular column, *Hometown Heroes* tells the story of fifty such people spanning ages fourteen to ninety-three. Capturing the true spirit of America—one of generosity, courage, and tireless devotion—these heroes warm our hearts and reveal a face of America we rarely hear about.

HarperOne
An Imprint of HarperCollinsPublishers